EYEWITNESS TRAVEL

LISBON

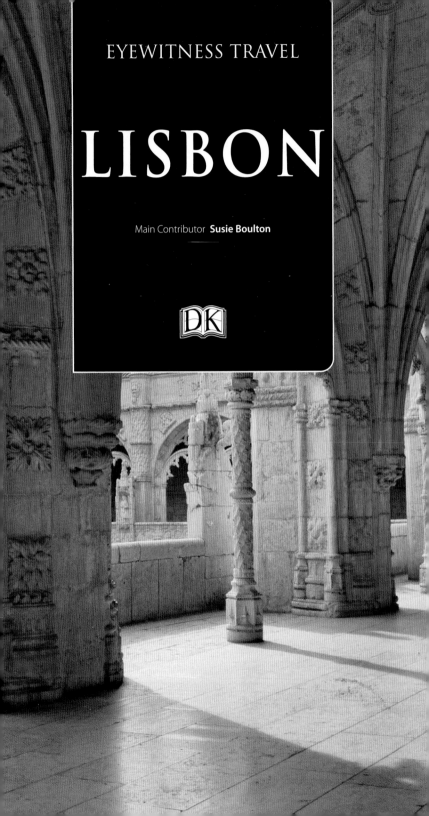

EYEWITNESS TRAVEL

LISBON

Main Contributor **Susie Boulton**

DK

LONDON, NEW YORK,
MELBOURNE, MUNICH AND DELHI
www.dk.com

Project Editors Claire Folkard, Ferdie McDonald

Art Editors Jim Evoy, Vanessa Hamilton

Editors Francesca Machiavelli, Rebecca Miles,
Alice Peebles, Alison Stäce

Designers Anthea Forlee, Carolyn Hewitson,
Nicola Rodway, Dooty Williams

Contributors and Consultants

Clive Gilbert, Peter Gilbert, Sarah McAlister, Norman Renouf,
Joe Staines, Martin Symington, Tomas Tranæus

Photographers

Linda Whitwam, Peter Wilson

Illustrators

Isidoro González-Adalid Cabezas/Acanto Arquitectura y Urbanismo S.L.,
Paul Guest, Claire Littlejohn, John Woodcock, Martin Woodward

Printed in China

First published in Great Britain in 1997
by Dorling Kindersley Limited
80 Strand, London WC2R 0RL

14 15 16 17 10 9 8 7 6 5 4 3 2 1

Reprinted with revisions 1999, 2000, 2001,
2002, 2003, 2004, 2006, 2008, 2011, 2013, 2015

**The information in this
DK Eyewitness Travel Guide is checked regularly.**
Every effort has been made to ensure that this book is as up-to-date as possible
at the time of going to press. Some details, however, such as telephone numbers,
opening hours, prices, gallery hanging arrangements and travel information are
liable to change. The publishers cannot accept responsibility for any consequences
arising from the use of this book, nor for any material on third party websites, and
cannot guarantee that any website address in this book will be a suitable source of
travel information. We value the views and suggestions of our readers very highly.
Please write to: Publisher, DK Eyewitness Travel Guides, Dorling Kindersley,
80 Strand, London, WC2R 0RL, UK, or email: travelguides@dk.com.

Front cover main image: Western face of the Padrão dos Descobrimentos

◀ The impressive cloister in the Mosteiro dos Jerónimos, Belém

Contents

Torre de Belém, one of the city's most
recognized landmarks

A statue of St Anthony, dressed up for his
feast day celebrations

View of São Vicente de Fora and the dome of Santa Engrácia

The multi-coloured marble interior beneath
Santa Engrácia's dome

The Monument to the Discoveries

Palácio da Pena, Sintra

HOW TO USE THIS GUIDE

This guide helps you get the most from a visit to Lisbon, providing expert recommendations as well as detailed practical information. The opening chapter *Introducing Lisbon* maps the city and sets it in its historical and cultural context. Each of the five area chapters, plus *The Lisbon Coast*, describe important sights, using maps, pictures and illustrations. Hotel and restaurant recommendations plus features on subjects such as entertainment and food and drink can be found in *Travellers' Needs*. The *Survival Guide* contains practical information on everything from transport to personal safety.

Lisbon

Lisbon has been divided into five main sightseeing areas. Each of these areas has its own chapter, which opens with a list of the major sights described. All sights are numbered and plotted on an *Area Map*. Information on the sights is easy to locate as the order in which they appear in the chapter follows the numerical order used on the map.

Sights at a Glance lists the chapter's sights by category: Churches, Museums and Galleries, Historic Buildings, Parks and Gardens.

1 Area Map
For easy reference, the sights covered in the chapter are numbered and located on a map. The sights are also marked on the *Street Finder* maps on pages 166–79.

A locator map shows clearly where the area is in relation to other parts of the city.

Each area is indicated by a colour-coded thumb tab (see inside front cover).

Stars indicate the sights that no visitor should miss.

2 Street-by-Street Map
This gives a bird's-eye view of the heart of each of the sightseeing areas.

A suggested route for a walk is shown in red.

3 Detailed Information
All the sights in Lisbon are described individually. Addresses and practical information are provided. The key to the symbols used in the information block is shown on the back flap.

1 Introduction to the Lisbon Coast

The Lisbon Coast has its own introduction, which provides an overview of the history and character of the coast and countryside around Lisbon and outlines what it has to offer the visitor today. The area covered by this section is highlighted on the map of Portugal shown on page 95. It covers coastal resorts and local wildlife, as well as beautiful palaces and historic towns.

2 Regional Map

This shows the main road network and gives an illustrated overview of the region. All entries are numbered and there are also useful tips on getting around the region.

The Lisbon Coast
chapter is indicated by a green thumb tab.

3 Detailed Information

All the important towns and other places to visit are described individually. They are listed in order, following the numbering given on the *Regional Map*. Within each entry, there is further detailed information on important buildings and other sights.

Story boxes explore specific subjects further.

For all the top sights, a Visitors' Checklist provides the practical information you need to plan your visit.

4 The Top Sights

These are given two or more full pages. Historic buildings are dissected to reveal their interiors; museums and galleries have colour-coded floorplans to help you locate the most interesting exhibits.

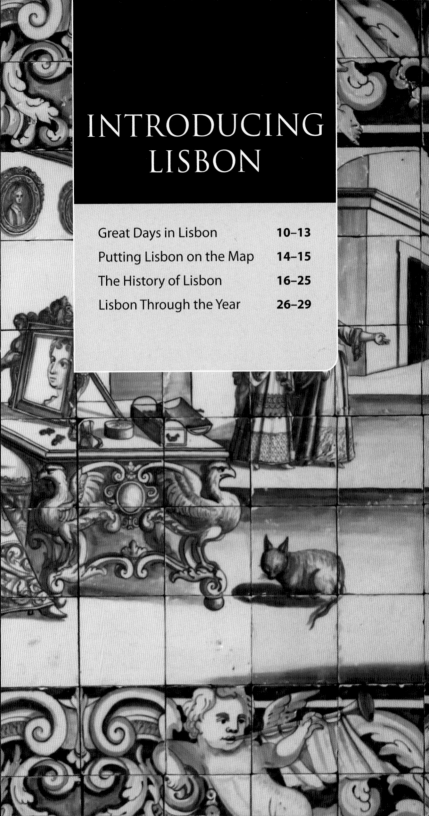

INTRODUCING LISBON

GREAT DAYS IN LISBON

Lisbon's many hidden nooks and crannies are home to numerous attractions that continue to surprise and seduce visitors. The city's charm lies in its inspiring architecture, enchanting squares and Moorish legacy. Sights listed here are cross-referenced to the rest of the guide

so you can learn more and tailor the day to your needs. The following itineraries are arranged first thematically and then by duration of stay. Prices shown include travel, food and admission for two adults or, in the case of the "Family Day" itinerary, for a family of four.

Panoramic view over the Castelo de São Jorge and Baixa from a vantage point in Alfama

Historic Lisbon

Two adults allow at least €80

- Charming Alfama and city views from the Castelo de São Jorge
- The Gothic ruins of Igreja do Carmo
- 16th- and 18th-century grandeur in São Roque

Morning
Begin the day at Lisbon's iconic Romanesque cathedral, the **Sé** *(p38)*, built by Portugal's first king and dating from the 12th century. From the quiet of the cathedral, set off into the intriguing warren of narrow lanes in **Alfama** *(pp34–5)*, then climb (or catch tram 28) to the **Castelo de São Jorge** *(pp40–41)* to spend an hour roaming the battlements and enjoying spectacular views of the city from the observation terrace and the periscope in Torre de Ulisses. Have lunch on the open-air patio of a restaurant in one of the area's oldest streets.

Afternoon
Head east from the castle to admire the grand Renaissance façade of **São Vicente de Fora** *(p36)*. The adjoining monastery has classic *azulejo* tiled panels, a stunning sacristy and an interesting, if eclectic, museum *(closed Mondays)*. The nearby **Santa Engrácia** *(p37; closed Mondays)* is also the National Pantheon and a fitting tribute to literary figures and legend-ary explorers. Climb to the roof for amazing river and city views. Next, catch tram 28 across town to **Chiado** *(pp54–5)*, where you can take a break from history and spend some time shopping, or take in the sombre but attractive ruins of the **Igreja do Carmo** *(p54)*. Walk south of the ruins to reach the viewing platform of the **Elevador de Santa Justa** *(p48)* to peer down at the patterned city pavements. Round off the day with a visit to the Igreja de **São Roque** *(p54)*, a shining example of Baroque architecture that miraculously survived the 1755 earthquake.

Art and Bulls

Two adults allow at least €60

- Restored Neo-Moorish bullring
- World-class art and treasures at the Gulbenkian
- Ancient art at the Museu Nacional de Arte Antiga

Morning
Visit the delightful Moorish pastiche that is **Campo Pequeno** *(p82)*, Lisbon's bullring since 1892. On the south side of the square is the impressive 17th-century Palácio Galveias, once the property of the ill-fated Távora family *(p73)*. This building now houses the Municipal Library. Reserve plenty of time to explore the exquisite **Museu Calouste Gulbenkian** *(pp78–81)*, which lies a short distance southwest. The museum houses one of the finest collections of art in the world, including works by Remembrandt and Houdon. You can also have lunch at the museum.

Classical marble statue in the Museu Calouste Gulbenkian

◀ A traditional *azulejo* tiled panel, dating back to the 17th-century

Intricately carved façade of the Mosteiro dos Jerónimos, Belém

Afternoon

After lunch, check out the **Centro de Arte Moderna** (p82), an excellent museum of contemporary art within the Gulbenkian complex. Later, spend time relaxing in the complex's pleasant gardens. Round off the day with a visit to the **Museu Nacional de Arte Antiga** (pp58–61), which houses a great collection of ancient art in all its forms. Alternatively, head for the wonderful **Museu Nacional do Azulejo** (pp84–5), a treat for ceramics fans that is well worth venturing further afield to discover.

A Day by the River

Two adults allow at least €70

- **Treasures old and new in Belém**
- **Ferry ride on the Tagus river**
- **Splendid river and city views from Elevador de Santa Justa**

Morning

Set at the mouth of the Tagus river, Belém is particularly rich in history and is home to many attractions. Take tram 15 to the 16th-century **Torre de Belém** (p72; closed Mondays), which served as the starting point for Lisbon's trade routes. The magnificent **Mosteiro dos Jerónimos** (pp68–9) is another of Lisbon's historic gems, as is the **Museu Colecção Berardo** (p71), the perfect place for contemporary art lovers. Just behind the monastery lies the **Jardim Botânico Tropical** (p67), a lush oasis peppered with ponds and grottoes. After this refreshing break, head back towards the river to the **Monument to the Discoveries** (pp70–71) to enjoy sweeping views of Belém from the viewpoint here.

Afternoon

Head for the Cais do Sodré ferry terminal and take a ferry across to Cacilhas to fully appreciate Lisbon's landmark suspension bridge, **Ponte 25 de Abril** (p76). On the south bank of the river stands the gigantic **Cristo Rei** monument (p76); go to the top of the statue for the finest views of Lisbon. Return to Cais do Sodré and take a short stroll along the Ribeira das Naus, a riverside walkway that connects this transport hub with the former royal square, **Praça do Comércio** (p49). Walk northwest of the square to reach the **Elevador de Santa Justa** (p48). Take the elevator to the top for a last look across the river before heading into the streets of the Baixa.

A Family Day

Family of four allow at least €150

- **The impressive Parque das Nações, a modern, self-contained riverside district**
- **Ocean life at the city's enormous oceanarium**
- **Exotic animals at Lisbon's popular zoo**

Morning

Begin the day with a visit to the **Parque das Nações** (p83), where you can ride a cable car, hire bikes or roller-skate. However, the park's main attraction is the immense **Oceanário de Lisboa** (p83) – buying tickets in advance is a good way to avoid long queues. Other highlights include the Pavilhão do Conhecimento – Ciencia Viva, a hands-on science museum, and the promenade along the river.

Afternoon

After lunch, take the train to Sete Rios, from where it is a short walk to the **Jardim Zoológico** (p86). Afternoon activities at the zoo include pelican- and sea lion-feeding sessions as well as free-flying birds in the Enchanted Forest. If the 2,000 animals are not enough to occupy a few hours, let off steam in the amusement park next door.

Modern art and architecture at Parque das Nações

Most museums are closed on Mondays.

2 Days in Lisbon

- Quaint Alfama, the oldest part of Lisbon
- The battlements of Castelo de São Jorge
- The architectural masterpieces in Belém

Day 1

Morning Catch tram 28 to **Castelo de São Jorge** (pp40–41) to soak in sweeping vistas of Lisbon. Then, walk down the narrow streets of Alfama to reach **Miradouro de Santa Luzia** (p36), from where there are gorgeous views over Alfama and the Tagus river. Afterwards, head to **São Vicente da Fora** (p36; closed Mondays) to admire the azulejo panels in the monastery cloisters.

Afternoon Go to the Elevador da Glória to take the funicular to **Miradouro de São Pedro de Alcântara** (p56). Walk to **Praça do Príncipe Real** (p56), then visit the ornate Igreja de **São Roque** (p54), before exploring the ruins of **Igreja do Carmo** (p54; closed Mondays) or taking a ride aboard the **Elevador de Santa Justa** (p48). End the day with a trip to **Chiado** (pp54–5) for some shopping.

Day 2

Morning Start the day with a visit to the **Torre de Belém** (p72; closed Mondays), one of the city's historical landmarks. Next, admire the stunning Manueline architecture of **Mosteiro dos Jerónimos** (pp68–9; closed Mondays). Follow it up with a stroll through the **Jardim Botânico Tropical** (p67).

Afternoon From Cais do Sodré, follow the Ribeira das Naus to **Praça do Comércio** (p49) and the interactive **Lisbon Story Centre** (p49). Take the elevator at **Rua Augusta** (p48) to enjoy panoramic views of the city. Next, head to **MUDE** (p48) for an insight into design. Round off the day with a visit to **Rossio** square (p47).

Imposing ramparts of the Castelo de São Jorge

3 Days in Lisbon

- Golden fairy-tale coaches at Museu Nacional dos Coches
- Unique art treasures at Museu Calouste Gulbenkian
- The extravagantly furnished Palácio Nacional da Ajuda

Day 1

Morning Start the day in Belém to see the splendid carriages at the **Museu Nacional dos Coches** (p66). Later, take a walk in the beautiful **Jardim Botânico Tropical** (p67), before visiting the cloisters of **Mosteiro dos Jerónimos** (pp68–9; closed Mondays).

Afternoon After lunch, check out the **Torre de Belém** (p72; closed Mondays), an impressive historical monument. Take a break from history at **Museu Colecção Berardo** (p71). Finally, head to the **Palácio Nacional da Ajuda** (p73) to admire its lavishly decorated rooms.

Day 2

Morning Spend the morning exploring the fabulous **Museu Calouste Gulbenkian** (pp78–81). Unwind in its pretty gardens, and then visit the **Centro de Arte Moderna** (p82) to see its superb collection of contemporary art.

Afternoon Enjoy the views from the top of **Parque Eduardo VII** (p77), then wander along **Avenida da Liberdade** (p46) to Rossio (p47). Take **Elevador de Santa Justa** (p48) to the haunting ruins of **Igreja do Carmo** (p54). Afterwards, go to the grandiose Igreja de **São Roque** (p54), followed by **Miradouro de São Pedro de Alcântara** (p56). Spend the evening exploring the trendy shops and cafés in **Praça do Príncipe Real** (p56).

Day 3

Morning Take tram 28 to **São Vicente da Fora** (p36) to see its eclectic monastery museum (closed Mondays), then visit the Baroque church of **Santa Engrácia** (p37; closed Mondays). Wind your way through the ancient streets of Alfama to **Castelo de São Jorge** (pp40–41).

Afternoon Amble downhill, stopping awhile at **Miradouro de Santa Luzia** (p36), to reach Lisbon's cathedral, the **Sé** (p38). Continue to **Rua Augusta** (p48) and take the elevator up the monumental archway leading onto **Praça do Comércio** (p49). Enjoy fashion and design highlights at **MUDE** (p48), before going to the fascinating **Lisbon Story Centre** (p49).

Baroque-style interiors of the Igreja de São Roque

5 Days in Lisbon

- Aquatic life at the Oceanário de Lisboa
- Ceramics galore at Museu dos Azulejos
- Spectacular palaces and scenery in Sintra

View of the ornate arch at Rua Augusta from the Praça do Comércio

Day 1

Morning Begin the·day in the verdant **Jardim Botânico** (p46). A 5-minute walk from here leads to the fashionable **Praça do Príncipe Real** (p56). Continue on foot to **Miradouro de São Pedro de Alcântara** (p56), pausing for city views, before being awe-inspired by the rich interior of **São Roque** (p54). Then explore the Gothic remains of **Igreja do Carmo** (p54). Don't miss the **Elevador de Santa Justa** (p48) nearby.

Afternoon After lunch, see the vast collection of artifacts at the **Museu Calouste Gulbenkian** (pp78–81), followed by contemporary art at the **Centro de Arte Moderna** (p82). Then stop at the viewpoint at the top of **Parque Eduardo VII** (p77) and visit the park's exotic Estufa Fria, before carrying on along **Avenida da Liberdade** (p46) towards **Restauradores** (pp44–5).

Day 2

Morning Discover 19th-century royal grandeur at the **Palácio Nacional da Ajuda** (p73; closed Wednesdays). Afterwards, head for Belém to wander in the pleasant **Jardim Botânico Tropical** (p67), before setting off for the magnificent **Mosteiro dos Jerónimos** (pp68–9; closed Mondays).

Afternoon Another one of Lisbon's "must see" monuments is the **Torre de Belém** (p72; closed Mondays). From here, go to **Museu Colecção Berardo** (p71) for some excellent contemporary art, and later climb the **Monument to the Discoveries** (pp70–71; closed Mondays). End the day with a visit to the **Museu Nacional dos Coches** (p66).

Day 3

Morning Dedicate the morning to the modern **Parque das Nações** (p83), dotted with pretty sculptures and gardens. While here, visit its main attraction, the **Oceanário de Lisboa** (p83), but be sure to buy tickets ahead of the visit.

Afternoon For a complete change of pace, explore the history of Portugal's renowned ceramics at the **Museu Nacional do Azulejo** (pp84–5). Then head back to the city centre, calling in at **Casa do Alentejo** (p45) before hitting the shops and cafés of **Baixa** and **Chiado** (pp54–5).

Day 4

Morning Walk from Cais do Sodré, along the pleasant Ribeira das Naus riverside path to **Praça do Comércio** (p49). Take the **Rua Augusta** archway elevator (p49) to appreciate the panoramic views. Afterwards, learn about the city's history at the thrilling **Lisbon Story Centre** (p49). Take a quick look at **MUDE** (p48) before walking to the cathedral, the **Sé** (p38).

Afternoon After lunch, relax at **Miradouro de Santa Luzia** (p36), then make your way to the monastery museum at **São Vicente da Fora** (p36; closed Mondays) to admire its splendid azulejo cloisters and enjoy spectacular views. See the magnificent marble pantheon at **Santa Engrácia**

(p37; closed Mondays). The last stop for the day is the medieval **Castelo de São Jorge** (pp40–41).

Day 5

Morning Make your way to **Rossio** (p47) and take the train to the forests and palaces of **Sintra** (pp102–, 7). Buy tickets in advance and head straight to the colourfully extravagant **Palácio da Pena** (pp106–7). Spend time relaxing amid the fountains and gazebos of the **Parque da Pena** (p103).

Afternoon After lunch, explore the **Palácio Nacional de Sintra** (pp104–5), whose delicate finery contrasts with the rugged appeal of the Moorish castle, **Castelo dos Mouros** (p103). Go shopping in the old town before returning to Lisbon.

Exterior of the kitsch Palácio da Pena in Sintra

Putting Lisbon on the Map

Lisbon, the capital of Portugal, is situated on the Atlantic coast, in the southwest of the country. It is approximately 300 km (180 miles) from the Algarve in the south and around 400 km (250 miles) from the Minho in the north. The political, economic and cultural centre of Portugal, the city lies on steep hills on the north bank of the Tagus. The Greater Lisbon area occupies around 1,000 sq km (300 sq miles) and has a population of 3.3 million. The city has become increasingly popular as a holiday destination and its proximity to the coast makes it an ideal choice for both sightseeing and sunbathing.

Key

- ▬▬ Motorway
- ▬▬ Major road
- ▭▭▭ Minor road
- ─── Main railway line
- ▬▬ National boundary

Rollogno deregido ao ſereniſſimo ı mujto pode
roſo prim[ci]pe elRey dom manuell noſſo ſen[or] ſobr
as vjdas ı excellentes feitos dos Reis de portugall
ſeus anteceſſores, bordenados ı eſcriptos per ſeu
mandado per duarte galluam fidallguo de ſua
caſa do ſeu cõſſelho noquall falla do grande lou
uor da preſente materia que he o proprio ı bordei
ro louuor deſtes meſmos Reis de portugall:-

Vito deuem ſereniſſimos ſenor trabalhar os homẽs po[r]
emſua uida obrarem uirtudes por que mereçã a d[eu]s no ou
tro mũdo ı neſte leirem de ſeu tempo memoria Ꝑ Nam ſoo
mẽte que uiueram o que as animallias tem per Jguall
com noſco. Mas que bem ı louuadamẽte bjueram que he proprio do
homem O quall teẽdo ainda em dias breue com aiuſtide a faz

THE HISTORY OF LISBON

Over the centuries, Lisbon has both flourished and suffered. The city is most famous for its history of maritime successes, in particular the voyages of Vasco da Gama, who first navigated a sea route to India. In recent years the city has flourished again, and it is now a major European centre of commerce.

According to myth, the Greek hero Odysseus (also known as Ulysses) founded Lisbon on his journey home from Troy. The Phoenicians are known to have established a trading post on the site in around 1200 BC. From 205 BC the town was in Roman hands, reaching the height of its importance when Julius Caesar became the governor in 60 BC.

With the collapse of the Roman Empire, barbarian tribes invaded from northern Europe. The Alans, who conquered the city in around AD 409, were superseded by the Suevi, who in turn were driven out by the Visigoths. None of these tribes were primarily town-dwellers and Lisbon began to decline. In 711 North African Muslim invaders, the Moors, overran the peninsula and occupied the city for almost 450 years. Lisbon was an important trading centre under the Moors and their legacy is evident today in the Castelo de São Jorge and the streets of the Alfama district.

The first king of Portugal, Afonso Henriques, finally ousted the Moors from Lisbon in 1147. Among those who helped was the English crusader Gilbert of Hastings, who became Lisbon's first bishop. A new cathedral was built below the castle and, shortly afterwards, the remains of St Vincent, the patron saint of Lisbon, were brought there. Lisbon received its charter early in the 13th century, but it was not until 1256, under Afonso III, that it became the capital.

Portuguese mariners' chart of the North Atlantic (c.1550)

◀ Illuminated page from the *Chronica de Dom Afonso Henriques*, showing Lisbon in the 16th century

The Reign of King Dinis

Under King Dinis, the son of Afonso III, the court at Lisbon became a centre of culture and in 1290 the University of Lisbon was founded. Dinis extended the city away from the castle, developing the Baixa, and Lisbon flourished as trade with Europe grew.

In the 14th century, the city continued to expand westwards along the river, despite the ruin caused by the Black Death, which spread throughout Portugal from Lisbon. In 1373, after Lisbon was sacked by Enrique II of Castile, Fernando I built a new line of fortifications to protect his 40,000 citizens

Statue of Manuel I and St Jerome on the Mosteiro dos Jerónimos

Musicians at the court of King Dinis

and to redefine the boundaries of the growing city. When Fernando died without an heir, the throne was claimed by his illegitimate half brother, João of Avis, who defeated Juan of Castile in 1385, at the famous Battle of Ajubarrota.

The Discoveries

Periodic outbreaks of plague continued to destabilize the economy and led to riots in Lisbon over grain shortages. Prosperity returned during the Age of Discovery *(see pp22–3)* when Vasco da Gama, setting out from Belém in 1497, successfully navigated a sea route to India. The resulting wealth from the spice trade made Lisbon the mercantile centre of Europe. In gratitude for this new-found prosperity, Manuel I ordered the building of the Torre de Belém *(see p72)* and the magnificent Mosteiro dos Jerónimos in Belém *(see pp68–9)*; their ornate late-Gothic style, known as Manueline after the king, reflects the Discoveries in the exotic and nautical nature of the detailed sculpture on the two monuments.

The 16th century saw major developments: a new square, the Terreiro do Paço (now the Praça do Comércio), was built on the waterfront, and a new district, the Bairro Alto, sprang up to house the many merchants drawn to Lisbon. The Inquisition, a Catholic movement which persecuted heretics and non-believers, began a reign of terror. Mass trials and executions of those that were condemned took place regularly in the Terreiro do Paço.

Spanish Control

The young King Sebastião I was killed at the battle of Alcácer-Quibir in a doomed attempt to invade Morocco in 1578. The lack of an heir led to conquest by Spain in 1580. Ignoring his advisers, Philip II of Spain refused to make Lisbon the capital of his extended kingdom and left the government of Portugal to a viceroy. The Spanish were ousted in 1640 and the Duke of Bragança was crowned João IV.

With the discovery of Brazilian gold in 1697, Lisbon enjoyed a new wave of prosperity. From 1706, João V began an ambitious building programme in the city. The most valuable addition to Lisbon at this time was the Águas Livres aqueduct *(see p86)*, which carried water across the Alcântara valley for just a few years before the devastating earthquake struck the city in 1755 *(see pp24–5)*.

The battle of Alcácer-Quibir in Morocco, where 8,000 men were killed and 15,000 captured

The Águas Livres aqueduct, completed in the 18th century

Pombal's Vision

Responsibility for rebuilding the ruined city fell to José I's chief minister, the Marquês de Pombal. Engineers drew up a plan that realigned Lisbon on a north–south axis and created a grid of streets with the Baixa at its heart. Pombal's vision was not continued by his successors; when the royal family fled to Brazil in 1807, ahead of Napoleon's invading army, Rio de Janeiro temporarily became the capital of the Portuguese empire, and Lisbon began to decline.

The Marquês de Pombal pointing to the new Lisbon, in a painting by Louis-Michel van Loo and Claude-Joseph Vernet

Regeneration

In the second half of the 19th century, a period of economic revival and industrialization commenced. Railways and new roads were built, trams were introduced, modern drains and sewers were constructed and work began on the embankment of the Tagus. In 1908 the king was assassinated, and two years later the monarchy was overturned. Under António Salazar's lengthy dictatorship (1926–68), Lisbon's modernization continued at the expense of the rest of the country.

A suspension bridge across the Tagus was completed in 1966. Initially called the Ponte Salazar, it was later renamed Ponte 25 de Abril in commemoration of the peaceful Carnation Revolution in 1974 which finally ended the totalitarian regime instituted by Salazar.

Modern Lisbon

The years following the Revolution were a period of both euphoria and political chaos. Then, in 1986, Portugal joined the European Community and foreign companies began to set up in Lisbon. Under the leadership of the Social Democratic prime minister Aníbal Cavaco Silva, Lisbon's economy recovered. Even the disastrous fire which swept through the Chiado district in 1988 failed to dampen the general optimism. To mastermind the rebuilding of this historic district, the city appointed Portugal's most prestigious architect, Álvaro Siza Vieira. Since then, Lisbon has enjoyed much prestige, and was voted European City of Culture in 1994. In 1998 the city hosted a World Exposition on the theme of the Oceans, in celebration of its maritime history. Today, Lisbon is a cosmopolitan city where the influence of its previous African and South American colonies is still widely evident.

The Rulers of Portugal

Afonso Henriques declared himself Portugal's first king in 1139, but his descendants' ties of marriage to various Spanish kingdoms led to dynastic disputes. João I's defeat of the Castilians in 1385 established the House of Avis, which presided over the golden age of Portuguese imperialism. Then in 1580, in the absence of a direct heir, Portugal was ruled by Spanish kings for 60 years before the Duke of Bragança became João IV. A Republican uprising ended the monarchy in 1910. However, in the first 16 years of the Republic there were 40 different governments, and in 1926 Portugal became a dictatorship under the eventual leadership of Salazar. Democracy was restored by the Carnation Revolution of 1974.

1557–78 Sebastião

1521–57 João III

1211–23 Afonso II

1185–1211 Sancho I

1248–79 Afonso III

1279–1325 Dinis

1481–95 João II

1100	1200	1300	1400	1500
House of Burgundy			Avis	
1100	1200	1300	1400	1500

1325–57 Afonso IV

1357–67 Pedro I

1223–48 Sancho II

1367–83 Fernando I

1139–85 Afonso Henriques (Afonso I)

1438–81 Afonso V

1578–80 Henrique

1433–8 Duarte

1580–9 Felipe I (Phili II of Spair

1385–1433 João I

1495–1521 Manuel I

1828–53 Maria II

2002–4 José Manuel Durão Barroso (prime minister)

2005–2011 José Sócrates Carvalho Pinto de Sousa (prime minister)

1932–68 António Salazar (prime minister)

1750–77 José I

1621–40 Felipe III (Philip IV of Spain)

1640–56 João IV

1656–83 Afonso VI

1683–1706 Pedro II (regent from 1668)

1816–26 João VI (regent from 1792)

1853–61 Pedro V

1861–89 Luís I

1976–8 & 1983–5 Mário Soares (prime minister)

2011– Pedro Manuel Mamede Passos Coelho (prime minister)

1700	1800	1900	2000

Bragança

Republic

1700	1800	1900	2000

98–1621 Felipe II (...ilip III of Spain)

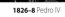

2006– Aníbal Cavaco Silva (president)

1985–95 Aníbal Cavaco Silva (prime minister)

2004–5 Pedro Miguel de Santana Lopes (prime minister)

1995–2001 António Guterres (prime minister)

1908–10 Manuel II

1777–1816 Maria I and Pedro III

1826–8 Pedro IV

1706–50 João V

1889–1908 Carlos I

The Age of Discovery

Portugal's astonishing period of conquest and exploration began in 1415 with the capture of the North African city of Ceuta. Maritime expeditions into the Atlantic and along the West African coast followed, motivated by conflict between Christianity and Islam and the desire for commercial gain. Great riches were earned from the gold and slaves taken from the Guinea coast, but the real breakthrough for Portuguese imperialism occurred in 1498 when Vasco da Gama *(see p70)* reached India. Portugal soon controlled the Indian Ocean and the spice trade, and established an eastern capital in Goa. With Pedro Álvares Cabral's "discovery" of Brazil, Portugal became a mercantile super-power rivalled only by her neighbour Spain.

Armillary Sphere
This celestial globe with the earth in its centre was used by navigators for measuring the positions of the stars. It became the personal emblem of Manuel I.

Magellan (c.1480–1521)
With Spanish funding, Portuguese sailor Fernão de Magalhães, known as Magellan, led the first circumnavigation of the globe (1519–22). He was killed in the Philippines before the voyage's end.

Key

— Discoverers' route

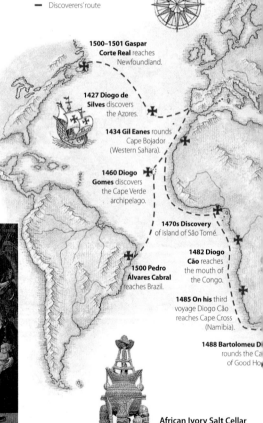

1500–1501 Gaspar Corte Real reaches Newfoundland.

1427 Diogo de Silves discovers the Azores.

1434 Gil Eanes rounds Cape Bojador (Western Sahara).

1460 Diogo Gomes discovers the Cape Verde archipelago.

1470s Discovery of island of São Tomé.

1482 Diogo Cão reaches the mouth of the Congo.

1500 Pedro Álvares Cabral reaches Brazil.

1485 On his third voyage Diogo Cão reaches Cape Cross (Namibia).

1488 Bartolomeu D[i] rounds the Ca[pe] of Good Ho[pe]

The Adoration of the Magi
Painted for Viseu Cathedral shortly after Cabral returned from Brazil in 1500, this panel is attributed to the artist Grão Vasco (c.1475–1540). King Baltazar is depicted as a Tupi Indian.

African Ivory Salt Cellar
This 16th-century ivory carving shows Portuguese warriors supporting a globe and a ship. A sailor peers out from the crow's nest at the top.

Japanese Screen (c.1600)
This screen shows traders unloading a *nau*, or great ship. Between 1575 and their expulsion in 1638, the Portuguese monopolized the carrying trade between China and Japan.

Henry the Navigator

Although he did not sail himself, Henry (1394–1460), the third son of João I, laid the foundations for Portugal's maritime expansion that were later built upon by João II and consolidated by Manuel I. As Master of the wealthy Order of Christ and Governor of the Algarve, Henry was able to finance expeditions along the African coast. By the time he died he had a monopoly on all trade south of Cape Bojador. Legend tells that he founded a school of navigation in the Algarve, at either Sagres or Lagos.

1543 Portuguese arrive in Japan.

1513 Trading posts set up in China at Macau and Canton.

1510 Capture of Goa.

1498 Vasco da Gama reaches Calicut in India.

1518 Fortress built in Colombo (Sri Lanka).

1512 Portuguese reach Ternate in the Moluccas (Spice Islands).

Cloves

Pepper

Nutmeg

Cinnamon

The Spice Trade
Exotic spices were a great source of wealth for Portugal. The much-disputed Moluccas, or Spice Islands, were purchased from Spain in 1528.

Portuguese Discoveries

The systematic attempt to find a sea route to India, which led to a monopoly of the spice trade, began in 1482 with the first voyage of Diogo Cão, who planted a padrão *(stone cross) on the shores where he landed.*

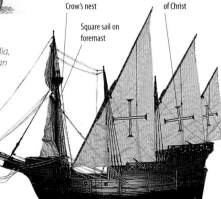

Crow's nest

Square sail on foremast

Cross of the Order of Christ

Lateen-rigged Caravel
These ships with three triangular sails were favoured by the first Portuguese explorers who sailed close to the African coast. For later journeys across the open ocean, square sails were found more effective.

The 1755 Lisbon Earthquake

The first tremor of the devastating earthquake was felt at 9:30am on 1 November. A few minutes later there was a second, far more violent shock, reducing over half the city to rubble. Although the epicentre was close to the Algarve, Lisbon, as the most populated area, bore the worst damage. Over 20 churches collapsed, crushing the crowds who had assembled for All Saints' Day. A third shock was followed by fires which quickly spread. An hour later, huge waves came rolling in from the Tagus and flooded the lower part of the city. Most of Portugal suffered damage and the shock was felt as far away as Italy. Perhaps 15,000 people lost their lives in Lisbon alone.

This anonymous painting of the arrival of a papal ambassador at cou in 1693 shows how Terreiro do Paço looked before the earthquake.

Some buildings that might have survived an earthquake alone were destroyed by the fire that followed.

The old royal palace, the 16th-century Paço da Ribeira, was utterly ruined by the earthquake and ensuing flood.

The royal family was staying at the palace in Belém, a place far less affected than Lisbon, and survived the disaster unscathed. Here the king surveys the city's devastation.

Ships crammed full of people fleeing the fire were wrecked and anchors thrown up to water level.

This detail is from a votive painting dedicated to Nossa Senhora da Estrela, given by a grateful father in thanks for the sparing of his daughter's life in the earthquake. The girl was found miraculously alive after being buried under rubble for 7 hours.

The Reconstruction of Lisbon

Marquês de Pombal (1699–1782)

No sooner had the tremors abated than Sebastião José de Carvalho e Melo, chief minister to José I and later to become Marquês de Pombal, was outlining ideas for rebuilding the city. While philosophers moralized, Pombal reacted with practicality. "Bury the dead and feed the living" is said to have been his initial response. He then began a progressive town-planning scheme. His efficient handling of the crisis won him almost total political control.

The ancient castle walls succumbed to the reverberating shock waves.

Reactions to the Disaster

The earthquake had a profound effect on European thought. Eyewitness accounts appeared in the papers, many written by foreigners living in Lisbon. A heated debate developed over whether the earthquake was a natural phenomenon or divine wrath. Pre-earthquake Lisbon had been a flourishing city, famed for its wealth – also for its Inquisition and idolatry. Interpreting the quake as punishment, preachers prophesied further catastrophes. Famous literary figures debated the significance of the event, among them the French writer Voltaire, who wrote a poem about the disaster, propounding his views that evil exists and man is weak and powerless, doomed to an unhappy fate on earth.

French author Voltaire

Flames erupted as the candles lit for All Saints' Day ignited the city's churches. The fire raged for seven days.

Some of Lisbon's finest buildings were destroyed, along with gold, jewellery, priceless furniture, archives, books and paintings.

At 11am, tidal waves rolled into Terreiro do Paço. The Alcântara docks, to the west, bore the brunt of the impact.

Churches, homes and public buildings all suffered in the disaster. The Royal Opera House, here shown in ruins, had only been completed in March the same year.

A Contemporary View of the Earthquake

This anonymous German engraving of 1775 gives a vivid picture of the scale of the disaster. Many who fled the flames made for the Tagus, but were washed away in the huge waves which struck the Terreiro do Paço. The human and material losses were incalculable.

The reconstruction of the centre of Lisbon took place rapidly. By the end of November the Marquês de Pombal had devised a strikingly modern scheme for a grid of parallel streets running from the waterfront to Rossio. The new buildings are shown in yellow.

Modern-day Lisbon holds many reminders of the earthquake. Pombal's innovative grid system is clearly visible in this aerial view of the Baixa (see pp42–9). The scheme took many years to complete, and the triumphal arch that spans Rua Augusta was not finished until over a century later, in 1873.

LISBON THROUGH THE YEAR

While the summer months are the most popular for visiting Lisbon and have many events on the calendar – the Festas dos Santos Populares, in June, are one of the highlights of the year – spring and autumn can also be rewarding if you want to tour the Lisbon Coast. In late winter, the colourful Carnaval celebrations attract many visitors to Lisbon. Other events during the year include music festivals, sporting fixtures and the many religious *festas*, which are great times of celebration for the Portuguese people.

Spring

With the arrival of spring-time in Lisbon, the café and restaurant terraces begin to fill with people. Many events, such as concerts, start to take place in the open air again as the weather improves. At the weekends the coastal resorts of Cascais and Estoril become livelier when on warm, bright days local people take day trips there to enjoy the seaside.

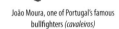

João Moura, one of Portugal's famous bullfighters (cavaleiros)

March

Moda Lisboa (mid-Mar). The first of two annual editions of Portugal's main fashion show (see p28).

World Poetry Day (3rd Sat). Literary events are held at the Centro Cultural de Belém, including debates, poetry workshops and music performances. Poets from all over the world present their latest works, and members of the public are encouraged to read their favourite poems.

Procissão dos Terceiros Franciscanos (4th Sun before Easter). This colourful procession through the streets of Mafra (see p98) starts at the convent. The ceremonial robes worn in the procession were given to the church by João V, in the 18th century.

Lisbon's Half Marathon (Mar or Apr – date varies). One of the city's most popular sporting events, the race draws inter-national runners.

April

Festa dos Merendeiros (Sun after Easter). This traditional festival and procession takes place in Santo Isidoro, near Mafra (see p98). There is a ceremony to bless the bread and the fields in the hope of a successful harvest later on in the year.

Formal military parade, held in Lisbon on Liberty Day

Liberty Day (25 Apr). A public holiday throughout Portugal, the annual celebration of the Carnation Revolution that ended 48 years of dictatorship in 1974 (see p19) is also known as the Dia da Revoluçaõ. Commemorations include a military parade and political speeches at the Praça do Império. The unions organize festivities that take place all over the city.

Portugal Open Tennis Championship (Apr/May). International players compete in Portugal's top tennis competition, which is held at the Jamor Tennis Courts.

Beginning of the bull-fighting season (Apr–Sep). The Campo Pequeno bullring in Lisbon is the usual venue for this traditional entertainment. Bullfights may also be seen in Montijo.

May

Dia do Trabalhador (1 May). Among the events organized by the unions on Labour Day are marches and political speeches throughout Lisbon.

Festival Estoril Jazz (May). A series of jazz concerts in and around Lisbon.

Feira do Livro (May–Jun – date varies). One of the main literary events in Lisbon, this book fair offers numerous bargains, such as second-hand books and signed copies. The event takes place at the Parque Eduardo VII, the city's largest park (see p77).

Exhibition of Horse-Riding at the Palácio Nacional de Queluz (May–Oct). Every Wednesday at 11am, riders from the Portuguese Equestrian School put on displays of their skills in the gardens of the Palácio Nacional de Queluz (see pp110–11).

Average Daily Hours of Sunshine

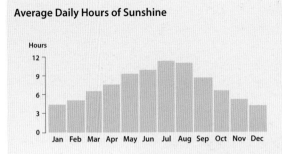

Hours

12
9
6
3
0

Jan Feb Mar Apr May Jun Jul Aug Sep Oct Nov Dec

Sunshine Chart
Although Lisbon enjoys a moderate amount of sunshine all year, the days are particularly hot and sunny in the summer months. Care should be taken to protect the skin against the sun, when walking around Lisbon itself and also when sunbathing on the beaches of Estoril or Cascais.

Summer

The summer months are a major holiday time in Lisbon, especially August when many Lisboetas retire to the coastal resorts, in particular Costa da Caparica and Cascais.

June

Festas da Cidade (*throughout Jun*). A celebration of the city of Lisbon itself, which includes a variety of events from rock concerts to drive-in films. A major highlight is the lively parade along Lisbon's Avenida da Liberdade on the evening of 12 June, which is followed by a party. The festa is in addition to the three saints' festivals listed below.
Santo António (*12–13 Jun*).
São João (*23–4 Jun*).
São Pedro (*28–9 Jun*). Santo António is the major festival in Lisbon, marking the beginning of the **Festas dos Santos Populares** (Feasts of the

Celebrating Santo António, one of Lisbon's most important festivals

The beach at Estoril, just one of the many popular bays along the Lisbon Coast

People's Saints). Locals decorate the Alfama and bring out chairs for the hundreds who come to enjoy the celebrations. The festivities continue throughout June with the *festas* of São João and São Pedro.
Arraial Lisboa Pride (*mid- to late Jun – date varies*). Events and celebrations are held in one of Lisbon's parks or squares.
Feira Grande de São Pedro (*29 Jun*). A market of crafts, antiques and local delicacies, in Sintra (*see pp102–7*).
Sintra Festival (*Jun–Jul*). A series of classical music concerts held in the parks and palaces of Sintra and Queluz (*see pp102–7*).
FIA-Lisbon International Handicraft Exhibition (*Jun–Jul*). This huge display of arts and crafts is held in the Parque de Nações.

July

Optimus Alive (*Jul*). A three-day pop and rock festival that takes place on the Algés riverside promenade in west Lisbon, featuring many of the world's most popular bands.
Feira de Artesanato (*Jul–early Sep*). This craft fair is held in Estoril (*see pp108–9*), and

features both folk music and dance performances.
Feira dos Alhos (*3rd Sun in Jul*). Annual market of crafts, delicacies and wine- and cheese-tasting, near the convent in the Palácio de Mafra (*see p98*).
Capuchos Summer Concerts (*Jul–Aug*). A series of musical events throughout the summer months, centred on the Capuchos Monastery on the south side of the Tagus.
Jazz in the Garden (*Jul*). The sounds of European jazz bands and the taste of German delicacies in the gardens of the Goethe Institute, Campo dos Mártires da Pátria.
Verão Em Sesimbra (*Jul–Sep*). Popular entertainment festival held in the town of Sesimbra (*see p112*).

August

Jazz em Agosto (*early Aug*). Jazz music is performed in the gardens of the Calouste Gulbenkian Cultural Centre.
Lisboa na Rua (*late Aug–Sep*). Com'Out Lisbon is a month-long festival of outdoor performances, featuring jazz and *fado* concerts, art exhibitions and a variety of street entertainment.
Romaria de São Mamede (*14–22 Aug*). Farmers lead their animals around the chapel of Janas, north of Colares (*see p99*), to be blessed. The tradition originates in the fact that the site of the church was once that of a Roman temple dedicated to the goddess Diana.

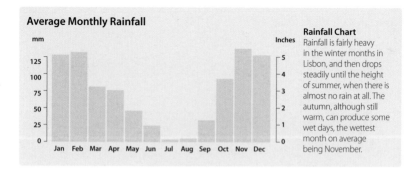

Average Monthly Rainfall

Rainfall Chart
Rainfall is fairly heavy in the winter months in Lisbon, and then drops steadily until the height of summer, when there is almost no rain at all. The autumn, although still warm, can produce some wet days, the wettest month on average being November.

Autumn

In many ways, this is the best season for touring and sightseeing. The strong heat of the summer has passed but the weather is still pleasantly warm. The countryside around Sintra is particularly beautiful with the changing colours of the trees.

September

Avante! *(1st weekend in Sep)*. This lively *festa* in Seixal, south of the Tagus, attracts large crowds. It includes rock and folk music, exhibitions and cultural events and an array of delicious food.
Nossa Senhora da Luz *(2nd weekend of Sep)*. A religious *festa* held in honour of Our Lady of the Light in Sampaio, near Sesimbra *(see p112)*.
Festa das Vindimas *(early Sep)*. At the foot of Palmela's medieval castle *(see p112)*, the first grape harvest is blessed, amid traditional entertainment, wine- and cheese-tasting and fireworks.

Nossa Senhora do Cabo Espichel *(last Sun of Sep)*. This event is held by local fishermen to honour the Virgin Mary with a procession up to the church at Cabo Espichel *(see p109)*.
Feira da Luz *(throughout Sep)*. This lively market focuses on arts and crafts, especially pottery and ceramics. It takes place in the Carnide district of Lisbon.
Festa da Senhora da Consolação *(throughout Sep)*. This festival, which is held in the Assafora area of Sintra *(see pp102–7)*, celebrates Portugal's patron saint with a month of street parties, music, food and colourful events.

October

Moda Lisboa *(Oct)*. This biannual fashion show attracts important designers from all over the world and is Portugal's main fashion event. Some catwalk shows take place in the Pátio da Galé, in Praça do Comércio. The autumn/winter

collections are shown in March *(see p26)*.
Rock 'n' Roll Lisbon Marathon *(5 Oct)*. Festive celebrations in the city as runners compete.
Republic Day *(5 Oct)*. The revolution that brought the monarchy to an end in 1910 *(see p19)* is commemorated annually in Lisbon with military parades.

An old lady laying flowers at a cemetery in Lisbon in honour of All Saints' Day

November

All Saints' Day *(1 Nov)*. An important festival in the Portuguese religious calendar, many families light candles and lay flowers in local cemeteries throughout the area, in honour of their dead relatives.
Feira de Todos os Santos *(1 Nov)*. Also known as the Dried Fruits' Market, this is a lively fair held in Azureira, near Mafra *(see p98)*.
Dia do Magusto e de São Martinho *(11 Nov)*. The celebration of Roast Chestnut Day is based on the tradition of preparing for winter and coincides with the first tastings of the year's wine.
Circus *(late Nov–early Jan)*. Before Christmas, circuses arrive in Lisbon. Check venues and dates with tourist offices.

Blessing the grape harvest at the Festa das Vindimas in Palmela

Average Monthly Temperature

°C   °F

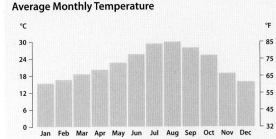

| | Jan | Feb | Mar | Apr | May | Jun | Jul | Aug | Sep | Oct | Nov | Dec |

Temperature Chart
Lisbon is rarely very cold, and maintains a pleasantly mild climate, even during the winter months, making it a good city to visit in any season. However, the summer months bring days of consistent heat, and although the city is quiet in high summer, it can become humid and stifling.

Winter

Those seeking mild, sunny climes and an escape from the winter cold will find this a good time of year to visit Lisbon. The nightlife is very lively and continues until the early hours, especially at weekends. Christmas is a time of great celebration and an important occasion for families to reunite and enjoy long meals together.

Colourful parades during the annual Carnaval celebrations in Lisbon

December

Festa da Imaculada Conceição
(8 Dec). This festival of the Immaculate Conception is a national holiday throughout Portugal. There are special church services and Lisbon's population celebrate with their usual festive spirit.

Christmas *(24–5 Dec)*. Throughout the Lisbon area, churches and shops display Nativity scenes and cribs. The main celebrations take place on Christmas Eve, when families get together and go to midnight Mass. They then return home for a large traditional meal of *bacalhau* (salted dried cod) and *sonhos* (small fried cakes similar to doughnuts, usually flavoured with pumpkin or orange).

Nossa Senhora da Conceição *(26 Dec)*. A traditional religious procession held in honour of Our Lady of the Immaculate Conception, the saint protector of Alfarim, near Sesimbra *(see p112)*.

The celebratory cake, *bolo rei*

January

New Year *(31 Dec–1 Jan)*. In Lisbon, a spectacular firework display is held in Praça do Comércio to welcome the New Year.

Epiphany *(6 Jan)*. The traditional cake baked for the Epiphany is *bolo rei* (king's cake), a small fruit cake made with a lucky charm and a bean inside. Crown-shaped, it is topped with crystallized fruit, resembling gems. The person who gets the bean must then buy the next cake. *Bolo rei* is also made at Christmas time.

Opera season *(Jan–Nov)*. The opera season starts at the Teatro Nacional de São Carlos *(see p55)*.

February

Carnaval *(date varies)*. This is celebrated throughout Portugal with spectacular costumes and floats; there is an especially colourful parade in Sesimbra *(see p112)*.

Procissão do Senhor dos Passos da Graça *(second Sun in Lent)*. The figure of Christ *(Senhor dos Passos)* is taken out of the Igreja da Graça *(see p39)* and carried through the streets of Graça, in Lisbon. The procession dates back to the 16th century.

Public Holidays

New Year's Day (1 Jan)
Carnaval (Feb)
Good Friday (Mar or Apr)
Dia 25 de Abril or **Liberty Day**, *commemorating 1974 revolution* (25 Apr)
Dia do Trabalhador, *Labour Day* (1 May)
Corpus Christi (date varies)
Camões Day (10 Jun)
Santo António (13 Jun)
Assumption Day (15 Aug)
Republic Day (5 Oct)
All Saints' Day (1 Nov)
Dia da Restauração, *commemorating independence from Spain, 1640* (1 Dec)
Immaculate Conception (8 Dec)
Christmas Day (25 Dec)

The Lisbon skyline, as seen from Almada ▶

LISBON AREA BY AREA

ALFAMA

It is difficult to believe that this humble neighbourhood was once the most desirable quarter of Lisbon. For the Moors, the tightly packed alleyways around the fortified castle comprised the whole city. The seeds of decline were sown in the Middle Ages when wealthy residents moved west for fear of earthquakes, leaving the quarter to fishermen and paupers. The buildings survived the 1755 earthquake *(see pp24–5)* and, although there are no Moorish houses still standing, the quarter retains its kasbah-like layout. Compact houses line steep streets and stairways, their façades strung with washing. Long overdue restoration is under way in the

most dilapidated areas, but daily life still revolves around local grocery stores and small, cellar-like tavernas.

Above the Alfama, the imposing Castelo de São Jorge crowns Lisbon's eastern hill. This natural vantage point, a defensive stronghold and royal palace until the 16th century, is today a popular promenade, with spectacular views from its reconstructed ramparts.

West of the Alfama stand the proud twin towers of the Sé. To the northeast, the domed church of Santa Engrácia and the white façade of São Vicente de Fora dominate the skyline.

Sights at a Glance

Museums and Galleries
2 Museu de Artes Decorativas
6 Museu Militar

Historic Buildings
7 Casa dos Bicos
10 *Castelo de São Jorge pp40–41*

Churches
3 São Vicente de Fora
5 Santa Engrácia

8 Sé
9 Santo António à Sé

Belvederes
1 Miradouro de Santa Luzia
11 Miradouro da Graça

Markets
4 Feira da Ladra

☐ **Restaurants** *p130*
1 Bica do Sapato
2 Casa do Leão
3 Casanova
4 Faz Figura
5 Hua-Ta-Li
6 Restô do Chapitô
7 Santo António de Alfama
8 Sr Fado de Alfama
9 Tentações de Goa
10 Via Graça

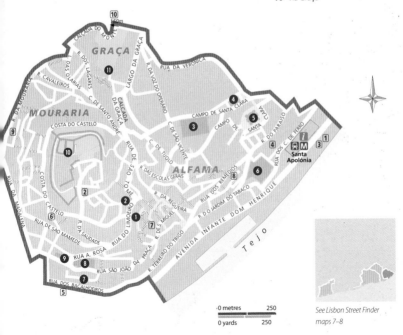

0 metres 250
0 yards 250

See Lisbon Street Finder
maps 7–8

◀ Painted ceiling of the 18th-century Baroque sacristy of São Vicente de Fora   For keys to symbols *see back flap*

Street-by-Street: Alfama

A fascinating quarter at any time of day, the Alfama comes to life in the late afternoon and early evening when the locals emerge at their doorways and the small tavernas start to fill. A new generation of younger residents has resulted in a small number of trendy shops and bars. Given the steep streets and steps of the quarter, the least strenuous approach is to start at the top and work your way down.

A walk around the maze of winding alleyways will reveal picturesque corners and crumbling churches as well as panoramic views from the shady terraces, such as the Miradouro de Santa Luzia.

Largo das Portas do Sol
Café tables look out over the Alfama towards the Tagus estuary. Portas do Sol was one of the entrance gates to the old city.

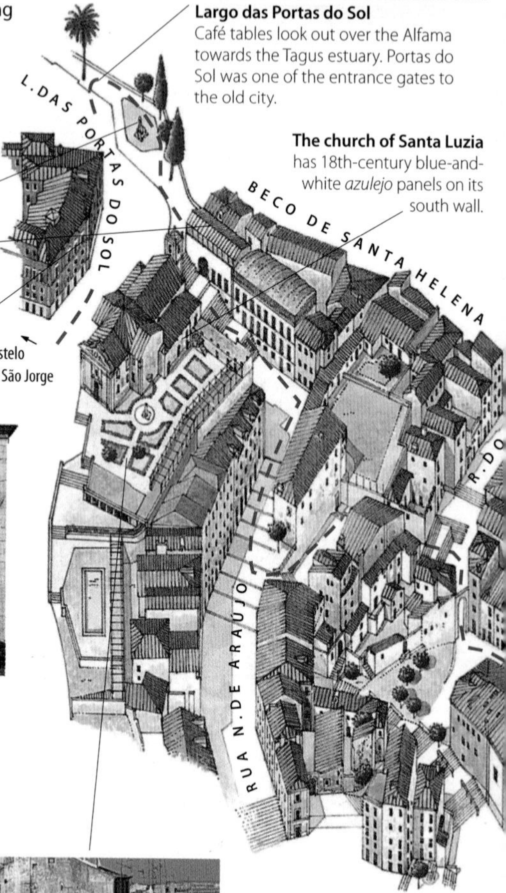

Statue of St Vincent

The church of Santa Luzia
has 18th-century blue-and-white *azulejo* panels on its south wall.

Largo das Portas do Sol
has its own terrace viewpoint on a converted rooftop on the east side of the Santa Luzia church.

Castelo de São Jorge

L. DAS PORTAS DO SOL

BECO DE SANTA HELENA

R. DO

RUA N. DE ARAUJO

❷ ★ **Museu de Artes Decorativas**
Set up as a museum by the banker Ricardo do Espírito Santo Silva, the 17th-century Palácio Azurara houses fine 17th- and 18th-century Portuguese furniture and decorative arts.

0 metres	25
0 yards	25

Key

 Suggested route

❶ ★ **Miradouro de Santa Luzia**
The view from this bougainvillea-clad terrace spans the tiled roofs of the Alfama toward the Tagus. This is a pleasant place to rest after a walk around the area's steep streets.

Beco das Cruzes

Like most of the alleyways *(becos)* that snake their way through the Alfama, this is a steep cobbled street. Locals often hang washing between the tightly packed houses.

Locator Map
See Lisbon Street Finder maps 7–8

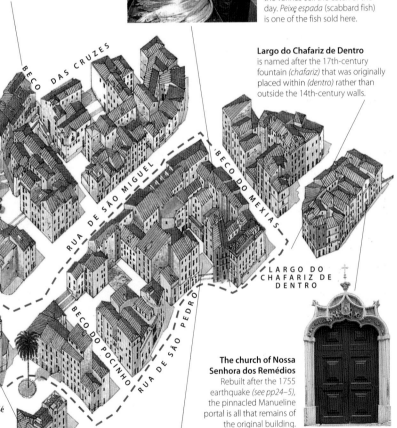

Rua de São Pedro

This street is the scene of a lively early-morning fish market where the *varinas* sell the catch of the day. *Peixe espada* (scabbard fish) is one of the fish sold here.

Largo do Chafariz de Dentro

is named after the 17th-century fountain *(chafariz)* that was originally placed within *(dentro)* rather than outside the 14th-century walls.

BECO DAS CRUZES

RUA DE SÃO MIGUEL

BECO DO MEXIAS

BECO DO POCINHO

RUA DE SÃO PEDRO

LARGO DO CHAFARIZ DE DENTRO

Sé

The church of Nossa Senhora dos Remédios

Rebuilt after the 1755 earthquake *(see pp24–5)*, the pinnacled Manueline portal is all that remains of the original building.

São Miguel was rebuilt after it was damaged in the 1755 earthquake. It retains a few earlier features, including a fine ceiling of Brazilian jacaranda wood.

Popular restaurants hidden in the labyrinth of alleyways spill out onto open-air patios. The Lautasco, in Beco do Azinhal, serves excellent Portuguese food.

Tile panel showing pre-earthquake Praça do Comércio, Santa Luzia

❶ Miradouro de Santa Luzia

Rua do Limoeiro. **Map** 8 D4. 🚋 28.

The terrace by the church of Santa Luzia provides a sweeping view over the Alfama and the Tagus river. Distinctive landmarks, from left to right, are the cupola of Santa Engrácia, the church of Santo Estêvão and the two startling white towers of São Miguel. While tourists admire the views, old men play cards under the bougainvillea-clad pergola. The south wall of Santa Luzia has two modern tiled panels, one of Praça do Comércio before it was flattened by the earthquake, the other showing the Christians attacking the Castelo de São Jorge *(see pp40–41)* in 1147.

❷ Museu de Artes Decorativas

Largo das Portas do Sol 2. **Map** 8 D3. **Tel** 218 881 991 or 218 814 600. 🚌 737. 🚋 12, 28. **Open** 10am–5pm Wed–Mon. **Closed** 1 Jan, 1 May, 25 Dec. 🅿 ♿ 🔲 fress.pt

Also known as the Ricardo do Espírito Santo Silva Foundation, the museum was set up in 1953 to preserve the traditions and increase public awareness of the Portuguese decorative arts. The foundation was named after a banker who bought the 17th-century Palácio Azurara in 1947 to house his fine collection of furniture, textiles, silver and ceramics. Among the

17th- and 18th-century antiques displayed in this handsome four-storey mansion are many fine pieces in exotic woods, including an 18th-century rosewood backgammon and chess table. Also of note are the collections of 18th-century silver and Chinese porcelain and hand-embroidered wool carpets from Arraiolos. The spacious rooms still retain some original ceilings and *azulejo* panels.

18th-century china cutlery case, Museu de Artes Decorativas

In the adjoining building are workshops where artisans preserve the techniques of cabinet-making, gilding, book-binding, wood-carving and other traditional crafts. Temporary exhibitions, lectures and concerts are also held in the palace.

Cloister of São Vicente de Fora, with tiled decorative panels

❸ São Vicente de Fora

Largo de São Vicente. **Map** 8 E3. **Tel** 218 824 400. 🚌 712, 734. 🚋 28. **Open** 9am–1pm, 2:30–5pm Tue–Sat, for Mass 10am Sun. Museum: **Open** 10am–6pm Tue–Sun. **Closed** public hols. ✝ 🕊 to museum.

St Vincent was proclaimed Lisbon's patron saint in 1173, when his relics were transferred from the Algarve, in southern Portugal, to a church on this site outside *(fora)* the city walls. Designed by the Italian architect Filippo Terzi, and completed in 1627, the off-white façade is sober and symmetrical, in Italian Renaissance style, with towers either side and three arches leading to the entrance hall. Statues of saints Augustine, Sebastian and Vincent can be seen over the entrance.

The adjoining former Augustinian monastery, reached via the nave, retains its 16th-century cistern and vestiges of the former cloister, but it is visited mainly for its 18th-century *azulejos*. Among the panels in the entrance hall off the first cloister there are lively, though historically inaccurate, tile scenes of Afonso Henriques attacking Lisbon and Santarém. Around the cloisters, the tiled rural scenes are surrounded by floral designs and cherubs, illustrating the fables of La Fontaine. A passageway leads behind the church to the old refectory, transformed into the Bragança Pantheon in 1885. The stone sarcophagi of almost every king and queen are here, from João IV, who died in 1656, to Manuel II, last king of Portugal. Only Maria I and Pedro IV are not buried here. A stone mourner kneels at the tomb of Carlos I and his son Luís Felipe, assassinated in Praça do Comércio in 1908. The church now operates as a museum, with access to the Bragança Pantheon.

❹ Feira da Ladra

Campo de Santa Clara. **Map** 8 F2.
Open 7:30am–1pm Tue & Sat.
🚌 712. 🚋 28.

The stalls of the so-called
"Thieves' Market" have occupied
this site on the edge of the
Alfama for over a century, laid
out under the shade of trees
or canopies. As the fame of this
flea market has grown, bargains
are increasingly hard to find
among the mass of bric-a-brac,
but a few of the vendors
have interesting wrought-iron
work, prints and tiles, as well as
second-hand clothes. Evidence
of Portugal's colonial past is
reflected in the stalls selling
African statuary, masks and
jewellery. Fish, vegetables and
herbs are sold in the central
wrought-iron marketplace.

Bric-a-brac for sale in the Feira da Ladra flea market

❺ Santa Engrácia

Campo de Santa Clara. **Map** 8 F2.
Tel 218 854 820. 🚌 712. 🚋 28. **Closed** 1
Jan, 25 Apr, Easter Sun, 25 Dec. 🅿 ♿

One of Lisbon's most striking
landmarks, the soaring dome of
Santa Engrácia punctuates the
skyline in the east of the city.
The original church collapsed
in a storm in 1681. The first
stone of the new Baroque
monument, laid in 1682,
marked the beginning of a 284-
year saga which led to the
invention of a saying that a
Santa Engrácia job was never
done. The church was not
completed until 1966.
  The interior is paved with
coloured marble and crowned
by a giant cupola. As the
National Pantheon, it houses
cenotaphs of Portuguese
heroes, such as Vasco da Gama

(*see p70*) and Afonso de
Albuquerque, Viceroy of India
(1502–15) on the left, and on
the right Henry the Navigator
(*see p23*). More contemporary
tombs include that of the
fadista Amália Rodrigues (*see
p145*). A lift up to the dome
offers a 360-degree panorama
of the city.

❻ Museu Militar

Largo do Museu de Artilharia. **Map** 8
D3. **Tel** 218 842 567. 🚌 728, 735, 759.
🚋 28. **Open** 10am–5pm Tue–Fri,
10am–noon, 1–5pm Sat & Sun.
Closed public hols. 🅿 🅆 **exercito.pt**

Located on the site of a
16th-century cannon foundry
and arms depot, the military
museum contains an extensive
collection. Visits begin in the
Vasco da Gama Room
with a collection of old
cannons and modern
murals depicting the
discovery of the sea
route to India. The Salas
da Grande Guerra, on
the first floor, display
exhibits related to
World War I. Other
rooms focus on the
evolution of weapons
in Portugal, from
primitive flints through
spears to rifles. The large
courtyard, flanked by cannons,
tells the story of Portugal in
tiled panels, from the Christian
reconquest to World War I. The
Portuguese artillery section in
the oldest part of the museum
displays the wagon used to
transport the triumphal arch to
Rua Augusta (*see p48*).

The multi-coloured marble interior beneath
Santa Engrácia's dome

❼ Casa dos Bicos

Rua dos Bacalhoeiros. **Map** 8 D4.
Tel 218 802 040. 🚌 728, 746, 759.
🚋 18, 25. **Open** 10am–6pm Mon–Sat.

Faced with diamond-shaped
stones (*bicos*), this house looks
rather conspicuous among the
other buildings in this area. It
was built in 1523 for Brás de
Albuquerque, illegitimate son
of Afonso, Viceroy of India and
conqueror of Goa and Malacca.
The façade is an adaptation of a
style that was popular in Europe
during the 16th century. The
two top storeys, ruined in the
earthquake of 1755 (*see pp24–5*),
were restored in the 1980s,
recreating the original from old
views of Lisbon in tile panels
and engravings. In the interim
the building was used for salting
fish (Rua dos Bacalhoeiros means
"street of the cod fishermen").
  It now has a permanent
exhibition on the life and work
of José Saramago (1922–2010),
winner of the 1998 Nobel Prize
for Literature, and also hosts
concerts, readings and seminars.

The curiously faceted Casa dos Bicos, and surrounding buildings

The façade of the Sé, the city's cathedral

❽ Sé

Largo da Sé. **Map** 8 D4.
Tel 218 866 752. 737. 12, 28.
Open 9am–7pm daily; cloister and
treasury: 10am–6:30pm Mon–Sat.
to Gothic cloister & treasury.

In 1150, three years after Afonso
Henriques recaptured Lisbon
from the Moors, he built a
cathedral for the first bishop
of Lisbon, the English crusader
Gilbert of Hastings, on the site
of the old mosque. Sé is short
for Sedes Episcopalis, the seat
(or see) of a bishop. Devasted
by three earth tremors in
the 14th century, as well as
the earthquake of 1755, and
renovated over the centuries,
the cathedral you see today
blends a variety of
architectural styles.
The façade, with
twin castellated
bell towers and
a splendid rose
window, retains its
solid Romanesque
aspect. The gloomy
interior, for the most
part, is simple and
austere, and hardly
anything remains of
the embellishment
lavished upon it by
King João V in the
first half of the 18th
century. Beyond the
Romanesque nave,
the ambulatory has
nine Gothic chapels.
The Capela de Santo
Ildefonso contains
the 14th-century sarcophagi
of Lopo Fernandes Pacheco,
companion in arms to King
Afonso IV, and his wife, Maria
Vilalobos. The bearded figure of
the nobleman, who is holding
a sword in his hand, and his
wife, clutching a prayer book,
are carved onto the tombs with
their dogs sitting faithfully at
their feet. In the adjacent

Tomb of the 14th-century nobleman Lopo Fernandes
Pacheco in the ambulatory

Detail of the Baroque Nativity scene by
Joaquim Machado de Castro

chancel are the tombs of Afonso
IV and his wife, Dona Beatriz.
The Gothic **cloister**,
reached via the third chapel
in the ambulatory, has elegant
double arches with some finely
carved capitals. One of the
chapels is still fitted with its
13th-century wrought-iron
gate. Ongoing archaeological
excavations in the cloister
have unearthed various
Roman, Moorish, Phoenician
and other remains.
To the left of the cathedral
entrance the Franciscan chapel
contains the font where
St Anthony was baptized in
1195 and is decorated
with a charming
tiled scene of him
preaching to the
fishes. The adjacent
chapel contains
a Baroque Nativity
scene made of cork,
wood and terracotta
by Machado de
Castro (1766).
The **treasury** is at the top
of the staircase on the right.
It houses silver, ecclesiastical
robes, statuary, illustrated
manuscripts and a few relics
associated with St Vincent
which were transferred to
Lisbon from Cape St Vincent
in southern Portugal in 1173.
Legend has it that two sacred
ravens kept a vigil over the
boat that transported the
relics. The ravens and the boat
became a symbol of the city
of Lisbon, still very much in
use today. It is also said that
the ravens' descendants
used to dwell in the cloisters
of the cathedral.

Santo Antonio (c.1195–1231)

To the chagrin of the Lisboetas, their best-loved saint is known
as St Anthony of Padua. Although born and brought up in Lisbon,
he spent the last months of his life in Padua, Italy.
St Anthony joined the Franciscan Order in 1220,
impressed by some crusading friars he had met at
Coimbra where he was studying. The Franciscan friar
was a learned and passionate preacher, renowned
for his devotion to the poor and his ability to
convert heretics. Many statues and paintings of
St Anthony depict him carrying the infant Jesus
on a book, while others show him preaching
to the fishes, as St Francis preached to the birds.
In 1934 Pope Pius XI declared St Anthony a patron
saint of Portugal. On 13 June, the anniversary
of his death, there are celebrations in the Alfama
district and a costumed procession along Avenida
da Liberdade.

❾ Santo António à Sé

Largo Santo António à Sé, 24.
Map 7 C4. **Tel** 218 869 145. 🚌 737.
🚋 12, 28. **Open** 8am–7pm daily (to
8pm Sat & Sun). 🏛 Museu Antoniano:
Tel 218 860 447. **Open** 10am–1pm,
2–6pm Tue–Sun. ♿

The popular little church of Santo António allegedly stands on the site of the house in which St Anthony was born. The crypt, reached via the tiled sacristy on the left of the church, is all that remains of the original church destroyed by the earthquake of 1755. Work began on the new church in 1757 headed by Mateus Vicente, architect of the Basílica da Estrela (see p57) and was partially funded by donations collected by local children with the cry "a small coin for St Anthony". Even today the floor of the tiny chapel in the crypt is strewn with euros and the walls are scrawled with devotional messages from worshippers.

The church's façade blends the undulating curves of the Baroque style with Neo-Classical Ionic columns on either side of the main portal. Inside, on the way down to the crypt, a modern *azulejo* panel commemorates the visit of Pope John Paul II in 1982. In 1995 the church was given a facelift for the saint's eighth centenary. It is traditional for young couples to visit the church on their wedding day

The Miradouro and Igreja da Graça seen from the Castelo de São Jorge

and leave flowers for St Anthony who is believed to bring good luck to new marriages.

Next door, the small **Museu Antoniano** houses artifacts relating to St Anthony as well as gold- and silverware which used to decorate the church. The most charming exhibit is a 17th-century tiled panel of St Anthony preaching to the fishes.

❿ Castelo de São Jorge

See pp40–41.

Tiled panel recording Pope John Paul II's visit to Santo António à Sé

⓫ Miradouro da Graça

Map 8 D2. 🚌 737. 🚋 12, 28.

The working-class quarter of Graça developed at the end of the 19th century. Today, it is visited chiefly for the views from its *miradouro* (belvedere). The panorama of rooftops and skyscrapers is less spectacular than the view from the castle, but it is a popular spot, particularly in the early evenings when couples sit at café tables under the pines. Behind the *miradouro* stands an Augustinian monastery, founded in 1271 and rebuilt after the earthquake. Once a flourishing complex, the huge building is nowadays used as barracks but the church, the **Igreja da Graça**, can still be visited. Inside, in the right transept, is the *Senhor dos Passos*, a representation of Christ carrying the cross on the way to Calvary. This figure, clad in brilliant purple clothes, is carried on a procession through Graça on the second Sunday in Lent. The *azulejos* on the altar front, dating from the 17th century, imitate the brocaded textiles usually draped over the altar.

⑩ Castelo de São Jorge

Following the recapture of Lisbon from the Moors in 1147, King Afonso Henriques transformed their hilltop citadel into the residence of the Portuguese kings. In 1511 Manuel I built a more lavish palace in what is now the Praça do Comércio and the castle was used variously as a theatre, prison and arms depot. After the 1755 earthquake the ramparts remained in ruins until 1938 when Salazar *(see p19)* began a complete renovation, rebuilding the "medieval" walls and adding gardens and wildfowl. The castle may not be authentic but the gardens and the narrow streets of the Santa Cruz district within the walls make a pleasant stroll and the views are the finest in Lisbon.

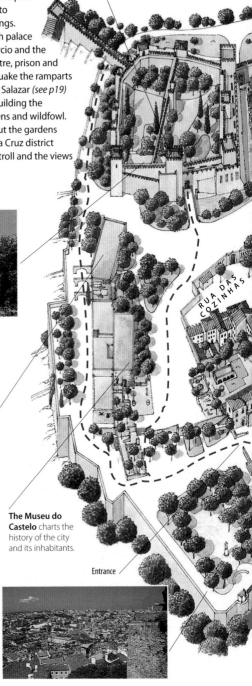

Torre de Ulisses has a camera obscura that projects views of Lisbon onto the inside walls of the tower.

RUA DAS COZINHAS

Entrance

★ Battlements
Visitors can climb the towers and walk along the reconstructed ramparts of the castle walls.

Casa do Leão Restaurant
Part of the former royal residence, it is now a restaurant with spectacular views (can be booked for evening meals only).

The Museu do Castelo charts the history of the city and its inhabitants.

Key

— Suggested route

★ Observation Terrace
This large shaded square affords spectacular views over Lisbon and the Tagus. Local men play backgammon and cards under the trees.

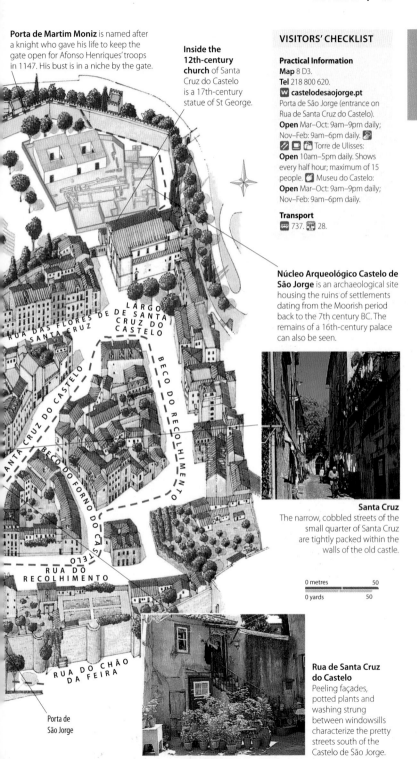

Porta de Martim Moniz is named after a knight who gave his life to keep the gate open for Afonso Henriques' troops in 1147. His bust is in a niche by the gate.

Inside the 12th-century church of Santa Cruz do Castelo is a 17th-century statue of St George.

VISITORS' CHECKLIST

Practical Information
Map 8 D3.
Tel 218 800 620.
🔲 castelodesaojorge.pt
Porta de São Jorge (entrance on Rua de Santa Cruz do Castelo).
Open Mar–Oct: 9am–9pm daily; Nov–Feb: 9am–6pm daily. 🅿️
🔲 🖥️ 🏠 Torre de Ulisses:
Open 10am–5pm daily. Shows every half hour; maximum of 15 people. 🎫 Museu do Castelo:
Open Mar–Oct: 9am–9pm daily; Nov–Feb: 9am–6pm daily.

Transport
🚌 737. 🚊 28.

Núcleo Arqueológico Castelo de São Jorge is an archaeological site housing the ruins of settlements dating from the Moorish period back to the 7th century BC. The remains of a 16th-century palace can also be seen.

RUA DAS FLORES DE SANTA CRUZ

LARGO DE SANTA CRUZ DO CASTELO

BECO DO RECOLHIMENTO

SANTA CRUZ DO CASTELO

BECO DO FORNO DO CASTELO

RUA DO RECOLHIMENTO

RUA DO CHÃO DA FEIRA

Porta de São Jorge

Santa Cruz
The narrow, cobbled streets of the small quarter of Santa Cruz are tightly packed within the walls of the old castle.

0 metres 50
0 yards 50

Rua de Santa Cruz do Castelo
Peeling façades, potted plants and washing strung between windowsills characterize the pretty streets south of the Castelo de São Jorge.

BAIXA AND AVENIDA

From the ruins of Lisbon, devastated by the earthquake of 1755 *(see pp24–5)*, the Marquês de Pombal created an entirely new centre. Using a grid layout of streets, he linked Praça do Comércio with the busy central square of Rossio. The streets were flanked by uniform, Neo-Classical buildings and named according to the shopkeepers and craftsmen who traded there. The Arco da Rua Augusta was built 80 years later.

The Baixa (lower town) is still the commercial hub of the capital, housing banks, offices and shops. At its centre, Rossio is a popular meeting point with cafés, theatres and restaurants. The geometric layout of the area has been retained, but most buildings constructed since the mid-18th century have not adhered to Pombaline formality. The streets are usually crowded, particularly the lively Rua Augusta, which serves as a thoroughfare to the Praça do Comércio and its numerous bars, restaurants and clubs.

Sights at a Glance

Museums and Galleries
4 Museu da Sociedade de Geografia

Churches
9 Nossa Senhora da Conceição Velha

Parks and Gardens
1 Jardim Botânico

Lifts
7 Elevador de Santa Justa

Historic Streets and Squares
2 Avenida da Liberdade
3 Praça dos Restauradores
5 Rossio
6 Praça da Figueira
8 Rua Augusta
10 Praça do Comércio

Restaurants *pp130–31*
1 Can the Can
2 Casa do Alentejo
3 Gambrinus
4 Marisqueira Santa Marta
5 Os Tibetanos
6 Restaurante 33A
7 Ribadouro
8 Solar dos Presuntos

See Lisbon Street Finder maps 7–8

0 metres 250
0 yards 250

◀ The Elevador de Santa Justa, a major tourist attraction in Lisbon

For keys to symbols *see back flap*

Street-by-Street: Restauradores

This is the busiest part of the city, especially the central squares of Rossio and Praça da Figueira. Totally rebuilt after the earthquake of 1755 *(see pp24–5)*, the area was one of Europe's first examples of town planning. Today, the large Neo-Classical buildings on the wide streets and squares house business offices. The atmosphere and surroundings are best absorbed from one of the busy pavement cafés. Rua das Portas de Santo Antão, a pedestrianized street where restaurants display tanks of live lobsters, is more relaxing for a stroll.

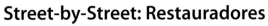

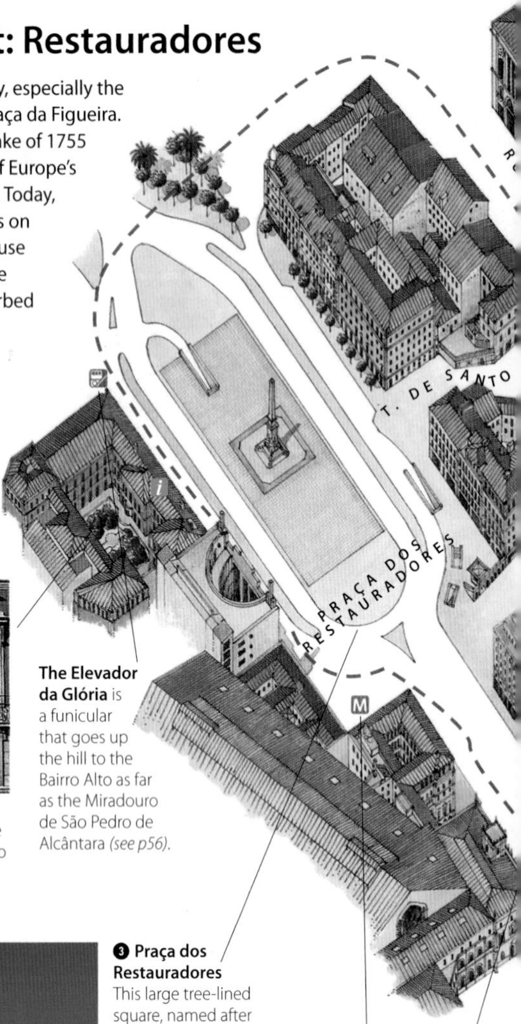

Palácio Foz
This magnificent 18th-century palace built by the Italian architect Francesco Fabri now houses a tourist office.

The Elevador da Glória is a funicular that goes up the hill to the Bairro Alto as far as the Miradouro de São Pedro de Alcântara *(see p56)*.

❸ Praça dos Restauradores
This large tree-lined square, named after the men who gave their lives during the War of Restoration, is a busy through road with café terraces on the patterned pavements.

Restauradores

Rossio station, designed by José Luís Monteiro, is an eye-catching late 19th-century Neo-Manueline building with two Moorish-style horseshoe arches

Key

— Suggested route

0 metres   50

0 yards   50

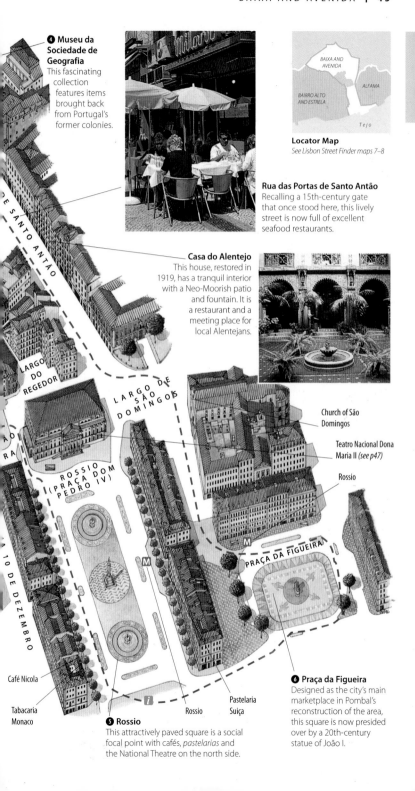

4 Museu da Sociedade de Geografia
This fascinating collection features items brought back from Portugal's former colonies.

Locator Map
See Lisbon Street Finder maps 7–8

Rua das Portas de Santo Antão
Recalling a 15th-century gate that once stood here, this lively street is now full of excellent seafood restaurants.

Casa do Alentejo
This house, restored in 1919, has a tranquil interior with a Neo-Moorish patio and fountain. It is a restaurant and a meeting place for local Alentejans.

Church of São Domingos

Teatro Nacional Dona Maria II *(see p47)*

Rossio

6 Praça da Figueira
Designed as the city's main marketplace in Pombal's reconstruction of the area, this square is now presided over by a 20th-century statue of João I.

5 Rossio
This attractively paved square is a social focal point with cafés, *pastelarias* and the National Theatre on the north side.

Pastelaria Suiça

Rossio

Café Nicola

Tabacaria Monaco

Bridge and pond shaded by trees in the Jardim Botânico

❶ Jardim Botânico

Rua da Escola Politécnica 58–60.
Map 4 F1. **Tel** 213 921 800. 🚍 758.
Ⓜ Rato. Gardens: **Open** 9am–8pm
daily (Nov–Mar: to 6pm). **Closed** 1 Jan,
25 Dec. 🐾 ♿ MUHNAC: **Open** 10am–
7pm Tue–Fri, 11am–6pm Sat &
Sun. **Closed** public hols. 🐾
Ⓦ mnhnc.ulisboa.pt

This complex comprises a museum and four hectares (10 acres) of gardens. The botanical gardens have a distinct air of neglect. However, it is worth paying the entrance fee to wander among the exotic trees and dense paths as the gardens descend from the main entrance towards Rua da Alegria. A magnificent avenue of lofty palms connects the two levels.

The **Museu Nacional de História Natural e da Ciência** or MUHNAC (National Museum of Natural History and Science) has collections on botany, zoology, anthropology, geology and palaeontology, as well as hosting temporary exhibitions on themes such as dinosaurs and local minerals. The museum also exhibits scientific instruments dating from the 16th to the 20th century and holds programmes that demonstrate basic scientific principles and are popular with school children.

❷ Avenida da Liberdade

Map 7 A2. 🚍 709, 711, 736 & many
other routes. Ⓜ Restauradores,
Avenida.

After the earthquake of 1755 (see pp24–5), the Marquês de Pombal created the Passeio Público (public promenade) in the area now occupied by the lower part of Avenida da Liberdade and Praça dos Restauradores. Despite its name, enjoyment of the park was restricted to Lisbon's high society and walls and gates ensured the exclusion of the lower classes. In 1821, when the Liberals came to power, the barriers were pulled down and the Avenida and square became open to all.

The boulevard you see today was built in 1879–82 in the style of the Champs-Elysées in Paris. The wide tree-lined avenue became a focus for pageants, festivities and demonstrations. A war memorial stands as a tribute to those who died in World War I. The avenue still retains a certain elegance with fountains and café tables shaded by trees; however, it no longer makes for a peaceful stroll. The once majestic thoroughfare, 90 m (295 ft) wide and decorated with abstract pavement patterns, is now divided by seven lanes of traffic linking Praça dos Restauradores and Praça Marquês de Pombal to the north. Some of the original mansions have been preserved, including the Neo-Classical Tivoli cinema at No. 188, with an original 1920s kiosk outside, and Casa Lambertini with its colourful mosaic decoration at No. 166. However, many of the Art Nouveau façades have given

19th-century monument in honour of the Restoration in Praça dos Restauradores

way to modern ones occupied by offices, hotels or shopping complexes.

❸ Praça dos Restauradores

Map 7 A2. 🚍 709, 711, 736 & many
other routes. Ⓜ Restauradores.

The square, distinguished by its soaring obelisk, erected in 1886, commemorates Portugal's liberation from the Spanish yoke in 1640. The bronze figures on the pedestal depict Victory, holding a palm and a crown, and Freedom. The names and dates that are inscribed on the sides of the obelisk are those of the battles of the War of Restoration.

On the west side, the Palácio Foz now houses a small tourist and other offices. It was built by Francesco Savario Fabri in 1755–77 for the Marquês de Castelo-Melhor and renamed after the Marquês de Foz, who lived here in the 19th century. The smart Avenida Palace Hotel, on the southwest side of the square, was designed by José Lúis Monteiro (1849–1942), who also built Rossio railway station (see p44).

Detail from the memorial to the dead of World War I in Avenida da Liberdade

❹ Museu da Sociedade de Geografia

Rua das Portas de Santo Antão 100.
Map 7 A2. **Tel** 213 425 401. 🚌 709,
711, 736. Ⓜ Restauradores.
🎥 compulsory, 3pm Tue &
by appointment. 🖥 ♿

Located in the Geographical
Society building, the museum
houses an idiosyncratic
ethnographical collection
brought back from Portugal's
former colonies. On display are
circumcision masks from Guinea
Bissau, musical instruments
and snake spears. From Angola
there are neckrests to sustain
coiffures and the original
padrão – the stone pillar erected
by the Portuguese in 1482
to mark their sovereignty over
the colony. Most of the exhibits
are arranged along the splendid
Sala Portugal.

❺ Rossio

Map 6 B3. 🚌 711, 732, 736, 759 &
many other routes. Ⓜ Rossio.

Formally called Praça de Dom
Pedro IV, this large square has
been Lisbon's nerve centre for
six centuries. During its history it
has been the stage of bullfights,
festivals, military parades and
the burning of heretics during
the Inquisition *(see p18)*. Today
there is little more than an
occasional political rally, and
the sober Pombaline buildings,

Teatro Nacional Dona Maria II in Rossio illuminated by night

disfigured on the upper level
by neon signs, are occupied at
street level by souvenir shops
and cafés. Centre stage is a
statue of Dom Pedro IV, the first
emperor of independent Brazil.
At the foot of the statue, the
four female figures are allegories
of Justice, Wisdom, Strength
and Moderation.

In the mid-19th century the
square was paved with wave-
patterned mosaics which gave
it the nickname of "Rolling
Motion Square". The hand-cut
grey and white stone cubes
were the first such designs to
decorate the city's pavements.
Today, only a small central
section of the design survives.

On the north side of Rossio is
the Teatro Nacional Dona Maria II,
named after Dom Pedro's

daughter. The Neo-Classical
structure was built in the
1840s by the Italian architect
Fortunato Lodi. The interior was
destroyed by fire in 1964 and
reconstructed in the 1970s.
On top of the pediment is
Gil Vicente (1465–1536), the
founder of Portuguese theatre.

Café Nicola, on the west side
of the square, was a favourite
meeting place among writers,
including the poet Manuel
du Bocage (1765–1805), who
was notorious for his satires.
Pastelaria Suiça, on the opposite
side, is popular with tourists
for its sunlit terrace.

❻ Praça da Figueira

Map 6 B3. 🚌 714, 759, 760 & many
other routes. 🚋 12, 15. Ⓜ Rossio.

Before the 1755 earthquake
(see pp24–5), the square next
to Rossio was the site of the
Hospital de Todos-os-Santos
(All Saints). In Pombal's new
design for the Baixa, the square
took on the role of the city's
central marketplace. In 1885 a
covered market was built, but
this was pulled down in the
1950s. Today, the four-storey
buildings are given over to
hotels, shops and cafés and the
square is no longer a marketplace. Perhaps its most eye-
catching feature is the multitude
of pigeons that perch on the
pedestal supporting Leopoldo
de Almeida's bronze equestrian
statue of João I, erected in 1971.

Bronze statue of King João I in Praça da Figueira

❼ Elevador de Santa Justa

Rua de Santa Justa & Largo do Carmo.
Map 7 B3. **Tel** 213 613 000. **Open** 7am–10pm daily (May–Sep: to 11pm). 🦽

Also known as the Elevador do Carmo, this Neo-Gothic lift was built at the turn of the 20th century by the French architect Raoul Mesnier du Ponsard, an apprentice of Alexandre Gustave Eiffel. Made of iron and embellished with filigree, it is one of the more eccentric features of the Baixa. The ticket office is located at the foot of the elevator.

Passengers can travel up and down inside the tower in one of two smart wood-panelled cabins with brass fittings; at the top of the elevator is a walkway, linking it to the Largo do Carmo in the Bairro Alto, 32 m (105 ft) above.

The very top of the tower, reached via an extremely tight spiral stairway, is given over to a viewing point. This high vantage point commands splendid views of Rossio, the Baixa, the castle on the opposite hill, the river and

View of the Elevador de Santa Justa

the nearby ruins of the Carmo church. The fire that gutted the Chiado district (*see p54*) was extinguished close to the lift.

❽ Rua Augusta

Map 7 B4. 🚌 711, 714, 732, 736, 759 & many other routes. Ⓜ Rossio. MUDE: Rua Augusta 24. **Tel** 218 886 117 or 218 171 892. **Open** 10am–6pm Tue–Sun. **Closed** 1 Jan, 25 Dec. 🆆 mude.pt

A lively pedestrianized street decorated with mosaic pavements and lined with boutiques and open-air cafés, Rua Augusta is the main tourist thoroughfare and the smartest street in the Baixa. Performers provide entertainment, while vendors sell lottery tickets, street art, books and souvenirs. The triumphal Arco da Rua Augusta (*see opposite*) frames the equestrian statue of José I in Praça do Comércio. Designed by the architect Santos de Carvalho to commemorate the city's recovery from the earthquake (*see pp24–5*), the arch was completed only in 1873. The **Museu do Design e da Moda (MUDE)** has an impressive collection of 20th-century design and fashion pieces from around the world.

The other main thoroughfares of the Baixa are Rua da Prata (silversmiths' street) and Rua do Ouro or Rua Aurea (goldsmiths' street). Cutting across these main streets full of shops and banks are smaller streets that give glimpses up to the Bairro Alto to the west and the Castelo de São Jorge (*see pp40–41*) to the east. Many of the streets retain shops that gave them their name: there are jewellers in Rua da Prata and Rua do Ouro and banks in Rua do Comércio.

The most incongruous sight in the heart of the Baixa is a small section of the Roman baths, located within the Banco Comercial Português in Rua dos Correeiros. The ruins and mosaics can be seen from the street window at the rear side of the bank; alternatively you can book ahead to visit the "museum" on 211 131 681.

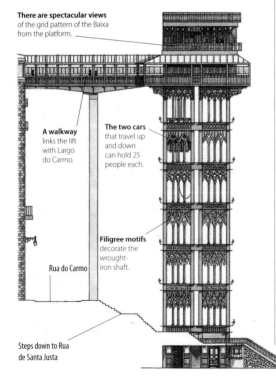

There are spectacular views of the grid pattern of the Baixa from the platform.

A walkway links the lift with Largo do Carmo.

The two cars that travel up and down can hold 25 people each.

Filigree motifs decorate the wrought-iron shaft.

Rua do Carmo

Steps down to Rua de Santa Justa

❾ Nossa Senhora da Conceição Velha

Rua da Alfândega. **Map** 7 C4.
Tel 218 870 202. 🚌 759, 794.
🚊 18. **Open** 9am–5pm Mon–Fri,
10am–2pm Sun. ✝ ♿

The elaborate Manueline doorway of the church is the only feature that has survived from the original 16th-century Nossa Senhora da Misericórdia, which stood here until the 1755 earthquake. The portal is decorated with a profusion of Manueline detail, including angels, beasts, flowers, armillary spheres and the cross of the Order of Christ. In the tympanum, the Virgin Mary spreads her protective mantle over various contemporary figures. These include Pope Leo X, Manuel I and his sister, Queen Leonor, widow of João II. It was Leonor who founded the original Misericórdia (alms house) on the site of a former synagogue.

Enjoyment of the portal is hampered by the constant stream of traffic along Rua da Alfândega and the cars parked right in front of the church. The interior has an unusual stucco ceiling; in the second chapel on the right is a statue of Our Lady of Restelo. This came from the Belém chapel where navigators prayed before embarking on their historic voyages east.

❿ Praça do Comércio

Map 7 C5. 🚌 711, 714, 759, 794 &
many other routes. 🚊 15, 18, 25. Arco
da Rua Augusta: Rua Augusta 2–10.
Open 9am–7pm daily. 🎫 Lisbon
Story Centre: Terreiro do Paço 78–81.
Tel 211 941 099. **Open** 10am–8pm
daily. 🎫 (combined ticket for arch &
museum.) 🌐 **lisboastorycentre.pt**

More commonly known by the locals as *Terreiro do Paço* (Palace Square), this huge open space was the site of the royal palace for 400 years. Manuel I transferred the royal residence from Castelo de São Jorge to this more convenient location by the river in 1511. The first palace, along with its library and 70,000 books, was destroyed in the 1755 earthquake. In rebuilding the city, the square became the *pièce de résistance* of Pombal's Baixa design. The new palace occupied spacious arcaded buildings extending around three sides of the square. After the 1910 revolution *(see p19)*, these were converted into government administrative offices and painted Republican pink. They have since been re-painted royal yellow.

The south side, graced by two square towers, looks across the wide expanse of the Tagus. This has ever been the finest gateway to Lisbon: royalty and ambassadors would alight and take the marble steps up from the river. Parts of the busy Avenida Infante Dom Henrique, which runs along the waterfront, are lined with restaurants and bars. Leading off the south side of the square, the Ribeiras das Naus promenade provides a pleasant waterside pathway for pedestrians and cyclists heading towards Cais do Sodré, from where ferries to Cacilhas depart. In the centre of Praça do Comércio is the equestrian statue of King José I erected in 1775 by Machado de Castro, the leading Portuguese sculptor of the 18th century. The bronze horse, depicted trampling on serpents, earned the square its third name of "Black Horse Square", used by English travellers and merchants. Over the years, however, the horse has acquired a green patina.

The impressive **Arco da Rua Augusta** on the north side of the square leads to Rua Augusta and is the gateway to the Baixa. An elevator ride to the top affords unparalleled views

Shaded arcades along the north side of Praça do Comércio

of Praça do Comércio and the Tagus river basin. In the northwest of the square, the Lisboa Welcome Centre has a tourist information service, gallery, restaurants and shops. In the opposite corner is Lisbon's oldest café, the Martinho da Arcada, formerly a haunt of the city's literati.

Located on the east side of the square, the **Lisbon Story Centre** is an interactive museum that highlights the many important events that have shaped the history of the city over the centuries.

On 1 February 1908, King Carlos and his son Luís Felipe were assassinated as they were passing through the square. In 1974 the square saw the first uprising of the Armed Forces Movement which overthrew the Caetano regime in a bloodless revolution *(see p19)*. Today the vast open space is used for cultural events and festivals.

Statue of King José I in Praça do Comércio

BAIRRO ALTO AND ESTRELA

Laid out in a grid pattern in the late 16th century, the hilltop Bairro Alto is one of the most picturesque districts of the city. First settled by rich citizens who moved out of the disreputable Alfama, by the 19th century it had become a run-down area frequented by prostitutes. Today, its small workshops and family-run *tascas* (cheap restaurants) exist alongside a thriving nightlife.

Very different in character to the heart of the Bairro Alto is the elegant commercial district known as the Chiado, where affluent Lisboetas do their shopping. To the northwest, the Estrela quarter is centred on the huge domed basilica and popular gardens. The mid-18th century district of Lapa, to the southwest, is home to foreign embassies and large, smart residences.

Sights at a Glance

Museums and Galleries

5 Museu Nacional de Arte Contemporânea do Chiado
6 Museu da Marioneta
11 *Museu Nacional de Arte Antiga pp58–61*

See Lisbon Street Finder maps 4 & 7–8

Churches

1 São Roque
2 Igreja do Carmo
13 Basílica da Estrela

Historic Buildings and Districts

3 Chiado
4 Teatro Nacional de São Carlos (Opera)
7 Solar do Vinho do Porto
10 Palácio de São Bento

Gardens and Belvederes

8 Miradouro de São Pedro de Alcântara
9 Praça do Príncipe Real
12 Jardim da Estrela

☐ Restaurants *pp131–2*

1 Belcanto
2 Bistro 100 Maneiras
3 Bota Alta
4 Café Buenos Aires
5 Café Fábulas
6 Cantinho Lusitano
7 Casanostra
8 Clube de Jornalistas
9 Decadente
10 Flor da Laranja
11 Grapes and Bites
12 Kais
13 La Brasserie de l'Entrecôte
14 Madragoa Café
15 Pap'Açorda
16 Pátio do Bairro
17 Picanha
18 Real Fábrica
19 Restaurante Lapa
20 Sea Me
21 Taberna Ideal
22 Trivial
23 Xapuri

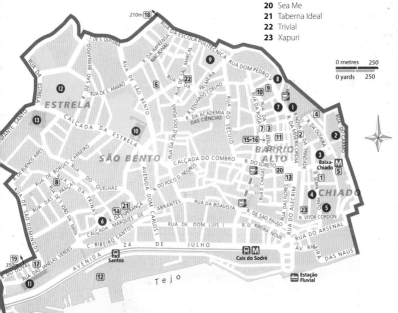

◄ Ruins of the Carmo church, which was destroyed in the earthquake of 1755

For keys to symbols *see back flap*

Street-by-Street: Bairro Alto and Chiado

The Bairro Alto (high quarter) is a fascinating area of cobbled streets adjacent to the Carmo and Chiado areas. Since the 1980s, this has been Lisbon's best-known nightlife zone, with countless small bars and restaurants alongside the older *casas de fado*. Much restoration work has taken place over the last few years, and many modern buildings now stand alongside old, peeling houses and tiny grocery shops. In contrast, the Chiado is an area of elegant shops and old-style cafés that extends down from Praça Luís de Camões towards Rua do Carmo and the Baixa. Major renovation work has taken place since a fire in 1988 *(see p54)* destroyed many of the buildings.

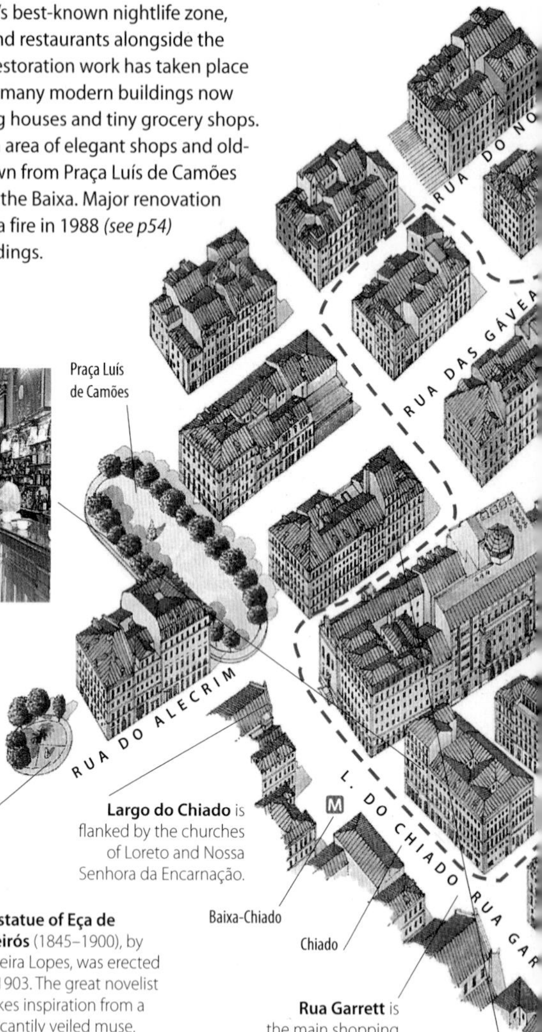

Praça Luís de Camões

Once a haunt of writers and intellectuals, Chiado is now an elegant shopping district. The A Brasileira café, on Largo do Chiado, is adorned with gilded mirrors.

RUA DO ALECRIM

Largo do Chiado is flanked by the churches of Loreto and Nossa Senhora da Encarnação.

Baixa-Chiado

Chiado

The statue of Eça de Queirós (1845–1900), by Teixeira Lopes, was erected in 1903. The great novelist takes inspiration from a scantily veiled muse.

Rua Garrett is the main shopping street of the Chiado.

Key

— Suggested route

Tavares, at No. 37 Rua da Misericórdia, first opened as a café in 1784. Today it is an elegant restaurant decorated at the turn of the 20th century with mirrors and elaborate stucco designs.

Elevador da Glória

The Museu de São Roque has an interesting exhibition of religious artifacts and explains the history of the treasures in the church of São Roque next door.

Locator Map
See Lisbon Street Finder maps 4 & 7–8

Cervejaria Trindade is a popular beer hall and restaurant decorated with *azulejo* panels.

❶ ★ São Roque
Opulent mosaics and semiprecious stones adorn the Baroque Capela de São João inside the 16th-century church of São Roque.

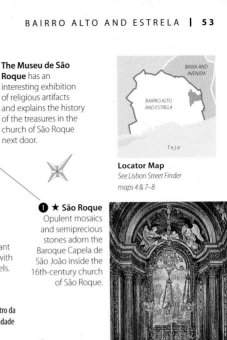

Teatro da Trindade

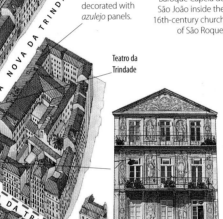

The tile decoration
on the façade of this house, erected in 1864 on Largo Rafael Bordalo Pinheiro, features allegorical figures of Science, Agriculture, Industry and Commerce.

❷ ★ Igreja do Carmo
The graceful skeletal arches of this Carmelite church, once the largest in Lisbon, stand as a reminder of the earthquake of 1755. The chancel and main body of the church house an archaeological museum.

Elevador de Santa Justa offers direct access from the Baixa to the Bairro Alto district.

The shops in Rua do Carmo have been restored and renewed after the devastating fire in 1988 *(see p54)*.

0 metres		50
0 yards		50

Ruins of the 14th-century Igreja do Carmo seen from the Baixa

❶ São Roque

Largo Trindade Coelho. **Map** 7 A3.
Tel 213 235 383. 🚌 758. **Open** 9am–
6pm daily (from 2pm Mon, to 7pm
summer). **Closed** public hols.
🏛 Museu de São Roque: **Tel** 213
235 380. **Open** 10am–6pm daily
(from 2pm Mon, to 7pm summer).
Closed public hols. 📷

São Roque's plain façade belies
a remarkably rich interior. The
church was founded at the
end of the 16th century by
the Jesuit Order, then at the
peak of its power. In 1742 the
Chapel of St John the
Baptist (last on the left)
was commissioned by
the prodigal João V
from the Italian
architects Luigi
Vanvitelli and Nicola
Salvi. Constructed
in Rome and
embellished with lapis
lazuli, agate, alabaster,
amethyst, precious
marbles, gold, silver
and mosaics, the chapel was
given the Pope's blessing in
the church of Sant'Antonio
dei Portoghesi in Rome,
dismantled and sent to
Lisbon in three ships.

Among the many tiles in the
church, the oldest and most
interesting are those in the third
chapel on the right, dating from
the mid-16th century and
dedicated to São Roque
(St Roch), protector against
the plague. Other features
of the church are the scenes of
the Apocalypse painted on the
ceiling, and the sacristy with
its coffered ceiling, as well as
painted panels of the life of

Tile detail, Chapel of
São Roque.

St Francis Xavier, the 16th-
century missionary. Treasures
from the Chapel of St John the
Baptist, including the silver and
lapis lazuli altar front, are in the
adjoining **Museu de São Roque**.

❷ Igreja do Carmo

Largo do Carmo. **Map** 7 B3. **Tel** 213
460 473. 🚌 758. 🚋 28. Ⓜ Baixa-
Chiado. 🏛 Igreja do Carmo & Museu
do Carmo: **Open** 10am–6pm Tue–Sat
(to 7pm Jun–Sep). **Closed** 1 Jan,
1 May, 25 Dec. 📷

The Gothic ruins of this
Carmelite church, built
on a slope overlooking
the Baixa, are evocative
reminders of the
devastation left by
the earthquake of 1755.
As the congregation
was attending Mass
the shockwaves caused
the church to collapse,
depositing tons of
masonry on to the people
below. Founded in the late 14th
century by Nuno Álvares Pereira,
the commander who became
a member of the Carmelite
Order, the church was at one
time the biggest in Lisbon.

Nowadays the main body
of the church and the chancel,
whose roof withstood the
earthquake, houses the
Museu do Carmo with
a small, heterogeneous
collection of sarcophagi,
statuary, ceramics and mosaics.

Among the more ancient
finds from Europe are a remnant
from a Visigothic pillar and a
Roman tomb carved with reliefs
depicting the Muses. There are
also impressive finds from
Mexico and South America,
including ancient mummies.

Outside the ruins, in the Largo
do Carmo, stands the Chafariz
do Carmo, an 18th-century
fountain designed by Ângelo
Belasco, elaborately decorated
with four dolphins.

❸ Chiado

Map 7 A4. 🚌 758. 🚋 28.
Ⓜ Baixa-Chiado.

Hypotheses abound for the
origin of the word Chiado, in
use since 1567. One of the
most interesting recalls the
creak *(chiar)* of the wheels of
the carts as they negotiated
the area's steep slopes.
A second theory refers to
the nickname given to the

The Chiado Fire

On 25 August 1988 a disastrous
fire began in a store in Rua do
Carmo, the street that links the
Baixa with the Bairro Alto. Fire
engines were unable to enter this
pedestrianized street and the fire
spread into Rua Garrett. Along
with shops and offices, many
important 18th-century
buildings were destroyed, the
worst damage being in Rua do
Carmo. The renovation project,
which is now complete, has
preserved many original
façades, and was headed by
the Portuguese architect
Álvaro Siza Vieira.

Firemen attending the raging fire
in Rua do Carmo

Stalls and circle of the 18th-century Teatro Nacional de São Carlos

16th-century poet António Ribeiro, "O Chiado". An area traditionally known for its intellectual associations, various statues of literary figures can be found here. Fernando Pessoa, Portugal's most famous 20th-century poet, is seated at a table outside the A Brasileira. Established in the 1920s, this was a favourite rendezvous of intellectuals.

The name Chiado is often used to mean just Rua Garrett, the main shopping street of the area, named after the author and poet João Almeida Garrett (1799–1854). This elegant street, which descends from Largo do Chiado towards the Baixa, is known for its clothes shops, cafés and bookshops. Devastated by fire in 1988, the former elegance of this quarter has now been restored.

On Largo do Chiado stand two Baroque churches: the Italian church, Igreja do Loreto, on the north side and opposite, Nossa Senhora da Encarnação, whose exterior walls are partly decorated with *azulejos*.

❹ Teatro Nacional de São Carlos

Rua Serpa Pinto 9. **Map** 7 A4. **Tel** 213 253 000. 🚌 758, 790. 🚃 28. Ⓜ Baixa-Chiado. **Open** 10:30am–6:30pm daily (to 4:30pm Sat & Sun). 🅿 Ⓦ **tnsc.pt**

Replacing a former opera house which was ruined by the earthquake of 1755, the Teatro de São Carlos was built in 1792–5 by José da Costa e Silva. Designed on the lines of La Scala in Milan, the building has a beautifully proportioned façade and an enchanting Rococo interior. Views of the exterior, however, are spoiled by the car park, invariably crammed, which occupies the square in front. The opera season lasts from September to June, but concerts and ballets are also staged here at other times of the year.

❺ Museu Nacional de Arte Contemporânea do Chiado

Rua Serpa Pinto 4–6. **Map** 7 A5. **Tel** 213 432 148. 🚌 758, 790. 🚃 28. Ⓜ Baixa-Chiado. **Open** 10am–6pm Tue–Sun. **Closed** 1 Jan, Easter, 1 May, 25 Dec. 🅿 Ⓦ **museuartecontem poranea.pt**

The National Museum of Contemporary Art, whose collection of 1850–1950 paintings could no longer be described as contemporary, moved to a stylishly restored warehouse in 1994 and started expanding its collection to the present day. The paintings and sculpture are arranged over three floors in 12 rooms. Each room has a different theme illustrating the development

from Romanticism to Modernism. The majority are Portuguese works, often showing a marked influence from other European countries. This is particularly noticeable in the 19th-century landscape painters who had contact with artists from the French Barbizon School. The few international works of art on display include a collection of drawings by Rodin (1840–1917) and some French sculpture from the late 19th century. There are also temporary exhibitions which are held for "very new artists, preferably inspired by the permanent collection".

Grotesque puppet in Museu da Marioneta

❻ Museu da Marioneta

Convento das Bernardas, Rua da Esperança 146. **Map** 4 D3. **Tel** 213 942 810. 🚌 713, 727, 760. 🚃 15, 25. Ⓜ Cais do Sodré. 🚊 Santos. **Open** 10am–1pm, 2–5:30pm Tue–Sun. **Closed** 1 Jan, 1 May, 24 & 25 Dec. 🅿 Ⓦ **museudamarioneta.pt**

This small puppet museum, housed in an elegantly refurbished convent building, includes characters from 17th- and 18th-century theatre and opera, including jesters, devils, knights and satirical figures. Many of the puppets possess gruesome, contorted features that are unlikely to appeal to small children. The museum explains the history of the art form and runs videos of puppet shows. Phone ahead to see if a live performance is being held on the small stage. There is also a space for pedagogical activities.

The popular A Brasileira café, in the Chiado

The wide selection of port at the Solar do Vinho do Porto

❼ Solar do Vinho do Porto

Rua de São Pedro de Alcântara 45. **Map** 4 F2. **Tel** 213 475 707. 758. 28, Elevador da Glória. **Open** 11am–midnight Mon–Fri, 2pm–midnight Sat. **Closed** public hols.

The Portuguese word *solar* means mansion or manor house, and the Solar do Vinho do Porto occupies the ground floor of an 18th-century mansion. The building was once owned by the German architect Johann Friedrich Ludwig (Ludovice), who built the monastery at Mafra *(see p98)*. The port wine institute of Oporto runs a pleasant if dated bar in the mansion's stylish interior for the promotion of port. Nearly 200 types of port are listed in the lengthy drinks menu, with every producer represented and including some rarities. Unfortunately, many of the listed wines are often unavailable. All but the vintage ports are sold by the glass, with prices ranging from 1 euro for the simplest ruby to €70 for a glass of 40-year-old tawny.

❽ Miradouro de São Pedro de Alcântara

Rua de São Pedro de Alcântara. **Map** 7 A2. 758. 28.

This belvedere *(miradouro)* commands a sweeping view of eastern Lisbon, across the Baixa. A tiled map, conveniently placed against the balustrade, helps you locate the landmarks in the city below. The panorama extends from the battlements of the Castelo de São Jorge *(see pp40–41)*, clearly seen surrounded by trees on the hill to the southeast, to the 18th-century church of Penha da França in the northwest. The large monastery complex of the Igreja da Graça *(see p39)* is also visible on the hill, and in the distance São Vicente de Fora *(see p36)* is recognizable by the symmetrical towers that flank its white façade.

Benches and ample shade from the trees make this terrace a pleasant stop after the steep walk up Calçada da Glória from the Baixa. Alternatively, the yellow funicular, Elevador da Glória, will drop you off nearby.

The memorial in the garden, erected in 1904, depicts Eduardo Coelho (1835–89), founder of the newspaper *Diário de Notícias*, and below him a ragged paper boy running with copies of the famous daily. This area was once the centre of the newspaper industry; however, the modern printing presses

have now moved to more spacious premises west of the city.

The view is most attractive at sunset and by night when the castle is floodlit and the terrace becomes a popular meeting point for young Lisboetas.

Playing cards under the shade in Praça do Príncipe Real

❾ Praça do Príncipe Real

Map 4 F1. 758.

Laid out in 1860 as a prime residential quarter, the square still retains an air of affluence. Smartly painted mansions surround a particularly pleasant park with an open-air café, statuary and some splendid robinia, magnolia and Judas trees. The branches of a huge cedar tree have been trained on a trellis, creating a wide shady spot for the locals who play cards beneath it. On the large square, at No. 26, the eye-catching pink-and-white Neo-Moorish building with domes and pinnacles is part of Lisbon university.

View across the city to Castelo de São Jorge from Miradouro de São Pedro de Alcântara

Attractive wrought-iron music pavilion in Jardim da Estrela

⓾ Palácio de São Bento

Largo das Cortes, Rua de São Bento. **Map** 4 E2. **Tel** 213 919 000. 🚌 790. 🚊 28. **Open** by appt only. 🎫 last Sat of the month, at 3pm & 4pm; call 213 919 446. 🌐 **parlamento.pt**

Also known as the Assembleia da República, this massive white Neo-Classical building started life in the late 1500s as the Benedictine monastery of São Bento. After the dissolution of the religious orders in 1834, the building became the seat of the Portuguese Parliament, known as the Palácio das Cortes. The interior is suitably grandiose with marble pillars and Neo-Classical statues.

⓫ Museu Nacional de Arte Antiga

See pp58–61.

⓬ Jardim da Estrela

Praça da Estrela. **Map** 4 D2. 🚌 720, 738. 🚊 25, 28. Ⓜ Rato. **Open** 7am–midnight daily.

Laid out in the middle of the 19th century, opposite the Basílica da Estrela, the popular gardens are a focal part of the Estrela quarter. Local families congregate here at weekends to feed the ducks and carp in the lake, sit at the waterside café or wander among the flower beds, plants and trees. The formal gardens are planted with herbaceous borders and shrubs surrounding plane trees and elms. The central feature of the park is a green wrought-iron bandstand, decorated with elegant filigree, where musicians strike up in the summer months. This was built in 1884 and originally stood on the Passeio Público, before the creation of Avenida da Liberdade (see p46).

The English Cemetery to the north of the gardens is best known as the burial place of Henry Fielding (1707–54), the English novelist and playwright who died in Lisbon at the age of 47. The *Journal of a Voyage to Lisbon*, published posthumously in 1775, recounts his last voyage to Portugal, made in a fruitless attempt to recover his failing health.

The tomb of the pious Maria I in the Basílica da Estrela

⓭ Basílica da Estrela

Praça da Estrela. **Map** 4 D2. **Tel** 213 960 915. 🚌 720, 738. 🚊 25, 28. **Open** 7:45am–1pm, 3–8pm daily (large groups by appointment). ♿

In the second half of the 18th century Maria I (see p111), daughter of José I, vowed she would build a church if she bore a son and heir to the throne. Her wish was granted and construction of the basilica began in 1779. Her son José, however, died of smallpox two years before the completion of the church in 1790. The huge domed basilica, set on a hill in the west of the city, is one of Lisbon's great landmarks. A simpler version of the basilica at Mafra (see p98), this church was built by architects from the Mafra School in late Baroque and Neo-Classical style. The façade is flanked by twin bell towers and decorated with an array of statues of saints and allegorical figures.

The spacious, somewhat awe-inspiring interior, where light streams down from the pierced dome, is clad in grey, pink and yellow marble. The elaborate Empire-style tomb of Queen Maria I, who died in Brazil, lies in the right transept. Locked in a room nearby is Machado de Castro's extraordinary Nativity scene, composed of over 500 cork and terracotta figures. (To see it, ask the sacristan.)

Neo-Classical façade and stairway of Palácio de São Bento

❶ Museu Nacional de Arte Antiga

Portugal's national art collection is housed in a 17th-century palace that was built for the counts of Alvor. In 1770 it was acquired by the Marquês de Pombal and remained in the possession of his family for over a century. Inaugurated in 1884, the museum is known to locals as the Museu das Janelas Verdes, referring to the former green windows of the palace. In 1940 a modern annexe (including the main façade) was added. This was built on the site of the St Albert Carmelite monastery, which was partially demolished between 1910 and 1920. The only surviving feature was the chapel, now integrated into the museum.

★ St Jerome
This masterly portrayal of old age by Albrecht Dürer expresses one of the central dilemmas of Renaissance humanism: the ephemeral nature of man (1521).

Gallery Guide

The ground floor contains 14th–19th-century European paintings as well as some decorative arts and furniture. Oriental and African art, Chinese and Portuguese ceramics, and silver, gold and jewellery are on display on the first floor. The top floor is dedicated to Portuguese art and sculpture.

The Temptations of St Anthony by Hieronymus Bosch

Stairs down to

St Augustine by Piero della Francesca

St Leonard
This statue is by the renowned Florentine Renaissance sculptor Andrea della Robbia (1435–1525), nephew of Luca della Robbia (1400–82).

Key to Floorplan

- European art
- Portuguese painting and sculpture
- Portuguese and Chinese ceramics
- Oriental and African art
- Silver, gold and jewellery
- Decorative arts
- Chapel of St Albert
- Furniture
- Temporary exhibitions
- Non-exhibition space

The Mystic Marriage of St Catherine
Hans Holbein the Elder's balanced composition of a *Sacra Conversazione* (1519) is set among majestic Renaissance architecture with saints clothed in detailed contemporary costumes sewing or reading.

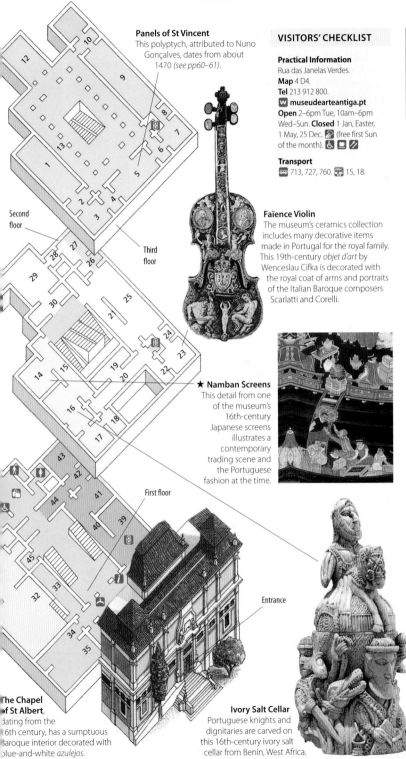

Panels of St Vincent
This polyptych, attributed to Nuno Gonçalves, dates from about 1470 *(see pp60–61)*.

VISITORS' CHECKLIST

Practical Information
Rua das Janelas Verdes.
Map 4 D4.
Tel 213 912 800.
W **museudearteantiga.pt**
Open 2–6pm Tue, 10am–6pm Wed–Sun. **Closed** 1 Jan, Easter, 1 May, 25 Dec. (free first Sun of the month).

Transport
713, 727, 760. 15, 18.

Second floor

Third floor

Faïence Violin
The museum's ceramics collection includes many decorative items made in Portugal for the royal family. This 19th-century *objet d'art* by Wenceslau Cifka is decorated with the royal coat of arms and portraits of the Italian Baroque composers Scarlatti and Corelli.

★ Namban Screens
This detail from one of the museum's 16th-century Japanese screens illustrates a contemporary trading scene and the Portuguese fashion at the time.

First floor

Entrance

The Chapel of St Albert, dating from the 16th century, has a sumptuous Baroque interior decorated with blue-and-white *azulejos*.

Ivory Salt Cellar
Portuguese knights and dignitaries are carved on this 16th-century ivory salt cellar from Benin, West Africa.

For keys to symbols *see back flap*

Exploring the Collections of the Museu Nacional de Arte Antiga

The museum has the largest collection of paintings in Portugal and is particularly strong on early religious works by Portuguese artists. The majority of exhibits came from convents and monasteries following the suppression of religious orders in 1834. There are also extensive displays of sculpture, silverware, porcelain and applied arts, giving an overview of Portuguese art from the Middle Ages to the 19th century, complemented by many fine European and Oriental pieces. The theme of the Discoveries is ever-present, illustrating Portugal's links with Brazil, Africa, India, China and Japan.

Panels of St Vincent

Cistercian monks from Alcobaça in central Portugal

Friar

Fisherman

European Art

Paintings by European artists, dating from the 14th to the 19th century, are arranged chronologically on the ground floor. Unlike the Portuguese art, which is located on the second floor, most of the works in this section were donated from private collections, contributing to the great diversity of works on display. The first rooms, dedicated to the 14th and 15th centuries, trace the transition from medieval Gothic taste to the aesthetic of the Renaissance.

Among the painters best represented in the European Art section are the 16th-century German and Flemish artists. Notable works are *St Jerome* by Albrecht Dürer (1471–1528), *Salomé* by Lucas Cranach the Elder (1472–1553), *Virgin and Child* by Hans Memling (c.1430–94) and *The Temptations of St Anthony* by the great Dutch master of fantasy, Hieronymus Bosch (1450–1516). Of the small number of Italian works, the finest include *St Augustine* by the Renaissance painter Piero della Francesca (c.1420–92) and a graceful early altar panel representing *The Miracle of St Eusebius of Cremona* by Raphael (1483–1520).

Portuguese Painting and Sculpture

Many of the earliest works of art are by the Portuguese primitive painters, who were influenced by the realistic detail of Flemish artists. There had always been strong trading links between Portugal and Flanders and in the 15th and 16th centuries several painters of Flemish origin, for example Frey Carlos of Évora, set up workshops in Portugal.

Pride of place, however, goes to the São Vicente de Fora polyptych, the most important painting of 15th-century Portuguese art and one that has become a symbol of national pride in the Age of Discovery. Painted around 1470–80, and generally believed to be by Nuno Gonçalves, the altarpiece shows St Vincent, patron saint of Lisbon, surrounded by dignitaries, knights and monks as well as beggars and fishermen *(see above)*. The accurate portrayal of contemporary figures makes the painting an invaluable historical and social document.

Later works include a 16th-century portrait of the young Dom Sebastião (1557–78) by Cristóvão de Morais and paintings by Neo-Classical artist Domingos António de Sequeira. The museum's sculpture collection has many Gothic polychrome stone and wood statues of Christ, the Virgin and saints. There are also statues from the 17th century and a late-18th-century Nativity scene by Barros Laborão in the Chapel of St Albert.

Portuguese and Chinese Ceramics

The extensive collection of ceramics enables visitors to trace the evolution of Chinese porcelain and Portuguese faïence

Central panel of *The Temptations of St Anthony* by Hieronymus Bosch

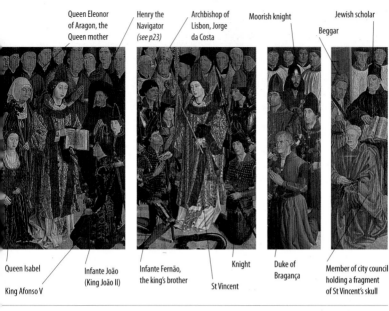

Queen Eleonor of Aragon, the Queen mother

Henry the Navigator (see p23)

Archbishop of Lisbon, Jorge da Costa

Moorish knight

Jewish scholar

Beggar

Queen Isabel

King Afonso V

Infante João (King João II)

Infante Fernão, the king's brother

Knight

St Vincent

Duke of Bragança

Member of city council holding a fragment of St Vincent's skull

and to see the influence of Oriental designs on Portuguese pieces, and vice versa. From the 16th century, Portuguese ceramics show a marked influence of Ming, and conversely the Chinese pieces bear Portuguese motifs such as coats of arms. By the mid-18th century individual potters had begun to develop an increasingly personal-ized, European style, with popular, rustic designs. The collection also includes ceramics from Italy, Spain and the Netherlands.

Chinese porcelain vase, 18th century

Oriental and African Art

The collection of ivories and furniture, with their European motifs, further illustrates the reciprocal influences of Portugal and her colonies. The 16th-century predilection for the exotic gave rise to a huge demand for items such as carved ivory hunting horns from Africa. The 16th- and 17th-century Japanese Namban screens show the Portuguese trading in Japan. *Namban-jin* (barbarians from the south) is the name the Japanese gave to the Portuguese.

Silver, Gold and Jewellery

Among the museum's fine collection of ecclesiastical treasures are King Sancho I's gold cross (1214) and the Belém monstrance (1506). Also on display is the 16th-century Madre de Deus reliquary, allegedly containing a thorn from the crown of Christ. High-light of the foreign collection is a sumptuous set of rare 18th-century silver tableware. Commissioned by José I from the Paris workshop of François-Thomas Germain, the 1,200 pieces include intricately decorated tureens, sauce boats and salt cellars. The rich collection of jewels came from the convents, originally donated by members of the nobility and wealthy bourgeoisie on entering the religious orders.

Applied Arts

Furniture, tapestries and textiles, liturgical vestments and bishops' mitres are among the wide range of objects on display. The furniture collection includes

many medieval and Renaissance pieces as well as Baroque and Neo-Classical items from the reigns of King João V, King José and Queen Maria I. Of the foreign furniture, French pieces from the 18th century are prominent.

The textiles include 17th-century bedspreads, tapestries (many of Flemish origin, such as the 16th-century *Baptism of Christ*), embroidered rugs and Arraiolos carpets.

Gold Madre de Deus reliquary inlaid with precious stones (c.1510–25)

BELÉM

At the mouth of the Tagus river, where the caravels set sail on their voyages of discovery, Belém is inextricably linked with Portugal's golden Age of Discovery. When Manuel I came to power in 1495 he reaped the profits of those heady days of expansion, building grandiose monuments and churches that mirrored the spirit of the time. Two of the finest examples of the exuberant and exotic Manueline style of architecture are the Mosteiro dos Jerónimos and the Torre de Belém. Today, Belém is a spacious, relatively green suburb with many museums, parks and gardens, as well as an attractive riverside setting with cafés and a promenade. On sunny days there is a distinct seaside feel to the river embankment.

Before the Tagus receded, the monks in the monastery used to look out onto the river and watch the boats set forth. In contrast today, several lanes of traffic along the busy Avenida da Índia cut central Belém off from the picturesque waterfront, and silver-and-yellow trains rattle regularly past.

Sights at a Glance

Museums and Galleries
2 Museu Nacional dos Coches
5 Museu Nacional de Arqueologia
6 Planetário Calouste Gulbenkian
7 Museu de Marinha
10 Museu Colecção Berardo

Parks and Gardens
3 Jardim Botânico Tropical
14 Jardim Botânico da Ajuda

Churches and Monasteries
4 Mosteiro dos Jerónimos pp68–9
12 Ermida de São Jerónimo
13 Igreja da Memória

Historic Buildings
1 Palácio de Belém
11 Torre de Belém p72
15 Palácio Nacional da Ajuda

Monuments
9 Monument to the Discoveries

Cultural Centres
8 Centro Cultural de Belém

Restaurants pp132–3
1 Belém 2 a 8
2 Nosolo Italia
3 Vela Latina

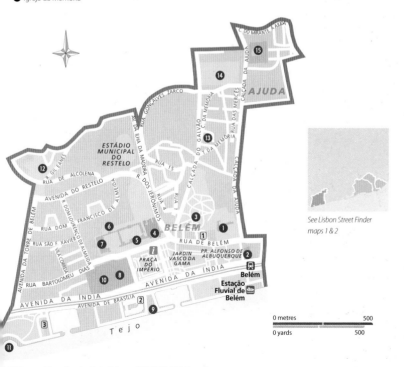

See Lisbon Street Finder maps 1 & 2

| 0 metres | | 500 |
| 0 yards | | 500 |

◄ The magnificent Mosteiro dos Jerónimos, a UNESCO World Heritage Site

For keys to symbols see back flap

Street-by-Street: Belém

Portugal's former maritime glory, expressed in the imposing, exuberant buildings such as the Jerónimos monastery, is evident all around Belém. In Salazar's *(see p19)* attempted revival of awareness of Portugal's Golden Age, the area along the waterfront, which had silted up since the days of the caravels, was restructured to celebrate the former greatness of the nation. Praça do Império was laid out for the Exhibition of the Portuguese World in 1940 and Praça Afonso de Albuquerque was dedicated to Portugal's first Viceroy of India. The royal Palácio de Belém, restored with gardens and a riding school by João V in the 18th century, briefly housed the royal family after the 1755 earthquake.

❹ ★ Mosteiro dos Jerónimos
Vaulted arcades and richly carved columns adorned with foliage, exotic animals and navigational instruments decorate the Manueline cloister of the Jerónimos monastery.

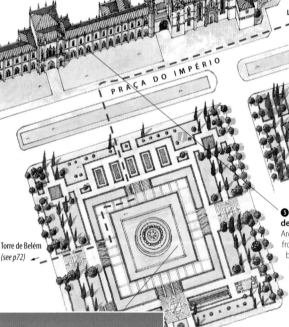

LARGO

DOS

JERÓNIMOS

PRAÇA DO IMPÉRIO

❺ Museu Nacional de Arqueologia
Archaeological finds ranging from an Iron Age gold bracelet to Moorish artifacts are among the interesting exhibits on display.

Torre de Belém
(see p72)

| 0 metres | 50 |
| 0 yards | 50 |

Praça do Império
is the great square in front of the monastery. The central fountain is lit up on special occasions.

Key

— Suggested route

❸ ★ Jardim Botânico Tropical
Exotic plants and trees gathered from Portugal's former colonies fill these peaceful gardens, which were once part of the Palácio de Belém.

Locator Map
See Lisbon Street Finder maps 1 & 2

Antiga Confeitaria de Belém, a 19th-century café, sells *pastéis de Belém*, rich custard in a flaky pastry cup.

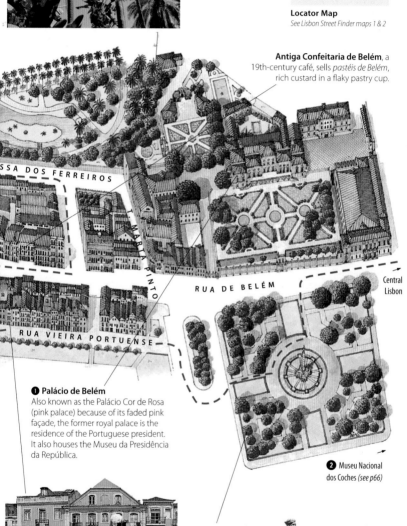

SSA DOS FERREIROS

T MARIA PINTO

RUA DE BELÉM

Central Lisbon

RUA VIEIRA PORTUENSE

❶ Palácio de Belém
Also known as the Palácio Cor de Rosa (pink palace) because of its faded pink façade, the former royal palace is the residence of the Portuguese president. It also houses the Museu da Presidência da República.

❷ Museu Nacional dos Coches *(see p66)*

Praça Afonso de Albuquerque
is named after the first Portuguese Viceroy of India. A Neo-Manueline column in the centre bears his statue, with scenes from his life carved on the base.

Rua Vieira Portuense runs along a small park. Its colourful 16th- and 17th-century houses contrast with the typically imposing buildings in Belém.

❶ Palácio de Belém

Praça Afonso de Albuquerque. **Map** 1
C4. **Tel** 213 614 600. 🚌 714, 727,
728, 729, 751. 🚊 15. 🚃 Belém.
Open 10am–6pm Sat. 🕐 10:30am &
4:30pm; compulsory for groups (213
414 660). Museu da Presidência da
República: **Open** 10am–6pm daily.
Closed Easter, 1 May, 25 Dec.
🅦 museu.presidencia.pt

Pink façade of the Palácio de Belém, official residence of the President of Portugal

Built by the Conde de Aveiras
in 1559, before the Tagus had
receded, this palace once had
gardens bordering the river. In
the 1700s it was bought by
João V, who made it suitably
lavish for his amorous liaisons.

When the 1755 earthquake
struck (see pp24–5), the king,
José I, and his family were
staying here and thus survived
the devastation of central
Lisbon. Fearing another tremor,
the royal family temporarily set
up camp in tents in the palace
grounds; the interior was used
as a hospital. Today the elegant
pink building is the residence
of the President of Portugal.

The Museu da Presidência
da República, located within
the palace, uses multimedia
systems to illustrate Portugal's
political history.

❷ Museu Nacional dos Coches

Praça Afonso de Albuquerque. **Map** 2
D4. **Tel** 213 610 850. 🚌 714, 727,
728, 729, 751. 🚊 15. 🚃 Belém.
Open 10am–6pm Tue–Sun. **Closed**
1 Jan, Easter, 1 May, 25 Dec. 🎫 (free
first Sun of the month). 🕐 for groups
by appt. 🛗 ground floor only.
🅦 museudoscoches.pt

The museum's unique
collection of coaches and
ceremonial vehicles from the
17th, 18th and 19th centuries
is arguably the finest in Europe.
It currently occupies the east
wing of the Palácio de Belém,
formerly the riding school
built by the Italian architect
Giacomo Azzolini in 1726.
Seated in the upper gallery,
the royal family used to watch
their beautiful Lusitanian
horses performing in the
arena. In 1905 the riding
school was turned into

a museum by King Carlos's
wife, Dona Amélia, whose
riding cloak is on show. In
2015, however, the museum
will shift to a new, more
spacious and purpose-built
building on the east side of
Praça Afonso de Albuquerque.

The original collection had
29 vehicles, dress uniforms,
harnesses and cavalry
accessories used by the Royal
Family. After the establishment
of the Republic in 1910,
the museum was renamed
the National Coach Museum,
and its collection was
extended with other vehicles
belonging to the Crown, the
Patriarchate of Lisbon and
some aristocratic families.

Made in Portugal, Italy,
France, Austria and Spain, the
coaches span three centuries
and range from the plain to
the preposterous. The main
gallery, in Louis XVI style with
a splendid painted
ceiling, is the setting for
two straight, regimented
rows of coaches created
for Portuguese royalty.

The collection starts
with the comparatively
plain 17th-century red-
leather and wood coach
of Philip II of Spain. The
coaches become more
sumptuous, the interiors
are lined with red velvet
and gold, the exteriors
are carved and decorated
with allegories and royal
coats of arms. The rows
end with three huge
Baroque coaches made in
Rome for the Portuguese
ambassador to the Vatican,
Dom Rodrigo Almeida e

Menezes, the Marquês de
Abrantes. The epitome of
pomp and extravagance,
these 5-tonne carriages are
embellished with life-size
gilded statues.

The neighbouring gallery
has further examples of royal
carriages, including two-
wheeled cabriolets, landaus
and pony-drawn chaises used
by young members of the
royal family. There is also
a 19th-century Lisbon cab,
painted black and green,
the colours of taxis right up
to the 1990s. The 18th-century
Eyeglass Chaise, whose black
leather hood is pierced by
sinister eye-like windows,
was made during the era of
Pombal (see p19) when lavish
decoration was discouraged.

The upper gallery has a
collection of harnesses, court
costumes and portraits of
members of the royal family.

Rear view of a coach built in 1716 for the
Marquês de Abrantes, the Portuguese
ambassador to Pope Clement XI

❸ Jardim Botânico Tropical

Rua da Junqueira 86 (entrance on Largo do Jerónimos). **Map** 1 C4. **Tel** 213 609 665. 🚌 727, 728, 751. 🚋 15. **Open** Mar & Oct: 10am–6pm daily; Apr & Sep: 10am–7pm daily; Jun–Aug: 10am–8pm daily; Nov–Jan: 10am–5pm daily. **Closed** 1 Jan, Easter, 25 Dec. 🐾 ♿

Also known as the Jardim do Ultramar, this peaceful park with ponds, waterfowl and peacocks, attracts surprisingly few visitors. Designed at the beginning of the 20th century as the research centre of the Institute for Tropical Sciences, it is more of an arboretum than a flower garden. The emphasis is on rare and endangered tropical and subtropical trees and plants. Among the most striking are dragon trees, native to the Canary Islands and Madeira, monkey puzzle trees from South America and an avenue of Washington palms. The Oriental garden with its streams and bridges is heralded by a large Chinese-style gateway that represented Macau in the Exhibition of the Portuguese World in 1940 *(see p64)*.

The research buildings are housed in the Palácio dos Condes da Calheta, whose interior walls are covered with *azulejos* spanning three centuries. Temporary exhibitions are held in the palace (closed 12:30–2pm).

❹ Mosteiro dos Jerónimos

See pp68–9.

❺ Museu Nacional de Arqueologia

Praça do Império. **Map** 1 B4. **Tel** 213 620 000. 🚌 714, 727, 728, 729, 751. 🚋 15. **Open** 10am–6pm Tue–Sun. **Closed** 1 Jan, Easter, 1 May, 25 Dec. 🐾 (free first Sun of the month). ♿ 🌐 **museuarqueologia.pt**

The long west wing of the Mosteiro dos Jerónimos *(see pp68–9)*, formerly the monks'

Washington palms in the Jardim Botânico Tropical

dormitory, has been a museum since 1893. Reconstructed in the middle of the 19th century, the building is a poor imitation of the Manueline original. The museum houses Portugal's main archaeological research centre and the exhibits, from sites all over the country, include a gold Iron Age bracelet, Visigothic jewellery found in the Alentejo in southern Portugal, Roman ornaments, some fine Roman mosaics and early 8th-century Moorish artifacts. The main Greco-Roman and Egyptian section is strong on funerary art, featuring figurines, tombstones, masks, terracotta amulets and funeral cones inscribed with hieroglyphics alluding to the solar system, dating from 6000 BC. The dimly lit Room of Treasures has a fine collection of coins, necklaces, bracelets and other jewellery dating from 1800 to 500 BC. This room has been refurbished to allow more of the magnificent jewellery, unseen by the public for decades, to be shown. In addition, the museum also holds temporary exhibitions from time to time.

Visigothic buckle, Museu Nacional de Arqueologia

❻ Planetário Calouste Gulbenkian

Praça do Império. **Map** 1 B4. **Tel** 213 620 002. 🚌 714, 727, 728, 751. 🚋 15. **Open** timings vary, check website for details. 🐾 ♿ 🌐 **planetario. marinha.pt**

Financed by the Gulbenkian Foundation *(see p81)* and built in 1965, this modern building sits incongruously beside the Jerónimos monastery. Inside, the Planetarium reveals the mysteries of the cosmos. There are shows in Portuguese, English, Spanish and French several times a week, explaining the movement of the stars and our solar system, as well as presentations on more specialist themes, such as the constellations or the Star of Bethlehem (Belém). A particular highlight is the 30-minute Hubble Vision show, which includes stunning images provided by the orbital telescope.

The dome of the Planetário Calouste Gulbenkian, near the Museu de Marinha

❹ Mosteiro dos Jerónimos

A monument to the wealth of the Age of Discovery (*see pp22–3*), this monastery is the culmination of Manueline architecture in this period. Commissioned by Manuel I in around 1501, after Vasco de Gama's return from his historic voyage, it was financed largely by "pepper money", a tax levied on spices, precious stones and gold. Various masterbuilders worked on the building, the most notable of whom was Diogo Boitac, replaced by João de Castilho in 1517. The monastery was cared for by the Order of St Jerome (Hieronymites) until 1834, when all religious orders were disbanded.

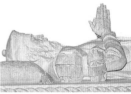

Tomb of Vasco da Gama
The 19th-century tomb of the navigator (*see p70*) is carved with armillary spheres and other seafaring symbols.

Refectory
The walls of the refectory are tiled with 18th-century *azulejos*. The panel at the northern end depicts the Feeding of the Five Thousand.

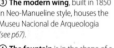

Entrance to church and cloister

KEY

① **Gallery**

② **The west portal** was designed by the French sculptor Nicolau Chanterène.

③ **The modern wing**, built in 1850 in Neo-Manueline style, houses the Museu Nacional de Arqueologia (*see p67*).

④ **The fountain** is in the shape of a lion, the heraldic animal of St Jerome.

⑤ **The chapterhouse** holds the tomb of Alexandre Herculano (1810–77), historian and first mayor of Belém.

⑥ **The chancel** was commissioned in 1572 by Dona Catarina, wife of João III.

⑦ **The tombs** of Manuel I, his wife Dona Maria, João III and Catarina are supported by elephants.

View of the Monastery
This 17th-century scene by Felipe Lobo shows women at a fountain in front of the Mosteiro dos Jerónimos.

★ Cloister
João de Castilho's pure Manueline creation was completed in 1544. Delicate tracery and richly carved images decorate the arches and balustrades.

VISITORS' CHECKLIST

Practical Information
Praça do Império. **Map** 1 B4.
Tel 213 620 034. **W** mosteiro jeronimos.pt. **Open** 10am–5pm Tue–Sun (May–Sep: to 6pm).
Closed public hols. 🎫 🗓 (free first Sun of the month; combined ticket for monastery & Torre de Belém available). ♿ cloisters.

Transport
🚌 714, 727, 728, 729, 751. 🚊 15.
🚇 Belém.

Nave
The spectacular vaulting in the church of Santa Maria is held aloft by slender octagonal pillars. These rise like palm trees to the roof creating a feeling of space and harmony.

★ South Portal
The strict geometrical architecture of the portal is almost obscured by the exuberant decoration. João de Castilho unites religious themes, such as this image of St Jerome, with the secular, exalting the kings of Portugal.

Tomb of King Sebastião
The tomb of the "longed for" Dom Sebastião stands empty. The young king never returned from battle in 1578.

Façade of the Museu de Marinha

❼ Museu de Marinha

Praça do Império. **Map** 1 B4. **Tel** 213
620 019. 🚌 727, 728, 729, 751. 🚊 15.
Open 10am–6pm Tue–Sun (Oct–Apr:
to 5pm). **Closed** 1 Jan, Easter, 1 May,
25 Dec. 🎟 (213 620 019). 🅿 (free
first Sun of the month). ♿
🌐 **museu.marinha.pt**

The Maritime Museum was
inaugurated in 1962 in the
west wing of the Jerónimos
monastery (see p68–9). It was
here, in the chapel built by
Henry the Navigator (see p23),
that mariners took Mass before
embarking on their voyages.
A hall devoted to the
Discoveries illustrates the

progress in shipbuilding
from the mid-15th
century, capitalizing on
the experience of long-
distance explorers.
Small replicas show the
transition from the bark
to the lateen-rigged
caravel, through
the faster square-
rigged caravel, to the
Portuguese *nau*. Also
here are navigational
instruments, astrolabes
and replicas of
16th-century maps
showing the world as
it was known then. The
stone pillars, carved with
the Cross of the Knights
of Christ, are replicas of
the types of *padrão* set
up as monuments to
Portuguese sovereignty
on the lands discovered.
    A series of rooms
displaying models of
modern Portuguese ships
leads on to the Royal Quarters,
where you can see the
exquisitely furnished wood-
panelled cabin of King Carlos
and Queen Amélia from the
royal yacht *Amélia*, built in
Scotland in 1900.
    The modern, incongruous
pavilion opposite houses
original royal barges, the
most extravagant of which
is the royal brig built in 1780
for Maria I. The collection ends
with a display of seaplanes,
including the *Santa Clara* which
made the first crossing of the
South Atlantic, from Lisbon to
Rio de Janeiro, in 1922.

Vasco da Gama (c.1460–1524)

In 1498 Vasco da Gama sailed around
the Cape of Good Hope and opened
the sea route to India (see pp22–3).
Although the Hindu ruler of Calicut, who
received him wearing diamond and ruby
rings, was not impressed by his humble
offerings of cloth and wash basins, da
Gama returned to Portugal with a cargo
of spices. In 1502 he sailed again to
India, establishing Portuguese trade
routes in the Indian Ocean. João III
nominated him Viceroy of India in 1524,
but he died of a fever soon after in the
town of Cochin.

16th-century painting of
Vasco da Gama in Goa

❽ Centro Cultural de Belém

Praça do Império. **Map** 1 B5.
Tel 213 612 400. 🚌 727, 728, 729,
751. 🚊 15. 🚇 Belém. **Open** 8am–
8pm Mon–Fri, 10am–6pm Sat, Sun &
public hols. 🅿 ♿ 🌐 **ccb.pt**

The construction of a stark
modern building between
the Manueline splendour of
the Jéronimos monastery and
the Tagus proved controversial.
Built as the headquarters of
the Portuguese presidency
of the European Community,
the Centro Cultural de Belém
opened as a cultural and
conference centre in 1993. It
stresses music, performing arts
and films. An exhibition centre
houses the Museu Colecção
Berardo (see opposite).
    Both the café and restaurant
spill out onto the ramparts of
the building, whose peaceful
gardens of olive trees and
geometric lawns look out
over the quay and the river.

The modern complex of the Centro Cultural
de Belém

❾ Monument to the Discoveries

Padrão dos Descobrimentos, Avenida
de Brasília. **Map** 1 C5. **Tel** 213 031
950. 🚌 727, 728, 729, 751. 🚊 15.
🚇 Belém. **Open** May–Sep: 10am–
7pm daily; Oct–Apr: 10am–6pm
Tue–Sun. **Closed** 1 Jan, 1 May,
25 Dec. 🛗 for lift. 🌐 **padraodos
descobrimentos.pt**

Standing prominently on the
Belém waterfront, this massive
angular monument, the Padrão
dos Descobrimentos, was built
in 1960 to mark the 500th
anniversary of the death of
Henry the Navigator (see p23).
The 52-m- (170-ft-) high
monument, commissioned
by the Salazar regime,
commemorates the mariners,

The huge pavement compass in front of the Monument to the Discoveries

⑩ Museu Colecção Berardo

Praça do Império. **Map** 1 B5.
Tel 213 612 878. 727, 728, 729, 751. 15. Belém.
Open 10am–7pm Tue–Sun.
W museuberardo.pt

The brainchild of business mogul and art collector José Manuel Rodrigues Berardo, this fascinating gallery, located in the Centro Cultural de Belém, boasts around 1,000 works by more than 500 artists. The Museu Colecção Berardo provides a rich compendium of a century of modern and contemporary art through a variety of media, from canvas to sculpture and from photography to video installations.

Among the highlights are Pablo Picasso's *Tête de Femme* (1909), a good example of the Spanish artist's Cubist style; several variants of Andy Warhol's famous *Brillo Box* (1964–8); Jeff Koons's *Poodle* (1991) and Balthus's *Portrait de Femme en Robe Bleue* (1935). Other artists on show include Piet Mondrian, Francis Bacon, Willem de Kooning, Richard Long and Henry Moore. There is also much Portuguese art on display, including Alberto Carneiro's sculptures, etchings by Paula Rego and dramatic black-and-white photographs by Fernando Lemos.

royal patrons and all those who took part in the development of the Portuguese Age of Discovery. The monument is designed in the shape of a caravel, with Portugal's coat of arms on the sides and the sword of the Royal House of Avis rising above the entrance. Henry the Navigator stands at the prow with a caravel in hand. In two sloping lines either side of the monument are stone statues of Portuguese heroes linked with the Age of Discovery. On the western face these include Dom Manuel I holding an armillary sphere, the poet Camões with a copy of *Os Lusíadas* and the painter Nuno Gonçalves with a paint pallet.

On the monument's north side, the huge mariner's compass cut into the paving stone was a present from the Republic of South Africa in 1960. The central map, dotted with galleons and mermaids, shows the routes of the discoverers in the 15th and 16th centuries. Inside the monument, a lift whisks you up to the sixth floor where steps then lead to the top for a splendid panorama of the river and Belém. The basement level is used for temporary exhibitions. The monument also functions as an educational centre where children can learn about Portugal's golden Age of Discovery and Lisbon's chequered history.

The Padrão is not to everyone's taste but the setting is undeniably splendid and the caravel design is imaginative. The monument looks particularly dramatic when viewed from the west in the light of the late afternoon sun.

Eastern Face of the Monument to the Discoveries

Afonso V (1432–81), patron of the first explorers

Henry the Navigator (1394–1460)

Pedro Álvares Cabral (1467–1520), discoverer of Brazil

Vasco da Gama (1460–1524)

Fernão Magalhães (Magellan), who crossed the Pacific in 1520–21

Padrão erected by Diogo Cão in the Congo in 1482

⓫ Torre de Belém

Commissioned by Manuel I, the tower was built as a fortress in the middle of the Tagus in 1514–20. The starting point for the navigators who set out to discover the trade routes, this Manueline gem became a symbol of Portugal's great era of expansion. The real beauty of the tower lies in the decoration of the exterior. Adorned with rope carved in stone, it has openwork balconies, Moorish-style watchtowers and distinctive battlements in the shape of shields. The Gothic interior below the terrace, which served as a storeroom for arms and a prison, is very austere, but the private quarters in the tower are worth visiting for the loggia and the panorama.

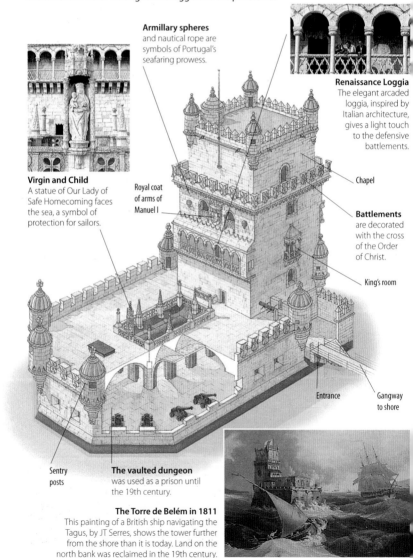

Armillary spheres
and nautical rope are symbols of Portugal's seafaring prowess.

Renaissance Loggia
The elegant arcaded loggia, inspired by Italian architecture, gives a light touch to the defensive battlements.

Virgin and Child
A statue of Our Lady of Safe Homecoming faces the sea, a symbol of protection for sailors.

Royal coat of arms of Manuel I

Chapel

Battlements
are decorated with the cross of the Order of Christ.

King's room

Sentry posts

The vaulted dungeon
was used as a prison until the 19th century.

Entrance

Gangway to shore

The Torre de Belém in 1811
This painting of a British ship navigating the Tagus, by JT Serres, shows the tower further from the shore than it is today. Land on the north bank was reclaimed in the 19th century.

The simple Manueline chapel, Ermida de São Jerónimo

⑫ Ermida de São Jerónimo

Praça de Itália. **Map** 1 A3. **Tel** 213 018 648. 🚌 714, 728, 729, 732, 751. **Open** Mon–Sat (by appt only).

Also known as the Capela de São Jerónimo, this elegant little chapel was constructed in 1514 when Diogo Boitac was working on the Jerónimos monastery (see pp68–9). Although a far simpler building, it is also Manueline in style and may have been built to a design by Boitac. The only decorative elements on the monolithic chapel are the four pinnacles, corner gargoyles and Manueline portal. Perched on a quiet hill above Belém, the chapel has fine views down to the Tagus river and a path from the terrace winds down the hill towards the Torre de Belém.

⑬ Igreja da Memória

Calçada do Galvão, Ajuda. **Map** 1 C3. **Tel** 213 635 295. 🚌 28, 732. 🚋 18. **Open** for Mass 6pm Mon–Sat, 10am Sun. 🕆 ♿

Built in 1760, the church was founded by King José I in gratitude for his escape from an assassination plot on this site in 1758. The king was returning from a secret liaison with a lady of the noble Távora family when his carriage was attacked and a bullet hit him in the arm. Pombal (see p19) used this as an excuse to get rid of his enemies in the Távora family, accusing them of conspiracy. In 1759 they were

savagely tortured and executed. Their deaths are commemorated by a pillar in Beco do Chão Salgado, off Rua de Belém.

The Neo-Classical domed church has a marble-clad interior and a small chapel, on the right, containing the tomb of Pombal. He died at the age of 83, a year after he had been banished from Lisbon.

⑭ Jardim Botânico da Ajuda

Calçada da Ajuda. **Map** 1 C2. **Tel** 213 622 503. 🚌 73, 714, 727, 728, 729, 732. 🚋 18. **Open** 10am–5pm daily. **Closed** 1 Jan, 25 Dec. 🎫 ♿ 🌐 jardimbotanicodajuda.com

Laid out on two levels by Pombal (see p19) in 1768, these Italian-style gardens provide a pleasant respite from the noisy suburbs of Belém. The entrance (wrought-iron gates in a pink wall) is easy to miss. The park comprises 5,000 plant species from Africa, Asia and America. Notable features are the 400-year-old dragon tree, native of Madeira, and the 18th-century fountain decorated with serpents, winged fish, sea horses and mythical creatures. A terrace looks out over the lower level of the gardens.

19th-century throne from the Palácio Nacional da Ajuda

⑮ Palácio Nacional da Ajuda

Calçada da Ajuda. **Map** 2 D2. **Tel** 213 620 264. 🚌 732, 742, 760. 🚋 18. **Open** 10am–5:45pm Thu–Tue. **Closed** 1 Jan, Easter, 1 May, 25 Dec. 🎫 (free first Sun of the month). ♿ 📷 🌐 palacioajuda.pt

The royal palace, destroyed by fire in 1795, was replaced in the early 19th century by this Neo-Classical building. It was left incomplete when the royal family was forced into exile in Brazil in 1807.

The palace only became a permanent residence of the royal family when Luís I became king in 1861 and married an Italian Princess, Maria Pia di Savoia. No expense was spared in furnishing the apartments, which feature silk wallpaper, Sèvres porcelain and crystal chandeliers.

A prime example of regal excess is the extraordinary Saxe Room, a wedding present to Maria Pia from the King of Saxony, in which every piece of furniture is decorated with Meissen porcelain. On the first floor, the huge Banqueting Hall, with crystal chandeliers, silk-covered chairs and an allegory of the birth of João VI on the frescoed ceiling, is truly impressive. At the other end of the palace, Luís I's Neo-Gothic painting studio is a more intimate display of intricately carved furniture.

Manicured formal gardens of the Jardim Botânico da Ajuda

FURTHER AFIELD

The majority of the outlying sights, which include some of Lisbon's finest museums, are easily accessible by bus or metro from the city centre. A 10-minute walk north from the gardens of the Parque Eduardo VII brings you to Portugal's great cultural complex, the Calouste Gulbenkian Foundation, set in a pleasant park. Few tourists go further north than the Gulbenkian, but the Museu da Cidade on Campo Grande is worth a detour for its fascinating overview of Lisbon's history.

The charming Palácio Fronteira, decorated with splendid tiles, is one of the many villas built for the aristocracy that now overlook the city suburbs. Those interested in tiles will also enjoy the Museu Nacional do Azulejo in the cloisters of the Madre de Deus convent. Visitors with a spare half day can cross the Tagus to the Cristo Rei monument. Northeast of Lisbon is the vast oceanarium, Oceanário de Lisboa, in the Parque das Nações, which includes other family-oriented attractions, hotels and shops.

Sights at a Glance

Museums and Galleries
- ❻ Museu Calouste Gulbenkian *pp78–81*
- ❼ Centro de Arte Moderna
- ❾ Museu da Água
- ❿ Museu Nacional do Azulejo *pp84–5*
- ⓭ Museu da Cidade

Modern Architecture
- ❶ Cristo Rei
- ❷ Ponte 25 de Abril
- ❸ Colombo Shopping Centre
- ⓫ Parque das Nações

Historic Architecture
- ❹ Praça Marquês de Pombal
- ❽ Campo Pequeno
- ⓯ Aqueduto das Águas Livres
- ⓰ Palácio Fronteira

Parks and Gardens
- ❺ Parque Eduardo VII
- ⓱ Parque do Monteiro-Mor

Zoos
- ⓬ Oceanário de Lisboa
- ⓮ Jardim Zoológico

Key

- ▨ Main sightseeing areas
- ▭ Motorway
- ▭ Major road
- ▭ Minor road

0 kilometres ————— 4

0 miles ————— 2

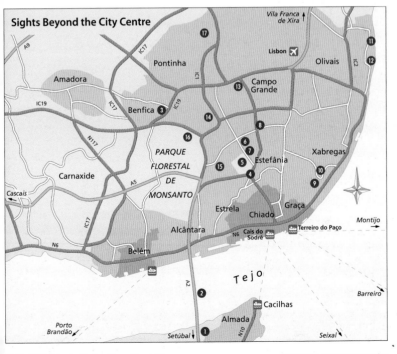

Sights Beyond the City Centre

◄ Breathtaking view from the top of Parque Eduardo VII

For keys to symbols *see back flap*

The towering monument of Cristo Rei overlooking the Tagus

❶ Cristo Rei

Santuário Nacional do Cristo Rei, Alto do Pragal, Almada. **Tel** 212 751 000. 🚢 from Cais do Sodré to Cacilhas then 🚌 101. **Open** 9:30am–6:15pm daily (Jul–Sep: to 6:30pm Mon–Fri, to 7pm Sat & Sun). 🚹

Modelled on the more famous Cristo Redentor in Rio de Janeiro, this giant-sized statue stands with arms outstretched on the south bank of the Tagus. The 28-m- (92-ft-) tall figure of Christ, mounted on a huge pedestal,

was sculpted by Francisco Franco in 1949–59 at the instigation of Prime Minister Salazar.

You can see the monument from various viewpoints in the city, but it is fun to take a ferry to the Outra Banda (the other bank, more popularly known as the Margem Sul), then a bus or taxi to the monument. A lift plus some steps take you up 82 m (269 ft) to the top of the pedestal, affording fine views of the city and river.

❷ Ponte 25 de Abril

Map 3 A5. 🚌 753.

Originally called the Ponte Salazar after the dictator who had it built in 1966, Lisbon's suspension bridge was renamed (like many other monuments) to commemorate the revolution of 25 April 1974 which restored democracy to Portugal (see p19).

Inspired by San Francisco's Golden Gate Bridge in the United States, this steel construction stretches for 1 km (half a mile). The lower tier was modified in 1999 to accommodate the Fertagus, a much-needed railway across the Tagus.

The bridge's notorious traffic congestion has been partly resolved by the opening of the 17-km (11-mile) Vasco da Gama bridge. Spanning the Tagus

river from Montijo to Sacavém, north of the Parque das Nações, this bridge was completed in 1998.

❸ Colombo Shopping Centre

Avenida Lusíada. **Tel** 217 113 600. 🚌 729, 764. Ⓜ Colégio Militar/Luz. **Open** 9am–midnight daily. **Closed** 1 Jan, 25 Dec. ♿ 🆆 colombo.pt

Colombo is the largest shopping centre in the Iberian Peninsula. This vast complex houses more than 420 shops, including fashion stores such as Mango, Zara, H&M and Timberland, a Disney Store and a branch of FNAC. It also offers ten cinema screens, a health club, an indoor amusement park, a bowling alley and over 60 restaurants, from American fast-food joints to traditional and typically Portuguese establishments.

❹ Praça Marquês de Pombal

Map 5 C5. 🚌 702, 711, 712, 720, 723, 727, 732, 736, 738 & many other routes. Ⓜ Marquês de Pombal.

At the top of the Avenida da Liberdade (see p46), traffic thunders round the "Rotunda" (roundabout), as the praça is also known. At the centre is the lofty monument to Pombal.

Ponte 25 de Abril bridge, linking central Lisbon with the Outra Banda, the south bank of the Tagus

Detail on the base of the monument in Praça Marquês de Pombal

The despotic statesman, who virtually ruled Portugal from 1750 to 77, stands on the top of the column, his hand on a lion (symbol of power) and his eyes directed down to the Baixa, whose creation he masterminded (see p19). Allegorical images depicting Pombal's political, educational and agricultural reforms decorate the base of the monument. Standing figures represent Coimbra University where he introduced a Faculty of Science. Although greatly feared, this dynamic politician propelled the country into the Age of Enlightenment. Broken blocks of stone at the foot of the monument and tidal waves flooding the city are an allegory of the destruction caused by the 1755 earthquake.

An underpass, which is not always open, leads to the centre of the square where the sculptures on the pedestal and the inscriptions relating to Pombal's achievements can be seen. Nearby, the well-tended Parque Eduardo VII extends northwards behind the square. The paving stones around the Rotunda are decorated with a mosaic of Lisbon's coat of arms. Similar patterns in small black and white cobbles decorate many of the city's streets and squares.

Many of the city's sightseeing operators have their main pick-up located at the bottom of Parque Eduardo VII. There is also a multi-lingual booth where visitors can buy tickets and plan excursions.

❺ Parque Eduardo VII

Praça Marquês de Pombal. **Map** 5 B4.
Tel 213 882 278. 711, 712, 738.
Ⓜ Marquês de Pombal. Estufa Fria:
Tel 213 882 278. **Open** Apr–Oct: 10am–7pm daily; Nov–Mar: 9am–5pm daily.

Central Lisbon's largest park was named after King Edward VII of England, who came here in 1902 to reaffirm the Anglo-Portuguese alliance. The wide grassy slope, which extends for 25 hectares (62 acres), was laid out as Parque da Liberdade, a continuation of Avenida da Liberdade (see p46), in the late 19th century. Neatly clipped box hedging, flanked by mosaic patterned walkways, stretches uphill from the Praça Marquês de Pombal to a belvedere at the top. Here are a flower-filled garden dedicated to the memory of Amália Rodrigues (see p145) and a pleasant café. From here there are fine views of the city. On clear days it is possible to see as far as the Serra da Arrábida (see p113).

Located at the northwest corner, the most inspiring feature of this rather monotonous park is the jungle-like **Estufa Fria**, or greenhouse, where exotic plants, streams and waterfalls provide an oasis from the city streets. There are in fact two greenhouses: in the Estufa Fria (cold greenhouse), palms push through the slatted bamboo roof and paths wind through a forest of ferns, fuchsias, flowering shrubs and banana trees; the warmer Estufa Quente, or hothouse, is a glassed-over garden with lush plants, water-lily ponds and cacti.

Near the *estufas*, a pond with carp and a galleon-shaped play area are popular with children. On the east side, the **Pavilhão Carlos Lopes**, named after the 1984 Olympic marathon winner, is now used for concerts and conferences.

Tropical plants in the Estufa Quente glasshouse, Parque Eduardo VII

❻ Museu Calouste Gulbenkian

Thanks to a wealthy Armenian oil magnate, Calouste Gulbenkian *(see p81)*, with wide-ranging tastes and an eye for a masterpiece, this museum has one of the finest collections of art in Europe. Inaugurated in 1969, the purpose-built museum was created as part of the charitable institution bequeathed to Portugal by the multimillionaire. The design of the building, set in a spacious park allowing natural light to fill some of the rooms, was devised to create the best layout for the founder's varied collection.

Mustard Barrel
This 18th-century silver mustard barrel was made in France by Antoine-Sébastien Durand.

Lalique Corsage Ornament
The sinuous curves of the gold and enamel snakes are typical of René Lalique's Art Nouveau jewellery. _____

★ **Diana**
This fine marble statue (1780) by the French sculptor Jean-Antoine Houdon was once owned by Catherine the Great of Russia but was considered too obscene to exhibit. The graceful Diana, goddess of the hunt, stands with a bow and arrow in hand.

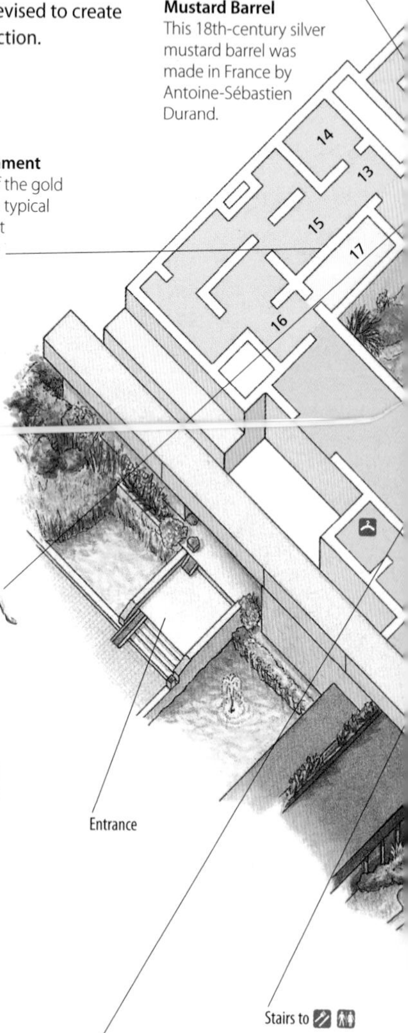

Entrance

Stairs to 🚻 👥

★ **St Catherine**
This serene bust, thought to be of St Catherine, was painted by the Flemish artist Rogier van der Weyden (1399– or 1400–64). The thin strip of landscape on the left of the wooden panel brings light and depth to the still portrait.

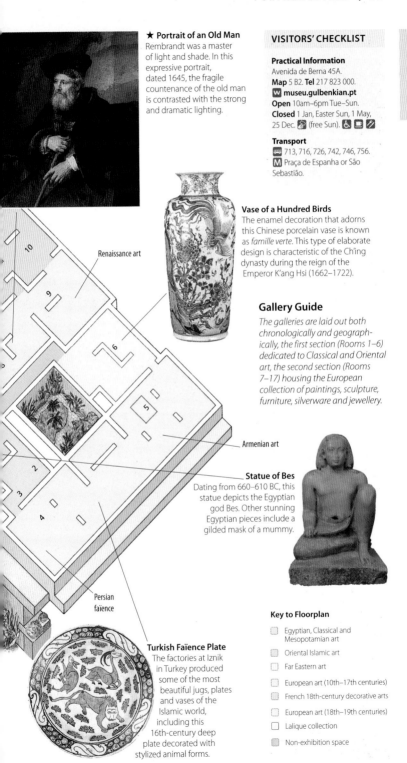

★ Portrait of an Old Man
Rembrandt was a master of light and shade. In this expressive portrait, dated 1645, the fragile countenance of the old man is contrasted with the strong and dramatic lighting.

Renaissance art

Vase of a Hundred Birds
The enamel decoration that adorns this Chinese porcelain vase is known as *famille verte*. This type of elaborate design is characteristic of the Ch'ing dynasty during the reign of the Emperor K'ang Hsi (1662–1722).

Gallery Guide

The galleries are laid out both chronologically and geographically, the first section (Rooms 1–6) dedicated to Classical and Oriental art, the second section (Rooms 7–17) housing the European collection of paintings, sculpture, furniture, silverware and jewellery.

Armenian art

Statue of Bes
Dating from 660–610 BC, this statue depicts the Egyptian god Bes. Other stunning Egyptian pieces include a gilded mask of a mummy.

Persian faïence

Turkish Faïence Plate
The factories at Iznik in Turkey produced some of the most beautiful jugs, plates and vases of the Islamic world, including this 16th-century deep plate decorated with stylized animal forms.

Key to Floorplan

- ☐ Egyptian, Classical and Mesopotamian art
- ☐ Oriental Islamic art
- ☐ Far Eastern art
- ☐ European art (10th–17th centuries)
- ☐ French 18th-century decorative arts
- ☐ European art (18th–19th centuries)
- ☐ Lalique collection
- ☐ Non-exhibition space

For keys to symbols *see back flap*

Exploring the Gulbenkian Collection

Housing Calouste Gulbenkian's unique collection of art, the museum ranks with the Museu de Arte Antiga (see pp58–61) as the finest in Lisbon. The exhibits, which span over 4,000 years from ancient Egyptian statuettes, through translucent Islamic glassware, to Art Nouveau brooches, are displayed in spacious and well-lit galleries, many overlooking the gardens or courtyards. The museum is quite small; however each individual work of art, from the magnificent pieces that make up the rich display of Oriental and Islamic art, to the selection of European paintings and furniture, is worthy of attention.

Early 17th-century Persian faïence tile from the School of Isfahan

Egyptian, Classical and Mesopotamian Art

Priceless treasures chart the evolution of Egyptian art from the Old Kingdom (c.2700 BC) to the Roman Period (Ist century BC). The exhibits range from an alabaster bowl of the 3rd Dynasty to a surprisingly modern-looking blue terracotta torso of a statuette of *Venus Anadyomene* from the Roman period.

Outstanding pieces in the Classical art section are a magnificent red-figure Greek vase and 11 Roman medallions, found in Egypt. These are believed to have been struck to commemorate the athletic games held in Macedonia in AD 242 in honour of Alexander the Great. In the Mesopotamian art section the large Assyrian

5th-century BC Greek vase

alabaster bas-relief represents the winged genius of Spring, carrying a container of sacred water (9th century BC).

Oriental Islamic Art

Being Armenian, Calouste Gulbenkian had a keen interest in art from the Near and Middle East. The Oriental Islamic gallery has a fine collection of Persian and Turkish carpets, textiles, costumes and ceramics. In the section overlooking the courtyard, the either Syrian or Egyptian mosque lamps and bottles, commissioned by princes and sultans, are beautifully decorated with coloured enamel on glass. The Armenian section has some exquisite illustrated manuscripts from the 17th century, produced by Armenian refugees in Istanbul, Persia and the Crimea.

Far Eastern Art

Calouste Gulbenkian acquired a large collection of Chinese porcelain between 1907 and 1947. One of the rarest pieces is the small blue-glazed bowl from the Yüan Dynasty (1279–1368), on the right as you go into the gallery. The majority of exhibits, however, are the later, more exuberantly decorated *famille verte* porcelain and the K'ang Hsi biscuitware of the 17th and 18th centuries. Further exhibits from the Far East are translucent Chinese jades and other semiprecious stones, Japanese prints, brocaded silk hangings, bound books and lacquerwork.

European Art (10th–17th Centuries)

Illuminated manuscripts, rare printed books and medieval ivories introduce the section on Western art. The delicately sculpted 14th-century ivory diptychs and triptychs, made in France, show scenes from the lives of Christ and the Virgin.

The collection of early European paintings starts with panels of possibly *St Joseph and St Catherine* by Rogier van der Weyden, leading painter of the mid-15th century in Flanders. Italian Renaissance painting is represented by Cima da Conegliano's *Sacra Conversazione* from the late 15th century and Domenico Ghirlandaio's *Portrait of a Young Woman* (c.1490).

The collection progresses to Flemish and Dutch works of the 17th century, including two works by Rembrandt: *Portrait of an Old Man* (1645),

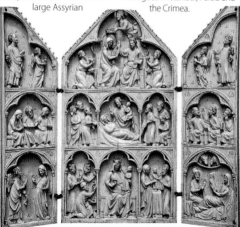

French ivory triptych of *Scenes from the Life of the Virgin* (14th century)

a masterpiece of psychological penetration, and *Pallas Athena* (c.1660–61), said to have been modelled on Rembrandt's son, Titus, and previously thought to have portrayed the Greek goddess Pallas Athena. Rubens is represented by three paintings, the most remarkable of which is the *Portrait of Hélène Fourment* (1630–2), the artist's second wife.

The gallery beyond the Dutch and Flemish paintings has tapestries and textiles from Italy and Flanders, Italian ceramics, rare 15th-century medallions and sculpture.

View of the Molo with the Ducal Palace (c.1780–90) by Francesco Guardi

French 18th-Century Decorative Arts

Some remarkably elaborate Louis XV and Louis XVI pieces, many commissioned by royalty, feature in the collection of French 18th-century furniture. The exhibits, many of them embellished with laquer panels, ebony and bronze, are grouped together according to historical style with Beauvais and "chinoiserie" Aubusson tapestries decorating the walls.

The French silverware from the same period, much of which once adorned the dining tables of Russian palaces, includes lavishly decorated soup tureens, salt-cellars and platters.

Louis XV chest of drawers inlaid with ebony and bronze

European Art (18th–19th Centuries)

The art of the 18th century is dominated by French painters, including Watteau (1684–1721), Fragonard (1732–1806) and Boucher (1703–70). The most celebrated piece of sculpture is a statue of *Diana* by Jean-Antoine Houdon.

Commissioned in 1780 by the Duke of Saxe-Gotha for his gardens, it became one of the principal exhibits in the Hermitage in Russia during the 19th and early 20th centuries.

One whole room is devoted to views of Venice by the 18th-century Venetian painter Francesco Guardi, and a small collection of British art includes works by leading 18th-century portraitists, such as Gainsborough's *Portrait of Mrs Lowndes-Stone* (c.1775) and Romney's *Portrait of Mrs Constable* (1787). There are also two stormy seascapes by JMW Turner (1775–1851). French 19th-century landscape painting is well represented here, reflecting Gulbenkian's preference for naturalism, with works by the Barbizon school and the Impressionists. The best-known paintings in the section, however, are probably Manet's *Boy with Cherries*, painted in about 1858 at the beginning of the artist's career,

and *Boy Blowing Bubbles*, painted in 1867. Renoir's *Portrait of Madame Claude Monet* was painted in about 1872–4 when the artist was staying with Monet at his country home in Argenteuil, in the outskirts of Paris.

Lalique Collection

The tour of the museum ends with an entire room filled with the flamboyant creations of French Art Nouveau jeweller, René Lalique (1860–1945). Gulbenkian was a close friend of Lalique's and he acquired many of the pieces of jewellery, glassware and ivory on display here directly from the artist. Inlaid with semiprecious stones and covered with enamel or gold leaf, the brooches, necklaces, vases and combs are decorated with the dragonfly, peacock or sensual female nude motifs characteristic of Art Nouveau.

Calouste Gulbenkian

Born in Scutari (Turkey) in 1869, Gulbenkian started his art collection at the age of 14 when he bought some ancient coins in a bazaar. In 1928 he was granted a 5 per cent stake in four major oil companies, including BP and Shell, in thanks for his part in the transfer of the assets of the Turkish Petroleum Company to those four companies. He thereby earned himself the nickname of "Mr Five Percent". With the wealth he accumulated, Gulbenkian was able to indulge his passion for fine works of art. During World War II, he went to live in neutral Portugal and, on his death in 1955, bequeathed his estate to the Portuguese in the form of a charitable trust. The Foundation supports many cultural activities and has its own orchestra, art library, concert halls and a modern art centre.

A light-filled gallery at the Centro de Arte Moderna

❼ Centro de Arte Moderna

Rua Dr Nicolau de Bettencourt. **Map** 5 B3. **Tel** 217 823 483. 🚌 716, 726, 742, 746, 756. Ⓜ São Sebastião. **Open** 10am–6pm Tue–Sun. **Closed** 1 Jan, Easter, 1 May, 25 Dec. 🅿 (free Sun). ♿ 🆆 cam.gulbenkian.pt

The Modern Art Museum lies across the gardens from the Calouste Gulbenkian museum and is part of the same cultural foundation (see p81).

The permanent collection features paintings and sculpture by Portuguese artists from the turn of the 20th century to the present day. The most famous painting is the striking portrait of poet Fernando Pessoa in the Café Irmãos Unidos (1964) by José de Almada Negreiros (1893–1970), a main exponent of Portuguese Modernism. Also of interest are paintings by Eduardo Viana (1881–1967), Amadeo de Sousa Cardoso (1887–1910) and contemporary artists such as Paula Rego, Rui Sanches, Graça Morais and Teresa Magalhães.

The museum is light and spacious, with pleasant gardens and a busy cafeteria.

❽ Campo Pequeno

Map 5 C1. 🚌 736, 744. Ⓜ Campo Pequeno. Bullring: **Tel** 217 998 450. **Open** 10am–11pm daily. 🅿 ♿

This square is dominated by the red-brick Neo-Moorish bullring built in the late 19th century. The building has undergone major development, and an underground car park and leisure centre have been added. Much of the bullring's distinctive architecture, such as keyhole-shaped windows and double cupolas, have been retained. Call the tourist office or the number listed above for information on this and other bullfight venues.

Renovated 19th-century steam pump in the Museu da Água

❾ Museu da Água

Rua do Alviela 12. **Tel** 218 100 215. 🚌 735. **Open** 10am–5:30pm Tue–Sat. **Closed** public hols. 🅿 Águas Livres aqueduct: **Open** Mar–Nov.

Dedicated to the history of Lisbon's water supply, this small but informative museum was imaginatively created around the city's first steam pumping station. It commemorates Manuel da Maia, the 18th-century engineer who masterminded the Águas Livres aqueduct (see p86). The excellent layout of the museum earned it the Council of Europe Museum Prize in 1990.

Pride of place goes to four lovingly preserved steam engines, one of which still functions (by electricity) and can be switched on for visitors. The development of technology relating to the city's water supply is documented with photographs. Particularly interesting are the sections on the Águas Livres aqueduct and the Alfama's 17th-century Chafariz d'El Rei, one of Lisbon's first fountains. Locals used to queue at one of six founts, depending on their social status.

❿ Museu Nacional do Azulejo

See pp84–5.

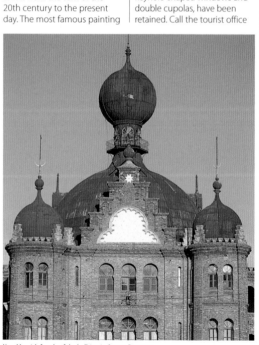

Neo-Moorish façade of the bullring in Campo Pequeno

The impressive Oriente Station, located next to Parque das Nações

⓫ Parque das Nações

Avenida Dom João II. **Tel** 218 919 898. 🚌 705, 725, 728, 744, 750, 782. 🇲 Oriente. 🚆 Gare do Oriente. **Open** 24 hours daily. ♿ 🚫 ⬛ Pavilhão do Conhecimento – Ciencia Viva: **Tel** 218 917 100. **Open** 10am–6pm Tue–Fri, 11am–7pm Sat & Sun. **Closed** 1 Jan, 24, 25 & 31 Dec. 🏛 Casino Lisboa: Alameda dos Oceanos. **Tel** 218 929 000. **Open** 3pm–3am Sun–Thu, 4pm–4am Fri & Sat. **Closed** 24 Dec. Cable car: **Tel** 218 956 143. **Open** Mar–May & Oct: 11am–7pm daily; Jun–Sep: 10:30am–8pm daily; Nov–Feb: 11am–6pm daily. **Closed** in adverse weather. 🏛 ⬛ **portaldasnacoes.pt**

Originally the site of Expo '98, Parque das Nações is now a Lisbon hub. With its contemporary architecture and family-oriented attractions, the park has renewed the eastern waterfront, which was once an industrial wasteland. The soaring geometry of the platform canopies over Santiago Calatrava's Oriente Station set the tone for the development. The **Portugal Pavilion**, designed by the Portuguese architect Álvaro Siza Vieira, has a large reinforced-concrete roof suspended like a sailcloth above its forecourt.

The **Pavilhão do Conhecimento – Ciencia Viva** (Knowledge and Science Pavilion) is a modern museum of science and technology that houses several interactive exhibitions. Also in the park is **Casino Lisboa**, with two floors of gaming tables, an auditorium hosting theatrical and musical performances and a range of restaurants. Spectacular views can be had from the **cable car** that links the Torre Vasco da Gama with the marina. The

promenade along the river also offers delightful views, including of the 17.5-km- (11-mile-) long **Vasco da Gama** bridge, the longest in Europe. Also in the area is the MEO Arena (see p143).

⓬ Oceanário de Lisboa

Esplanada Dom Carlos 1, Parque das Nações. **Tel** 218 917 002. 🚌 705, 725, 728, 744, 750, 782. 🇲 Oriente. 🚆 Oriente. **Open** Apr–Oct: 10am–8pm daily; Nov–Mar: 10am–7pm daily. 🏛 ♿ ⬛ **oceanario.pt**

Centrepiece of Expo '98 and now the main attraction at Parque das Nações, the somewhat futuristic oceanarium was designed by American architect Peter Chermayeff, and is perched on the end of a pier, surrounded by water. It is the second-largest aquarium in the world, and holds an impressive array of species – birds and some mammals as well as fish and

18th-century Indian toy, Museu da Cidade

other underwater dwellers.

Four separate sea- and landscapes represent the habitats of the Atlantic, Pacific, Indian and Antarctic oceans, with suitable fauna and flora. The main attraction for most visitors, though, is the vast central tank with a dazzling variety of fish, large and small, swimming round and round. Sharks co-exist peaceably with bream, barracudas with rays. The softly lit waters can be

viewed through any number of glass panes, on two levels.

⓭ Museu da Cidade

Campo Grande 245. **Tel** 217 513 200. 🚌 736, 747, 750. 🇲 Campo Grande. **Open** 10am–1pm, 2–6pm Tue–Sun. **Closed** public hols. 🏛 (free Sun until 1pm). ♿ ⬛ **museudacidade.pt**

Palácio Pimenta was allegedly commissioned by João V (see p18) for his mistress Madre Paula, a nun from the nearby convent at Odivelas. When the mansion was built, in the middle of the 18th century, it occupied a peaceful site outside the capital. Nowadays it has to contend with the traffic of Campo Grande. The house itself, however, retains its period charm and the city museum is one of the most interesting in Lisbon.

The displays follow the development of the city, from prehistoric times, through the Romans, Visigoths and Moors, traced by means of tiles, drawings, paintings, models and historical documents. Some of the most fascinating exhibits are those depicting the city before the earthquake of 1755, including a highly detailed model made in the 1950s and an impressive 17th-century oil painting by Dirk Stoop (1610–86) of Terreiro do Paço, as Praça do Comércio was known then (see p49). One room is devoted to the Águas Livres aqueduct (see p86), with detailed architectural plans for its construction as well as prints and watercolours of the completed aqueduct.

The earthquake theme is resumed with pictures of the city amid the devastation and various plans for its reconstruction. The museum brings you into the 20th century with a large colour poster celebrating the Revolution of 1910 and the proclamation of the new republic (see p19).

❿ Museu Nacional do Azulejo

Dona Leonor, widow of King João II, founded the Convento da Madre de Deus in 1509. Originally built in Manueline style, the church was restored under João III using simple Renaissance designs. The striking Baroque decoration was added by João V. The convent cloisters provide a stunning setting for the National Tile Museum. Decorative panels and individual tiles trace the evolution of tile-making from its introduction by the Moors, through Spanish influence and the development of Portugal's own style up to the present day.

Level 2

Panorama of Lisbon
A striking 18th-century panel, located on the top floor, depicts Lisbon before the 1755 earthquake (see pp24–5). This detail shows the royal palace on Terreiro do Paço.

Hunting Scene
Artisans rather than artists began to decorate tiles in the 17th century. This detail shows a naive representation of a hunt.

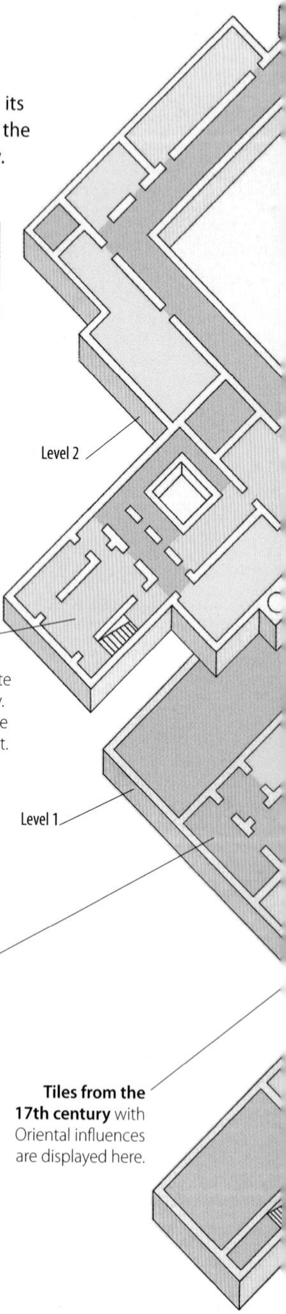

Level 1

Key to Floorplan

- ▢ Moorish tiles
- ▢ 16th-century tiles
- ▢ 17th-century tiles
- ▢ 18th-century tiles
- ▢ 19th-century tiles
- ▢ 20th-century tiles
- ▢ Temporary exhibition space
- ▢ Non-exhibition space

Tiles from the 17th century with Oriental influences are displayed here.

★ **Nossa Senhora da Vida**
This detail showing St John is part of a fine 16th-century majolica altarpiece. The central panel of the huge work depicts *The Adoration of the Shepherds*.

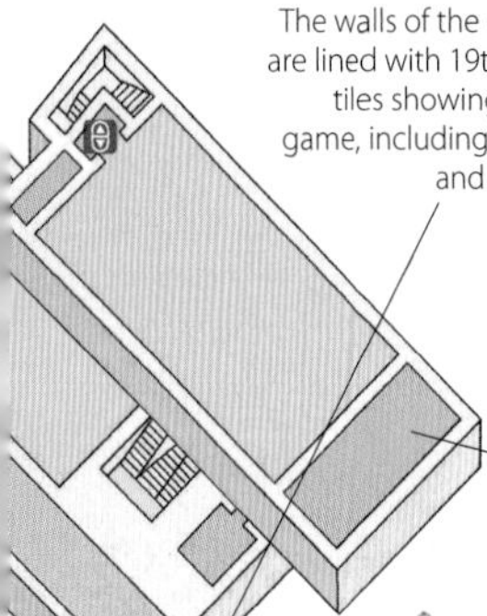

Kitchen Tiles
The walls of the restaurant are lined with 19th-century tiles showing hanging game, including wild boar and pheasant.

Level 3

VISITORS' CHECKLIST

Practical Information
Rua da Madre de Deus 4.
Tel 218 100 340.
Ⓦ museudoazulejo.pt
Open 10am–6pm Tue–Sun (last adm: 30 mins before closing).
Closed public hols. (free first Sun of the month).

Transport
🚌 718, 728, 742, 759, 794.

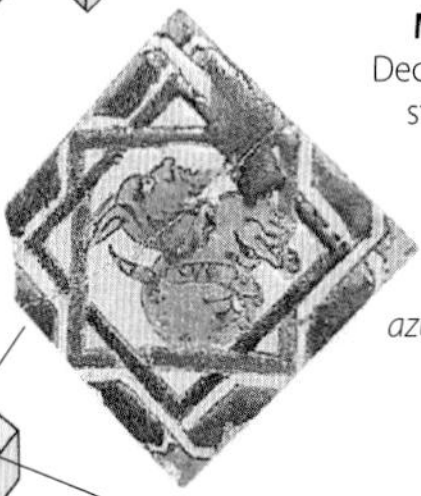

Moorish Tiles
Decorated with a stylized animal motif, this 15th-century tile is typical of Moorish *azulejo* patterns.

Entrance

The Renaissance cloister
is the work of Diogo de Torralva (1500–66).

★ **Madre de Deus**
Completed in the mid-16th century, it was not until two centuries later, under João V, that the church of Madre de Deus acquired its ornate decoration. The sumptuous Rococo altarpiece was added after the earthquake of 1755.

Gallery Guide

The rooms around the central cloister are arranged chronologically with the oldest tiles on the ground floor. Access to the Madre de Deus is via the ground floor. The front entrance of the church is used only during religious services.

The carved Manueline portal
was recreated from a 16th-century painting.

★ **Manueline Cloister**
This cloister is an important surviving feature of the original convent. Fine geometrical patterned tiles dating from the 17th century were added to the walls in the 19th century.

For keys to symbols *see back flap*

⓮ Jardim Zoológico

Praça Marechal Humberto Delgado.
Tel 217 232 910. 📠 716, 731, 755, 758
and other routes. Ⓜ Jardim
Zoológico. **Open** 10am–6pm daily
(Apr–Sep: to 8pm). 🅿 W zoo.pt

The gardens of the Jardim
Zoológico are as much a
feature as the actual zoo.
Opened in 1905, the zoo has
been revamped, and the
majority of its aviaries and
cages now provide more
comfortable conditions for the
specimens. It has an impressive
collection of 2,000 animals
comprising 400 different

A dolphin show at Dolphin's Bay in Lisbon's Jardim Zoológico

species. Current attractions
of the zoo include a cable
car touring the park, a reptile
house, dolphin shows and an
amusement park. The area is
divided into four zones and
the admission ticket provides
access to all of the attractions.

⓯ Aqueduto das Águas Livres

Best seen from Calçada da Quintinha.
Tel 213 251 652. 📠 702, 712, 713,
742, 758. **Open** Mar–Nov: 10am–6pm
Tue–Sat. **Closed** public hols. Mãe
d'Água das Amoreiras: Praça das
Amoreiras. **Tel** 213 251 644.
Open 10am–6pm Mon–Sat.
Closed public hols. 🅿

Considered the most beautiful
sight in Lisbon at the turn of
the 20th century, the Aqueduto
das Águas Livres looms over
the Alcântara valley northwest
of the city. The construction
of an aqueduct gave João V
(see p18) the opportunity to

indulge his passion for
grandiose building schemes, as
the only area of Lisbon with
fresh drinking water was the
Alfama. A tax on meat, wine,
olive oil and other comestibles
funded the project, and
although not complete until
the 19th century, it was already
supplying the city with water
by 1748. The main pipeline
measures 19 km (12 miles), but
the total length, including all
the secondary channels, is
58 km (36 miles). The most
visible part of this imposing
structure, classified a National
Monument in 2002, are
the 35 arches crossing the
Alcântara valley, the tallest
of which rise to a spectacular
65 m (213 ft) above ground.

The public walkway along
the aqueduct has been closed
since 1853. This is partly due
to Diogo Alves, the infamous
robber who threw his victims
over the edge. Today, it is
possible to take lively guided

tours over the Alcântara
arches. There are also tours
of the Mãe d'Água reservoir
and trips to the Mãe d'Água
springs, the source of the
water supply. These tours can
be irregular, so it is best to
contact the Museu da Água
(see p82) for details of the
trips on offer.

At the end of the aqueduct,
the **Mãe d'Água das Amoreiras**
is a castle-like building which
once served as a reservoir for
the water supplied from the
aqueduct. The original design
of 1745 was by the Hungarian
architect Carlos Mardel, who
worked under Pombal (see
pp24–5) in the rebuilding
of the Baixa. Completed in
1834, it became a popular
meeting place and acquired
a reputation as the rendezvous
for kings and their mistresses.
Today the space is used for art
exhibitions, fashion shows and
other events. There are great
views from the roof.

Imposing arches of the Aqueduto das Águas Livres spanning the Alcântara valley

⑯ Palácio Fronteira

Largo São Domingos de Benfica 1.
Tel 217 782 023. 🚌 770. Ⓜ Jardim
Zoológico. 🚊 Benfica. **Open** Mon–
Sat: 🕐 Jun–Sep: 10:30, 11am,
11:30am, noon; Oct–May: 11am, noon.
Closed public hols. 🖾

This delightful country
manor house was built as a
hunting pavilion for João de
Mascarenhas, the first Marquês
de Fronteira, in 1640. Although
skyscrapers are visible in the
distance, it still occupies a quiet
spot, by the Parque Florestal
de Monsanto. Both house
and garden have *azulejo*
decoration whose subjects
include battle scenes and
trumpet-blowing monkeys.

Although the palace is still
occupied by the 12th Marquis,
some of the living rooms and
the library, as well as
the formal gardens,
are included in the
tour. The Battles
Room has lively tiled
panels depicting
scenes of the War of
Restoration (1640–
68), with a detail of
João de Fronteira
fighting a Spanish
general. It was his
loyalty to Pedro II
during this war that
earned him the title of Marquis.
Interesting comparisons can
be made between these naive
17th-century Portuguese tiles
and the Delft ones from the
same period in the dining
room, depicting naturalistic
scenes. The dining room is also
decorated with frescoed panels
and portraits of Portuguese
nobility by artists such as
Domingos António de Sequeira
(1768–1837).

The late-16th-century chapel
is the oldest part of the house.
The façade is adorned with
stones, shells, broken glass and
bits of china. These fragments
of crockery are believed to
have been used at the feast
inaugurating the palace and
then smashed to ensure no one
else could sup off the same set.
Visits to the **garden** start at the
chapel terrace, where tiled
niches are decorated with

Tiled terrace leading to the chapel of the Palácio Fronteira

figures personifying the arts
and mythological creatures.

In the formal Italian garden
the immaculate box hedges are
cut into shapes
to represent the
seasons of the year.
To one end, tiled
scenes of dashing
knights on horse-
back, representing
ancestors of the
Fronteira family,
are reflected in the
waters of a large
tank. On either side
of the water, a grand
staircase leads
to a terrace above. Here,
decorative niches contain the
busts of Portuguese kings and
colourful majolica reliefs adorn
the arcades. More blue-and-
white tiled scenes, realistic and
allegorical, decorate the wall at
the far end of the garden.

Bust of João I in the gardens
of Palácio Fronteira

Entrance to the theatre museum in Parque
do Monteiro-Mor

⑰ Parque do Monteiro-Mor

Largo Júlio Castilho. **Tel** 217 567 620.
🚌 703, 736, 796. Ⓜ Lumiar. Park:
Open 2–6pm Tue, 10am–10pm Wed–
Sun. **Closed** 1 Jan, Easter, 1 May,
25 Dec. Museu Nacional do Traje:
Tel 217 567 620. **Open** 2–6pm Tue,
10am–6pm Wed–Sun. 🖾 (free first
Sun of the month). Museu Nacional
do Teatro: **Tel** 217 567 410. **Open**
10am–6pm Tue–Sun. 🖾 (combined
ticket for park & museums). ♿

Monteiro-Mor Park was sold
to the state in 1975 and the
18th-century palace buildings
were converted to museums.
The gardens are attractive and
rather more romantic than the
manicured box-hedge gardens
so typical of Lisbon. Much of
the land is wooded, though the
area around the museums has
gardens with flowering shrubs,
duck ponds and tropical trees.

The rather old-fashioned
Museu Nacional do Traje
(Costume Museum) has a vast
collection of textiles, accessories
and costumes worn by
musicians, politicians, poets,
aristocrats and soldiers.

The **Museu Nacional do
Teatro** has two buildings,
one devoted to temporary
exhibitions, the other
containing a small permanent
collection. Photos, posters
and cartoons feature famous
20th-century Portuguese actors,
and one section is devoted to
Amália Rodrigues, the famous
fado singer (see p145).

TWO GUIDED WALKS

The folds and creases of Lisbon's many hills demand to be explored on foot, yet they can also be quite demanding on the walker. It is possible to plan routes that avoid most steep inclines, but such routes often miss many of the hidden treasures of the city's *bairros*.

The two walks described here give a true taste of Lisbon's topography and of the rich mix of the city's lifestyles via some of the most charming neighbourhoods. The first walk takes you from lofty Estrela in

northwest Lisbon through picturesque *bairros*, passing the grandiose Palácio de São Bento (Portuguese Parliament building), towards the historic centre. The second walk begins in the Baixa and leads walkers through one of the many narrow entrances into the labyrinthine alleyways of Alfama before climbing to Castelo de São Jorge for spectacular views. In addition to these walks, each of the four areas of Lisbon described in the *Area-by-Area* section of this book has a walk on its *Street-by-Street* map.

CHOOSING A WALK

The Two Walks
This map shows the location of the two guided walks in relation to the main sightseeing areas of Lisbon.

Steep, narrow street typical of Alfama
(see pp32–41)

West Central
(p89)

Baixa & Avenida

Alfama

Baixa, Alfama, Castelo and Mouraria
(pp90–91)

Bairro Alto & Estrela

Tejo

0 metres 800
0 yards 800

Key

• • • Walk route

Neo-Classical façade of the Palácio de São Bento *(see p57)*

A 45-Minute Walk Around West Central Lisbon

The mainly residential Estrela neighbourhood is typical of well-to-do west Lisbon. The Portuguese Parliament lies to the east, then the terrain rises to Praça do Príncipe Real. This sloping neighbourhood with its small, bustling streets and energetic nightlife is typically Lisboetan. On the other side of the ridge, the Jardim Botânico descends steeply towards the city centre.

Tips for Walkers

Starting point: Basílica da Estrela
Length: 2.5 km (1.5 miles).
Getting there: Catch tram 25 or 28 or bus 709, 720 or 738.
Stopping off points: Pão de Canela in Praça das Flores is a pleasant café with outdoor seating. Another good spot is the café in Praça do Príncipe Real. Stop for a glass of wine at Enoteca ⑩.

① Inside Lisbon's 18th-century Basílica da Estrela

da Piedade to Praça das Flores ⑤, a typical Lisbon square with several appealing cafés. Cross the square to Rua do Monte Olivete, home of the British Council in its handsome palace ⑥. The grand polytechnic building, on Rua da Escola Politécnica, now houses the Museu Nacional de História Natural e da Ciência. Behind this is the Jardim Botânico ⑦ (see p46). Turn right and head

the side of a grand marble water reservoir, now the excellent Enoteca wine bar ⑩. Continue down Rua da Mãe

Begin at Basílica da Estrela ① (see p57), one of Lisbon's landmarks, then enjoy a stroll through the pleasant Jardim da Estrela ② (see p57). On leaving the park, head down Rua de Santo Amaro which descends steeply to Rua de São Bento ③. Turn right past attractive tiled façades and a number of antique shops and head to the Palácio de São Bento ④ (see p57), the seat of the Portuguese Parliament. Retrace your steps and turn right down Rua Nova

to Praça do Príncipe Real ⑧ (see p56), with its delightful magnolia-shaded garden and café. Opposite is the striking Neo-Moorish Palácio Ribeiro da Cunha ⑨. Cross the street and walk down the narrow lane to a flight of steps. These lead down

d'Água to Rua da Alegria, passing the famous jazz venue, Hot Clube ⑪ (see p143). From there, Travessa do Salitre will take you past atmospheric Parque Mayer ⑫, the city's old vaudeville park, before you reach the splendid, tree-lined Avenida da Liberdade (see p46), where you can catch the metro.

Key

• • • Walk route

② Peaceful Jardim da Estrela

For keys to symbols see back flap

A 90-Minute Walk Around Baixa, Alfama, Castelo and Mouraria

From the late-18th-century splendour of the Baixa, this walk takes you into the alleyways of Alfama, a much older and humbler neighbourhood. Castelo de São Jorge crowns the hill, standing on a site that has been fortified for thousands of years. Behind it, Mouraria was the quarter to which Lisbon's remaining Moors were relegated after Afonso Henriques conquered the city in 1147. Their legacy is believed to survive most notably in the cadences of *fado*, which is at its most authentic here.

① Equestrian statue of José I in Praça do Comércio

Begin the walk at Praça do Comércio ① *(see p49)*, which was once the grand maritime entrance to Lisbon. The statue at the centre of the vast square is of José I, king at the time of the great 1755 earthquake which destroyed the palace and most of lower-lying Lisbon *(see pp24–5)*. The grand arcades of the post-earthquake buildings surrounding the square ② faintly echo the palace, creating a somewhat ghostly atmosphere.

Tips for Walkers

Starting point: Praça do Comércio
Length: 3 km (1.9 miles)
Getting there: Catch tram 25 or bus 709 or 711
Stopping off points: Pois, Café ⑤ is well worth a visit. Alfama has several cheerful eateries, including Santo António de Alfama ⑧ and Mesa de Fradesis on Rua dos Remédios. The café by the statue of São Vicente ⑪ is a popular drinking spot, as is Bar Cerca Moura across the street.

Walk along Rua da Alfândega and turn left on to Rua da Madalena. The first street on your right is Rua dos Bacalhoeiros ③, named after the cod merchants who once dominated it. Continue along Rua dos Bacalhoeiros to the unmistakable Casa dos Bicos ④ *(see p37)* and pass through the arch at Arco de Jesus, which leads via steps up to Rua de São João da Praça. Now you have entered Alfama proper, protected by the hulking Sé to the left and with a gradually winding web of small streets, steps and alleys to the right. Head left and enjoy a coffee at Pois, Café ⑤ *(see pp136–7)*. Then head back and follow Rua de São João da Praça until it becomes Rua de São Pedro ⑥. The stalls selling fresh fish along here are an Alfama institution. The narrow street empties into Largo do Chafariz de Dentro, with the Restaurante do Museu do Fado ⑦ *(see p145)* across the street. To re-enter the small alleyways, cross the square and head up Rua dos Remédios. Stop for lunch at Santo António de Alfama ⑧ *(see p130)*, in nearby Beco de São Miguel. Next, find Escadinhas de Santo Estêvão or Calçadinha de Santo Estêvão and climb up to Santo Estêvão church ⑨. Lisbon is a city of viewing points, and this is one

of the best. From the square by the church, take Rua Guilherme Braga and then the steps on the left (Beco do Loureiro). These lead to a small square which opens on Rua da Regueira; turn right here and follow it to Rua do Castelo Picão, which takes you back into the heart of

⑥ The lively fish market on Rua de São Pedro

Sweeping views over the rooftops of Alfama

Across the square is the Museu de Artes Decorativas ⑫ *(see p36)*. Find Beco do Maldonado on the far side of the square and climb its steps until you can turn left into Pátio de Dom Fradique ⑬. Walk down Rua do Chão da Feira, the main access to the Castelo de São Jorge *(see pp40–41)*. In a corner here is a single-booth urinal whose ornate iron sign makes it a much-photographed work of art ⑭. In a niche inside the gateway to the citadel is a statue of St George ⑮. The steep incline up to the castle entrance is lined with tourist shops ⑯ as well as the ticket office. From the castle gate, head south down Rua Bartolomeu de Gusmão, turning right into Rua do Milagre de Santo António. Follow Costa do Castelo all the way around the back of the castle, which brings you to

Calçada de Santo André. A small gate here ⑰ is said to have been the scene of a decisive event during Afonso Henriques' 1147 siege of the castle. According to legend, the knight Martim Moniz prevented the gate from closing with his own body, sacrificing his life to allow Afonso Henriques and his men to storm the castle.

Next, follow the path round into Largo Rodrigues Freitas on the left. Take this past Beco da Laje on the right and turn left into a small square, then left again out of it. Now you are at the top of Calçada de Santo André and the Mouraria quarter. Head down the *calçada* and take the first left, Rua da Amendoeira. Descend this street to a small square and bear left into Rua Marquês de Ponte do Lima. Turn right at the junction with Escadinhas da Saúde and then immediately left into Rua das Fontainhas de São Lourenço. This is the heart of Mouraria ⑱. Stay on the charming Rua de São Lourenço, which becomes Largo das Farinhas. Turn right down the steps to Largo dos Trigueiros and follow this down to Beco do Rosendo. Descend down the steps and cross Rua da Madalena to Rua dos Condes de Monsanto. From the warren of Mouraria you have arrived in the Baixa. Ahead is Praça da Figueira ⑲ *(see p47)*, with an impressive equestrian statue of João I. Take the metro from Rossio station or one of the many buses that run from the square.

Key

• • • Walk route

Alfama. Follow its 45-degree turn to the right at Beco das Cruzes and continue walking to Calçadinha de São Miguel ⑩. Pass through the narrow arch here and onto Escadinhas de São Miguel. Then turn right and climb up Beco da Corvinha, passing through another arch up to Rua Norberto Araújo. Turn right and follow the street up steps and around the corner to Largo das Portas do Sol and the statue of the city's patron saint, São Vicente ⑪.

View from the battlements of Castelo de São Jorge

The Palácio da Pena, the oldest surviving palace in Portugal ▶

THE LISBON COAST

THE LISBON COAST

Within an hour's drive northwest of Lisbon you can reach the rocky Atlantic coast, the wooded slopes of Sintra or countryside dotted with villas and royal palaces. South of Lisbon you can enjoy the sandy beaches and fishing towns along the coast or explore the lagoons of the Tagus and Sado river estuaries.

Traders and invaders, from the Phoenicians to the Spanish, have left their mark in this region, in particular the Moors, whose forts and castles, rebuilt many times over the centuries, can be found all along this coast. After Lisbon became the capital in 1256, Portuguese kings and nobles built summer palaces and villas in the country-side west of the city, particularly on the cool, green heights of the Serra de Sintra.

Across the Tagus, the less fashionable southern shore (Outra Banda, more popularly known as the Margem Sul) could be reached only by ferry until the suspension bridge was built in 1966. Now, the long sandy beaches of the Costa da Caparica, the coast around the fishing town of Sesimbra and even the remote Tróia peninsula have become popular resorts during the summer months. Fortunately, large stretches of coast and unspoilt countryside are being protected as conservation areas and nature reserves.

Despite the region's rapid urbanization, small fishing and farming communities still survive. Lively fish markets offer a huge variety of fresh fish and seafood; Palmela and the Sado region are noted for their wine; sheep still roam the unspoilt Serra da Arrábida, providing milk for Azeitão cheese; and rice is the main crop in the Sado estuary. Traditional industries also survive, such as salt panning near Alcochete and marble quarries at Pero Pinheiro.

Though the sea is cold and often rough, especially on west-facing coasts, the beaches are among the cleanest in Europe. As well as surfing, fishing and scuba diving, the region provides splendid golf courses, horse-riding facilities and a motor-racing track. Arts and entertainment range from music and cinema festivals to bullfights and country fairs where regional crafts, such as hand-painted pottery, lace and baskets, are on display.

View of the town of Sesimbra, lying at the foothills of the Serra da Arrábida

◄ Rocky cliffs along the coast at the Cabo da Roca, the westernmost point of both mainland Portugal and continental Europe

Exploring the Lisbon Coast

North of the Tagus, the beautiful hill town of Sintra is dotted with historic palaces and surrounded by wooded hills, at times enveloped in an eerie sea mist. On the coast, cosmopolitan Cascais and the traditional fishing town of Ericeira are both excellent bases from which to explore the rocky coastline and surrounding countryside. South of the Tagus, the Serra da Arrábida and the rugged coast around Cabo Espichel can be visited from the small port of Sesimbra. Inland, the nature reserves of the Tagus and Sado estuaries offer a quiet retreat.

Sights at a Glance

1. Palácio de Mafra
2. Ericeira
3. Colares
5. Monserrate
6. *Sintra pp102–7*
7. Cascais
8. Estoril
9. *Palácio Nacional de Queluz pp110–11*
10. Alcochete
11. Costa da Caparica
12. Cabo Espichel
13. Sesimbra
14. Palmela
15. Serra da Arrábida
16. Setúbal
17. Península de Tróia
18. Alcácer do Sal

Tours

4. Serra de Sintra

Key

▬▬	Motorway
▬	Major road
▭▭▭	Minor road
▬	Scenic route
▬▬	Main railway
▬	Minor railway
▬▬	Regional border

Cabo da Roca on the western edge of the Serra de Sintra

Convento da Arrábida in the hills of the Serra da Arrábida

Getting Around

Motorways give quick access from Lisbon to Sintra, Estoril, Palmela and Setúbal. Main roads are generally well signposted and surfaced, though traffic congestion can be a problem. Watch out for potholes on smaller roads. Fast, frequent trains run west from Lisbon's Cais do Sodré station to Estoril and Cascais, and from Rossio, Roma Areeiro and Entrecampos stations to Queluz and Sintra. For trains south to Setúbal, Alcácer do Sal and beyond, use either the Fertagus service or Barreiro station on the southern bank of the Tagus. There are good bus services to all parts of the region, which leave mainly from Sete Rios.

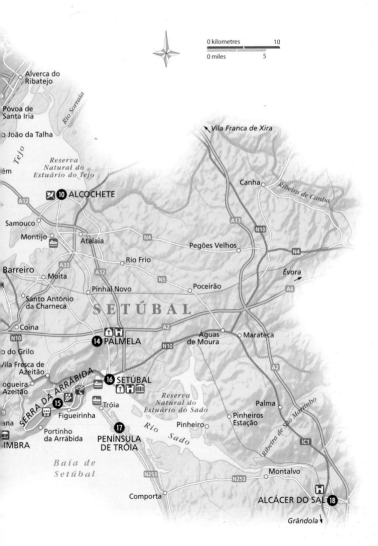

For keys to symbols *see back flap*

The stunning library in the Palácio de Mafra, paved with chequered marble

❶ Palácio de Mafra

Terreiro de Dom João V, Mafra.
Tel 261 817 550. 🚌 from Lisbon.
Ⓜ Campo Grande, then 🚌 Ericeira.
Open 9am–6pm Wed–Mon (last adm:
1 hr before closing). **Closed** 1 Jan,
Easter, 1 May, 25 Dec. 🎫 🚫 (free first
Sun of the month). 🎫 compulsory.
Ⓦ palaciomafra.pt

This massive Baroque palace
and monastery dwarfs the small
town of Mafra. It was built
during the reign of João V, and
began with a vow by the young
king to build a new monastery
and basilica, supposedly in
return for an heir (but more
likely, to atone for his well-
known sexual excesses). Work
began in 1717 on a modest
project to house 13 Franciscan
friars but, as the wealth began
to pour into the royal coffers
from Brazil, the king and his
Italian-trained architect, Johann
Friedrich Ludwig (1670–1752),

The king's bedroom in the Royal Palace

made ever more extravagant
plans. No expense was spared:
52,000 men were employed
and the finished project
eventually housed not 13, but
330 friars, a royal palace and
one of the finest libraries in
Europe, decorated with
precious marble, exotic
wood and countless
works of art. The
magnificent basilica was
consecrated on the
king's 41st birthday,
22 October 1730.

The palace was only
popular with those
members of the royal
family who enjoyed
hunting deer and wild
boar. Today, a wolf
conservation project
runs here. Most of the
finest furniture and art
works were taken to Brazil when
the royal family escaped the
French invasion in 1807.

The monastery was
abandoned in 1834
following the
dissolution of all
religious orders, and
the palace itself was
finally abandoned in
1910, when the last
Portuguese king,
Manuel II, escaped
from here to the
royal yacht anchored
off Ericeira.

Allow at least an
hour for the lengthy
tour, which starts in

the rooms of the monastery,
through the pharmacy, with
fine old medicine jars and some
alarming medical instruments,
to the hospital, where
16 patients in private cubicles
could see and hear Mass in the
adjoining chapel without
leaving their beds.

Upstairs, the sumptuous
palace state rooms extend
across the whole of the
monumental west façade,
with the King's apartments
at one end and the Queen's
apartments at the other, a
staggering 232 m (760 ft) apart.
Halfway between the two,
the long, imposing façade is
relieved by the twin bell towers
of the domed basilica. The
interior of the church is
decorated in contrasting
colours of marble and furnished
with six early-19th-century
organs. Fine Baroque
sculptures,
executed by
members of the
Mafra School of
Sculpture, adorn the
atrium of the basilica.
Begun by José I in
1754, many renowned
Portuguese and
foreign artists trained
in the school under
the directorship of
the Italian sculptor
Alessandro Giusti
(1715–99). Further
on, the Sala da Caça
has a grotesque
collection of
hunting trophies
and boars' heads. Mafra's
greatest treasure, however,
is its magnificent library,
which has a patterned marble
floor, Rococo-style wooden
bookcases and a collection
of over 40,000 books in gold-
embossed leather bindings,
including a prized first edition
of *Os Lusíadas* (1572) by the
celebrated Portuguese poet,
Luís de Camões (1524–80).

Statue of St Bruno
in the atrium of
Mafra's basilica

Environs
Once a week, on Thursday
mornings, the small country
town of **Malveira**, 10 km
(6 miles) east of Mafra, has the
region's biggest market, selling

Tractor pulling a fishing boat out of the sea at Ericeira

clothes and household goods as well as food.
At the village of **Sobreiro**, 6 km (4 miles) west of Mafra, Zé Franco's model village is complete with houses, farms, a waterfall and a windmill.

❷ Ericeira

🏠 7,500. 🚌 🛈 Rua Dr Eduardo Burnay 46 (261 863 122). 🗓 Jun–Sep daily.

Ericeira is an old fishing village which keeps its traditions despite an ever-increasing influx of summer visitors, from Lisbon and abroad, who enjoy the bracing climate, clean, sandy beaches and fresh seafood. In July and August, when the population leaps to 30,000, pavement cafés, restaurants and bars around the tree-lined Praça da República are buzzing late into the night. Red flags warn when swimming is dangerous; alternative attractions include a crazy golf course in Santa Marta park and a local history museum, the **Museu da Ericeira**, exhibiting model boats and traditional regional fishing equipment.
The unspoilt old town, a maze of whitewashed houses and narrow, cobbled streets, is perched high above the ocean. From Largo das Ribas, at the top of a 30-m (100-ft) stone-faced cliff, there is a bird's-eye view over the busy fishing harbour below, where tractors haul the boats out of reach of the tide. On 16 August, the annual fishermen's festival is celebrated with a candlelit procession to the harbour at the foot of the cliffs for the blessing of the boats.

On 5 October 1910, Manuel II, the last king of Portugal (see p19), finally sailed into exile from Ericeira as the Republic was declared in Lisbon; a tiled panel in the fishermen's chapel of Santo António above the harbour records the event. The banished king settled in Twickenham, southwest London, where he died in 1932.

🏛 Museu da Ericeira
Largo da Misericórdia. **Tel** 261 862 536. **Open** 10am–1pm & 2–6pm Tue. 🗲

❸ Colares

🏠 7,500. 🚌 🛈 Cabo da Roca, (219 280 081).

On the lower slopes of the Serra de Sintra, this lovely village faces towards the sea over a green valley, the Várzea de Colares. A leafy avenue winds its way up to the village, lined with pine and chestnut trees. Small quantities of the famous Colares wine are still made, but current vintages lack the character and ageing

potential of classic Colares and growers face a financial struggle to survive. Their hardy old vines grow in sandy soil, with their roots set deep below in clay; these were among the few vines in Europe to survive the disastrous phylloxera epidemic brought from America in the late 19th century with the first viticultural exchanges. The insect, which destroyed vineyards all over Europe by eating the vines' roots, could not penetrate the dense sandy soil of the Atlantic coast. Wine can be sampled at the Adega Regional de Colares on Alameda de Coronel Linhares de Lima.

Environs
There are several popular beach resorts west of Colares. From the village of Banzão you can ride 3 km (2 miles) to **Praia das Maçãs** on the old tramway, which opened in 1910 and still runs daily in July and August and on Fridays, Saturdays and Sundays from September to June. Just north of Praia das Maçãs is the picturesque village of **Azenhas do Mar**, clinging to the cliffs; to the south is the larger resort of **Praia Grande**. Both have natural pools in the rocks, which are filled by sea water at high tide and are now closed to swimmers. The unspoilt **Praia da Adraga**, 1 km (half a mile) further south, has a delightful beach café and restaurant. In the evenings and off-season, fishermen catch bass, bream and flat fish.

Natural rock pool at Azenhas do Mar, near Colares

❹ Serra de Sintra Tour

This round trip from Sintra follows a dramatic route over the top of the wooded Serra. The first part is a challenging drive with hazardous hairpin bends on steep, narrow roads that are at times poorly surfaced. It passes through dense forest and a surreal landscape of giant moss-covered boulders, with breathtaking views over the Atlantic coast, the Tagus estuary and beyond. After dropping down to the rugged, windswept coast, the route returns along small country roads, passing through hill villages and large estates on the cool, green northern slopes of the Serra de Sintra.

Atlantic coastline seen from Peninha

⑥ **Colares** The village of Colares rests on the lower slopes of the wooded Serra, surrounded by gardens and vineyards (see p99).

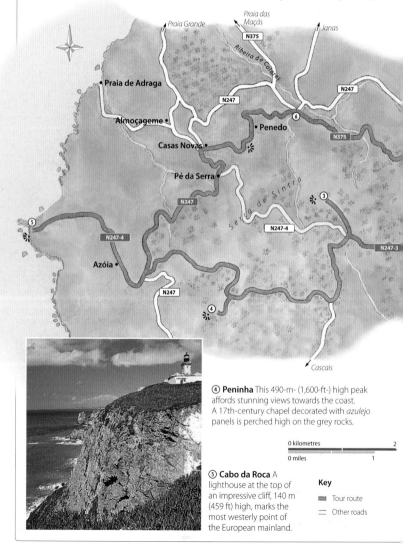

④ **Peninha** This 490-m- (1,600-ft-) high peak affords stunning views towards the coast. A 17th-century chapel decorated with *azulejo* panels is perched high on the grey rocks.

0 kilometres		2
0 miles		1

⑤ **Cabo da Roca** A lighthouse at the top of an impressive cliff, 140 m (459 ft) high, marks the most westerly point of the European mainland.

Key

▬ Tour route

═ Other roads

Tips for Drivers

Length: 36 km (22 miles).
Stopping-off points: There are cool springs of drinking water and fountains along the mountain roads. At Cabo da Roca you will find a café, restaurant and souvenir shops; at Colares there are several delightful restaurants and bars.

⑧ **Seteais** The elegant palace, now a luxury hotel and restaurant (see p123 & p135) was built in the 18th century for the Dutch Consul, Daniel Gildemeester.

⑦ **Monserrate** The cool forest park and elaborate 19th-century palace epitomize the romanticism of Sintra.

② **Sintra** From the centre of the old town the road winds steeply upwards past magnificent *quintas* (country estates) hidden among the trees.

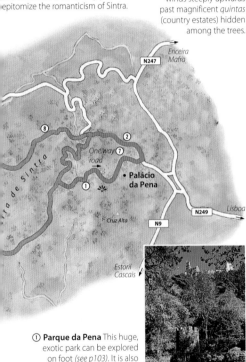

① **Parque da Pena** This huge, exotic park can be explored on foot (see p103). It is also possible to visit the beautiful Palácio da Pena (see pp106–7).

③ **Convento dos Capuchos** Two huge boulders guard the entrance to this remote Franciscan monastery, founded in 1560, where the friars lived in tiny rock-hewn cells lined with cork. There are stunning views of the coast from the hill above this austere, rocky hideaway.

Palace of Monserrate, an example of Romantic architecture

❺ Monserrate

Rua Barbosa du Bocage. **Tel** 219 237 300. 🚂 to Sintra, then taxi or bus 435. **Open** daily (last adm: 1 hour before closing); 30 Mar–25 Oct: 9:30am–8pm (to 7pm for the palace); 26 Oct–29 Mar: 10am–6pm (to 5pm for the palace). **Closed** 1 Jan, 25 Dec. 🅿
Ⓦ parquesdesintra.pt

The wild, romantic garden of this once magnificent estate is full of exotic trees and flowering shrubs. Among the subtropical foliage and valley of tree ferns, the visitor will come across a waterfall, a small lake and a chapel, built as a ruin, tangled in the roots of a giant *Ficus* tree. Its history dates back to the Moors but it takes its name from a small 16th-century chapel dedicated to Our Lady of Montserrat in Catalonia, Spain. The gardens were landscaped in the late 1700s by a wealthy young Englishman, William Beckford. They were later immortalized by Lord Byron in *Childe Harold's Pilgrimage* (1812).

In 1856, the abandoned estate was bought by another Englishman, Sir Francis Cook, who built a fantastic Moorish-style palace (which has now been restored) and transformed the gardens with a large sweeping lawn, camellias and subtropical trees from all over the world. These include the giant *Metrosideros* (Pacific Islands Christmas tree, covered in a blaze of red flowers in July), the native *Arbutus* (known as the strawberry tree because of its juicy red berries), from which the *medronho* firewater drink is distilled, and cork oak, with small ferns growing on its bark.

The Parques de Sintra maintains the house and gardens.

❻ Sintra

Sintra's stunning setting on the north slopes of the granite Serra, among wooded ravines and freshwater springs, made it a favourite summer retreat for the kings of Portugal. The tall, conical chimneys of the Palácio Nacional de Sintra *(see pp104–5)* and the fabulous Palácio da Pena *(see pp106–7)*, eerily impressive on its peak when the Serra is blanketed in mist, are unmistakable landmarks.

Today, the town (recognized as a UNESCO Cultural Landscape site in 1995) draws thousands of visitors all through the year. Even so, there are many quiet walks in the wooded hills around the town, especially beautiful in the long, cool evenings of the summer months.

Exploring Sintra

Present-day Sintra is in three parts, Sintra Vila, Estefânia and São Pedro, joined by a confusing maze of winding roads scattered over the surrounding hills. In the pretty cobbled streets of the old town, Sintra Vila, which is centred on the **Palácio Nacional de Sintra**, are the museums and beautifully tiled **post office**. The curving **Volta do Duche** leads from the old town, past the lush **Parque da Liberdade**, north to the Estefânia district and the striking Neo-Gothic **Câmara Municipal** (Town Hall). To the south and east, the hilly village of São Pedro spreads over the slopes of the Serra. The Sunday **market**, held on the second and fourth Sunday of every month, extends across the broad market square.

Exploring Sintra on foot involves a lot of walking and climbing up and down its steep hills. For a more leisurely tour, take one of the horse-and-carriage rides around the town. The **Miradouro da Vigia** in São Pedro offers impressive views, as does the cosy **Casa de Sapa** café, where you can sample *queijadas*, the local sweet speciality.

The many fountains dotted around the town are used by locals for their fresh spring drinking water. Two of the most striking are the tiled **Fonte Mourisca** (Arab Fountain), named for its Neo-Moorish decoration, and **Fonte da Sabuga**, where the water spouts from a pair of breasts.

Fonte Mourisca on Volta do Duche

🏛 Museu do Brinquedo

Rua Visconde de Monserrate 26.
Tel 219 242 171. **Open** 10am–6pm Tue–Sun. **Closed** 1 Jan, 1 May, 25 Dec
🅿 ⚏ 🆆 museu-do-brinquedo.pt

This small museum has a fine collection of toys, ranging from model planes, cars and trains, to dolls and dolls' houses, tin toys and clockwork models of cars and soldiers. There is also a restoration workshop and a playroom with puppets and storytellers.

Toy Alfa Romeo, Museu do Brinquedo

🏛 Museu das Artes de Sintra

Avenida Heliodoro Salgado. **Tel** 965 233 692. **Open** 10am–8pm Tue–Fri (to 6pm winter), 2–8pm Sat & Sun. **Closed** public hols. 🅿 ⚏

This museum displays the works of Portuguese and international artists, with the permanent exhibition featuring the private collections of Emílio Paula Campos and Dórita Castel-Branco, and several landscapes of Sintra dating from the mid-18th century.

🏛 Quinta da Regaleira

Rua Barbosa du Bocage. **Tel** 219 106 650. ▦ 435. **Open** 10am–6:30pm daily (to 8pm Apr–Sep, to 5:30pm Nov–Jan). 🅿 📷 🖉 🅿 🆆 regaleira.pt

Built between 1904 and 1910, this palace and extensive gardens are a feast of historical and religious references, occult symbols and mystery. The obsession of the eccentric millionaire António Augusto Carvalho Monteiro, they are a must for anyone interested in esoterica.

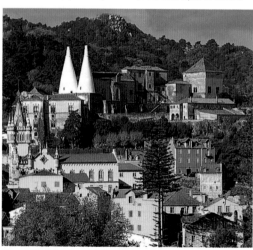
Chimneys of the Palácio Nacional de Sintra above the old town

Parque da Pena
Estrada da Pena. **Tel** 219 237 300.
Open daily; 30 May–25 Oct:
9:30am–8pm; 26 Oct–29 Mar:
10am–6pm (last entrance: 1 hour
before closing). **Closed** 25 Dec.
parquesdesintra.pt

A huge park surrounds the
Palácio da Pena and hidden
among the foliage are gazebos,
follies and fountains, and a chalet
built by Fernando II for his
second wife in 1869. Cruz Alta,
the highest point of the Serra at
529 m (1,740 ft), commands
spectacular views of the Serra
and surrounding plain. On a

nearby crag is a statue known
as *The Warrior*, supposedly
symbolizing the king watching
over his park and palace.

Castelo dos Mouros
Estrada da Pena. **Tel** 219 237 300.
Open daily; May–Oct: 9:30am–8pm;
Nov–Apr: 10am–6pm (last entrance
1 hour before closing). **Closed** 25 Dec.

Standing above the old town,
the ramparts of the 8th-century
Moorish castle conquered by
Afonso Henriques in 1147 snake
over the top of the Serra. On a
fine day, there are great views
from the castle walls over the old

town to Palácio da Pena, on a
neighbouring peak, and along
the coast. Hidden inside the walls
is an ancient Moorish cistern,
while just outside are
the ruins of Sintra's first church.
A steep footpath threads up
through wooded slopes from the
12th-century church of **Santa
Maria**. Follow the signs to a dark
green swing gate where the
footpath begins. The monogram
"DFII" carved on the gateway is
a reminder that the castle walls
were restored by Fernando II
(see p107) in the 19th century.

VISITORS' CHECKLIST

Practical Information
25,000. Praça da República
23 (219 231 157) ; Sintra station
(211 932 545) . 2nd & 4th Sun
of month in São Pedro. Sintra
Festival (Jun–Jul).

Transport
Avenida Dr Miguel Bombarda.
Buses run by Scotturb also run
regularly, check www.scotturb.
com for details.

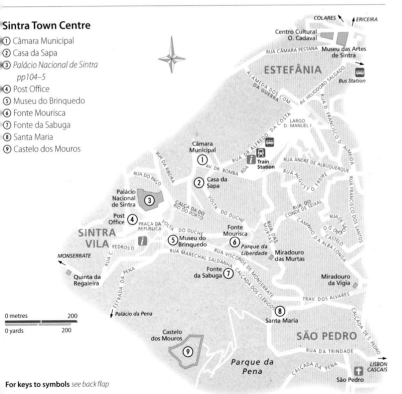

Battlements of the Castelo dos Mouros perched on the slopes of the Serra

Sintra Town Centre

① Câmara Municipal
② Casa da Sapa
③ *Palácio Nacional de Sintra*
    pp104–5
④ Post Office
⑤ Museu do Brinquedo
⑥ Fonte Mourisca
⑦ Fonte da Sabuga
⑧ Santa Maria
⑨ Castelo dos Mouros

0 metres   200
0 yards   200

For keys to symbols *see back flap*

Palácio Nacional de Sintra

At the heart of the old town of Sintra (Sintra Vila), a pair of strange conical chimneys rise high above the Royal Palace. The main part of the palace, including the central block with its plain Gothic façade and the large kitchens beneath the chimneys, was built by João I in the late 14th century, on a site once occupied by the Moorish rulers. The Paço Real, as it is also known, became the favourite summer retreat for the court, and continued as a residence for Portuguese royalty until 1910. Additions to the building by the wealthy Manuel I, in the early 16th century, echo the Moorish style. Gradual rebuilding of the palace has resulted in a fascinating amalgamation of various different styles.

★ **Sala das Pegas**
It is said that King João I had the ceiling panels painted as a rebuke to the court women for indulging in idle gossip like chattering magpies (pegas).

★ **Sala dos Brasões**
The domed ceiling of this majestic room is decorated with stags holding the coats of arms (brasões) of 72 noble Portuguese families. The lower walls are lined with 18th-century Delft-like tiled panels.

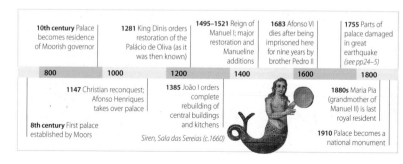

800	1000	1200	1400	1600	1800
10th century Palace becomes residence of Moorish governor	**1281** King Dinis orders restoration of the Palácio de Oliva (as it was then known)	**1495–1521** Reign of Manuel I; major restoration and Manueline additions	**1683** Afonso VI dies after being imprisoned here for nine years by brother Pedro II	**1755** Parts of palace damaged in great earthquake (see pp24–5)	

1147 Christian reconquest; Afonso Henriques takes over palace

1385 João I orders complete rebuilding of central buildings and kitchens

8th century First palace established by Moors

Siren, Sala das Sereias (c.1660)

1880s Maria Pia (grandmother of Manuel II) is last royal resident

1910 Palace becomes a national monument

VISITORS' CHECKLIST

Practical Information
Largo Rainha Dona Amélia.
Tel 219 237 300.
Open 30 Mar–25 Oct: 9:30am–
7pm daily; 26 Oct–29 Mar:
9:30am–6pm daily (last ticket:
30 mins before closing).
Closed 1 Jan, Easter, 25 Dec.
(free 10am–2pm Sun).

★ Sala dos Cisnes
The magnificent ceiling of the former banqueting hall, painted
in the 16th century, is divided into octagonal panels decorated
with swans *(cisnes)*.

Sala das Sereias
Intricate Arabesque
designs on 16th-
century tiles frame
the door of the
Room of the Sirens.

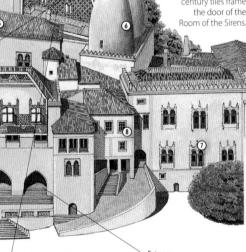

Entrance

KEY

① **Sala de Dom Sebastião**,
the bedroom of the young king

② **Jardim da Preta**, a walled
garden

③ **Sala das Galés** (galleons)

④ **The Torre dos Brasões** has
dovecotes below the cornice
decorated with nautical rope.

⑤ **The Sala dos Árabes** is
decorated with fine *azulejos*.

⑥ **The kitchens**, beneath the huge
conical chimneys, have spits and
utensils once used for preparing
royal banquets.

⑦ **The *ajimene* windows**, a
distinctive Moorish design with a
slender column dividing two arches,
were added by Manuel I.

⑧ **Sala dos Archeiros**, the
entrance hall

Chapel
Symmetrical Moorish
patterns decorate the
original 15th-century
chestnut and oak ceiling
and the mosaic floor of
the private chapel.

Sintra: Palácio da Pena

On the highest peaks of the Serra de Sintra stands the spectacular palace of Pena, an eclectic medley of architectural styles built in the 19th century for the husband of the young Queen Maria II, Ferdinand Saxe-Coburg-Gotha. It stands over the ruins of a Hieronymite monastery founded here in the 15th century on the site of the chapel of Nossa Senhora da Pena. Ferdinand appointed a German architect, Baron Von Eschwege, to build his summer palace filled with oddities from all over the world and surrounded by a park. With the declaration of the Republic in 1910, the palace became a museum, preserved as it was when the royal family lived here. Allow at least an hour and a half to visit this enchanting place.

Entrance Arch
A studded archway with crenellated turrets greets the visitor at the entrance to the palace. The palace buildings are painted the original daffodil yellow and strawberry pink.

Manuel II's Bedroom
The oval-shaped room is decorated with green walls and stuccoed ceiling. A portrait of Manuel II, the last king of Portugal, hangs above the fireplace.

KEY

① **In the kitchen** the copper pots and utensils still hang around the iron stove. The dinner service bears the coat of arms of Ferdinand II.

② **The Triton Arch** is encrusted with Neo-Manueline decoration and is guarded by a fierce sea monster.

③ **The cloister**, decorated with colourful patterned tiles, is part of the original monastery buildings.

★ **Great Hall**
The spacious hall is sumptuously furnished with German stained-glass windows, precious Oriental porcelain and four life-size turbaned torchbearers holding giant candelabra.

★ **Arab Room**
Marvellous trompe-l'oeil frescoes cover the walls and ceiling of the Arab Room, one of the loveliest in the palace. The Orient was a great inspiration to Romanticism.

VISITORS' CHECKLIST

Practical Information
Estrada da Pena, 5 km (3 miles) South of Sintra.
Tel 219 237 300.
W parquesdesintra.pt
Open 30 Mar–25 Oct: 9:45am–7pm; 26 Oct–29 Mar: 10am–6pm; last adm: 30 mins before closing.
Closed 1 Jan, 25 Dec.

Transport
434 from Avenida Dr Miguel Bombarda, Sintra.

★ **Chapel Altarpiece**
The impressive 16th-century alabaster and marble retable was sculpted by Nicolau Chanterène. Each niche portrays a scene of the life of Christ, from the manger to the Ascension.

Entrance

Ferdinand: King Consort

Ferdinand was known in Portugal as Dom Fernando II, the "artist" king. Like his cousin Prince Albert, who married the English Queen Victoria, he loved art, nature and the new inventions of the time. He was himself a watercolour painter. Ferdinand enthusiastically adopted his new country and devoted his life to patronizing the arts. In 1869, 16 years after the death of Maria II, Ferdinand married his mistress, the opera singer Countess Edla. His life-long dream of building the extravagant palace at Pena was completed in 1885, the year he died.

Outdoor café in the popular holiday resort of Cascais

❼ Cascais

🏠 27,800. 🚌 🚃 🛈 Rua Visconde da Luz 14 (214 822 327). 🗓 1st & 3rd Sun of the month.

Having been a holiday resort for well over a century, Cascais possesses a certain illustriousness that younger resorts lack. Its history is most clearly visible in the villas along the coast, built as summer residences by wealthy Lisboetas during the late 19th century, after King Luís I had moved his summer activities to the 17th-century fortress here.

The sandy, sheltered bay around which the modern suburb has sprawled was a fishing harbour in prehistoric times. Fishing still goes on, and was recently given a municipal boost with the decision to build a quay for the landing and initial auctioning of the fishermen's catch. But Cascais today is first of all a favoured suburb of Lisbon. It may sometimes seem more defined by its ceaseless construction boom than by any historic or even touristic qualities, but the beautiful, windswept coastline beyond the town has been left relatively undeveloped.

The **Museu Condes de Castro Guimarães** is perhaps the best place to get a taste of Cascais as it was just over a century ago. A castle-like villa on a small creek by a headland, its grounds are today part of a park.

Across the road from the museum is the marina, one of the most emblematic developments in Cascais. With its small shopping centre, restaurants and cafés, it is a weekend magnet for today's car-borne Cascais residents and tourists.

The **Casa das Histórias**, designed by Eduardo Souto de Moura, was established by the artist Paula Rego to exhibit her works, which range from paintings and drawings to illustrations and lithographs.

🏛 **Museu Condes de Castro Guimarães**
Avenida Rei Humberto de Itália. **Tel** 214 825 401. Museum: **Open** 10am–5pm Tue–Sun. Library: Casa da Horta de Santa Clara. **Open** 10am–6pm Mon–Sat. **Closed** 1–2pm Mon, Sun & public hols.

🏛 **Casa das Histórias**
Avenida da República 300. **Tel** 214 826 970. **Open** 10am–6pm daily (to 7pm in summer).

Environs
At **Boca do Inferno** (Mouth of Hell), about 1.5 km (1 mile) west on the coast road, the sea rushes into clefts and caves in the rocks making an ominous booming sound and sending up spectacular spray in rough weather. The place is almost obscured by a roadside market and cafés but a small platform gives a good view of the rocky arch with the sea below.

The magnificent sandy beach of **Guincho**, 10 km (6 miles) further west, is backed by sand dunes with clumps of umbrella pines and a cycle path. A small fort (now a luxury hotel) stands perched on the rocks above the sea. Atlantic breakers rolling in make this a paradise for experienced windsurfers and surfers, but beware of the strong currents.

Spectacular view of the weatherbeaten coastline at Boca do Inferno, near Cascais

❽ Estoril

🏠 24,000. 🚌 🚃 🛈 Rua Visconde da Luz 14, Cascais (214 822 327).

Despite once being the haunt of exiled royalty fleeing European republicanism, the lovely resort town of Estoril does not rest on its historical laurels. Today it is a tourist and business resort, and a place for comfortable retirement. As such, it relies equally on its historical reputation and on the natural attractiveness it has always possessed. There are also a number of good golf courses.

What separates Estoril from Cascais, besides a pleasant beach promenade of 3 km (2 miles) and a mansion-covered ridge known as Monte Estoril, is its sense of place. The heart of Estoril is immediately accessible from the train station. On one side of

Sandy beach and promenade along the bay of Estoril

the tracks is the riviera-like, but relaxed beach, on the other a palm-lined park flanked by grand buildings, stretching up past fountains to what is said to be Europe's biggest casino. Dwarfing the casino is the Estoril Congress Centre, a vast multipurpose edifice that speaks confidently of Estoril's contemporary role.

9 Palácio Nacional de Queluz

See pp110–11.

10 Alcochete

🏠 8,000. 🚌 ℹ️ Largo da Misericórdia (212 348 655).

This delightful old town overlooks the wide Tagus estuary from the southern shore. Salt has long been one of the main industries here, and saltpans can still be seen to the north and south of the town, while in the town centre a large statue of a muscular salt worker has the inscription: "Do Sal a Revolta e a Esperança" (From Salt to Rebellion and Hope). On the outskirts of town is a statue of Manuel I *(see p18)*, who was born here on 1 June 1469 and granted the town a Royal Charter in 1515.

Environs
The **Reserva Natural do Estuário do Tejo** covers a vast area of estuary water, salt marshes and small islands around Alcochete and is a very important breeding ground for water birds. Particularly interesting are flocks of flamingos that gather here during the autumn and spring migration, en route from colonies such as the Camargue in France and Fuente de Piedra in Spain. Ask at the tourist office about boat trips to see the wildlife of the estuary, which includes wild bulls and horses.

🏛️ **Reserva Natural do Estuário do Tejo**
Avenida dos Combatentes da Grande Guerra 1. **Tel** 212 348 021.

18th-century pilgrims' lodgings, Cabo Espichel

11 Costa da Caparica

🏠 12,000. 🚌 to Cacilhas or Trafaria then bus. 🚊 to Pragal then bus. ℹ️ Avenida General Humberto Delgado (212 900 071).

Long beaches backed by sand dunes make this a popular holiday resort for Lisboetas, who come to sunbathe, swim, and enjoy the beach cafés and seafood restaurants. A railway with open carriages runs for 10 km (6 miles) along the coast in summer. The first beaches reached from the town are popular with families with children, while the furthest beaches suit those seeking quiet isolation. Further south, sheltered by pine forests, **Lagoa de Albufeira** is a peaceful windsurfing and kiteboarding centre and camp site.

Statue of a salt worker in Alcochete (1985)

12 Cabo Espichel

🚌 from Sesimbra.

Sheer cliffs drop straight into the sea at this windswept promontory where the land ends dramatically. The Romans named it Promontorium Barbaricum, alluding to its dangerous location, and a lighthouse warns sailors of the treacherous rocks below. Stunning views of the ocean and the coast can be enjoyed from this bleak outcrop of land but beware of the strong gusts of wind on the cliff edge.

In this desolate setting is the impressive **Santuário de Nossa Senhora do Cabo**, a late-17th-century church with its back to the sea. On either side of the church, a long line of dilapidated 18th-century pilgrims' lodgings, facing inwards, form an open courtyard. Baroque paintings, *ex votos* and a frescoed ceiling decorate the church's interior. Nearby, a domed chapel has tiled blue-and-white *azulejo* panels depicting fishing scenes. The site became a popular place of pilgrimage in the 13th century when a local man had a vision of the Madonna rising from the sea on a mule. Legend has it that the mule tracks can be seen embedded in the rock. The large footprints, on Praia dos Lagosteiros below the church, are actually believed to be fossilized dinosaur tracks.

Spring flowers by the saltpans of the Tagus estuary near Alcochete

Palácio Nacional de Queluz

In 1747, Pedro, younger son of João V, commissioned Mateus Vicente to transform his 17th-century hunting lodge into a Rococo summer palace. The central section, including a music room and chapel, was built, but after Pedro's marriage in 1760 to the future Maria I, the palace was again extended. The French architect Jean-Baptiste Robillion added the sumptuous Robillion Pavilion and gardens, cleared space for the Throne Room and redesigned the Music Room. During Maria's reign, the royal family kept a menagerie and went boating on the *azulejo*-lined canal.

Corridor of the Sleeves
Painted *azulejo* panels (1784) representing the continents and the seasons, as well as hunting scenes, line the walls of the bright Corredor das Mangas (*sleeves*).

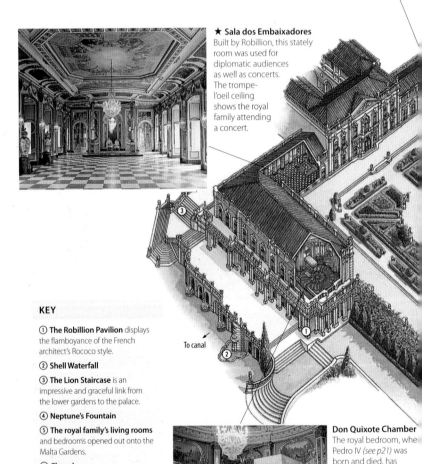

★ Sala dos Embaixadores
Built by Robillion, this stately room was used for diplomatic audiences as well as concerts. The trompe-l'oeil ceiling shows the royal family attending a concert.

To canal

KEY

① **The Robillion Pavilion** displays the flamboyance of the French architect's Rococo style.

② **Shell Waterfall**

③ **The Lion Staircase** is an impressive and graceful link from the lower gardens to the palace.

④ **Neptune's Fountain**

⑤ **The royal family's living rooms** and bedrooms opened out onto the Malta Gardens.

⑥ **Chapel**

⑦ **Malta Gardens**

⑧ **The Hanging Gardens**, designed by Robillion, were built over arches, raising the ground in front of the palace above the surrounding gardens.

Don Quixote Chamber
The royal bedroom, where Pedro IV (*see p21*) was born and died, has a domed ceiling and magnificent floor decoration in exotic woods, giving the square room a circular appearance. Painted scenes in the room tell the story of *Don Quixote*.

Music Room

Operas and concerts were performed here by Maria I's orchestra, "the best in Europe" according to English traveller William Beckford. A portrait of the queen hangs above the fortepiano.

VISITORS' CHECKLIST

Practical Information
Largo do Palácio, Queluz.
Tel 219 237 300.
🆆 parquesdesintra.pt
Open 30 Mar–25 Oct: 9am–7pm daily (last adm: 1 hr before closing); 26 Oct–29 Mar: 9am–5:30pm daily (last adm: 30 mins before closing). **Closed** 1 Jan, 25 Dec. 🎟 (free 10am–2pm Sun; check website for details on combined tickets). ♿ 🖥 ▨

Transport
🚌 from Lisbon (Colégio Militar). 🚉 Queluz-Belas or Queluz-Massama.

Entrance

★ **Throne Room**
The elegant state room (1770) was the scene of splendid balls and banquets. The gilded statues of Atlas are by Silvestre Faria Lobo.

Maria I (1734–1816)

Maria, the eldest daughter of José I, lived the palace in Queluz after her marriage her uncle, Pedro, in 1760. Serious and evout, she conscientiously filled her role as ueen, but suffered increasingly from bouts melancholia. When her son José died om smallpox in 1788, she went hopelessly ad. Visitors to Queluz were dismayed by r agonizing shrieks as she suffered visions d hallucinations. After the French invasion of 807, her younger son João (declared regent in 1792) ok his mad mother to Brazil.

★ **Palace Gardens**
The formal gardens, adorned with statues, fountains and topiary, were often used for entertaining. Concerts performed in the Music Room would spill out into the Malta Gardens.

⓭ Sesimbra

🏙 42,000. 🚌 ℹ️ Largo da Marinha 26–7 (212 288 540). 🛒 Wed–Sat.

A steep narrow road leads down to this busy fishing village in a sheltered south-facing bay. Protected from north winds by the slopes of the Serra da Arrábida, the town has become a popular holiday resort with Lisboetas. It was occupied by the Romans and later the Moors until King Sancho II *(see p20)* conquered its heavily defended forts in 1236. The old town is a maze of steep narrow streets, with the **Santiago Fort** (now a customs post) in the centre overlooking the sea. From the terrace, which is open to the public during the day, there are views over the town, the Atlantic and the unspoilt wide sandy beach that stretches out on either side. Sesimbra is fast developing as a resort, with holiday flats mushrooming on the surrounding hillsides and plentiful pavement cafés and bars that are always busy on sunny days, even in winter, and offer a surprisingly lively nightlife.

The fishing fleet of brightly painted boats is moored in the **Porto do Abrigo** to the west of the main town. The harbour is reached by taking Avenida dos Náufragos, a sweeping

Colourful fishing boats in the harbour at Sesimbra

promenade that follows the beach out of town. On the large trawlers *(traineiras)*, the catch is mainly sardines, sea bream, whiting and swordfish; on the smaller boats, octopus and squid. In the late afternoon, when the fishing boats return from a day at sea, a colourful, noisy fish auction takes place on the quayside. The day's catch can be tasted in the town's excellent fish restaurants along the shore.

High above the town is the **Moorish castle**, greatly restored in the 18th century when a church and small, flower-filled cemetery were added inside the walls. There are wonderful views from the ramparts, especially at sunset.

⓮ Palmela

🏙 57,000. 🚌 🚉 ℹ️ Castelo de Palmela (212 332 122). 🛒 every other Tue.

The formidable castle at Palmela stands over the small hill town, high on a northeastern spur of the wooded Serra da Arrábida. Its strategic position dominates the plain for miles around, especially when floodlit at night. Heavily defended by the Moors, it was finally conquered in the 12th century and given by Sancho I *(see p20)* to the Knights of the Order of Santiago. In 1423, João I transformed the castle into a monastery for the Order, which has been restored and converted into a splendid *pousada (see p123)*, with a restaurant in the monks' refectory and a swimming pool for residents, hidden inside the castle walls. From the castle terraces, and especially from the top of the 14th-century keep, there are fantastic views all around, over the Serra da Arrábida to the south and on a clear day across the Tagus to Lisbon. In the town square below, the church of **São Pedro** contains 18th-century tiles of scenes from the life of St Peter.

The annual wine festival, the Festa das Vindimas, is held on the first weekend of September in front of the 17th-century Paços do Concelho (town hall). Traditionally dressed villagers press the wine barefoot and on the final day of celebrations there is a spectacular firework display from the castle walls.

The castle at Palmela with views over the wooded Serra da Arrábida

⓯ Serra da Arrábida

🚌 from Setúbal. 🛈 Parque Natural da Arrábida, Avenida Luísa Todi (265 545 010).

The Parque Natural da Arrábida covers the small range of limestone mountains that stretches east–west along the coast between Sesimbra and Setúbal. It was established to protect the wild, beautiful landscape and rich variety of birds and wildlife, including eagles, wildcats and badgers.

The name Arrábida is from Arabic, meaning a place of prayer, and the wooded hillsides are indeed a peaceful, secluded retreat. The sheltered, south-facing slopes are thickly covered with aromatic and evergreen shrubs and trees, such as pine and cypress, more typical of the Mediterranean. Vineyards also thrive on the sheltered slopes and the town of **Vila Nogueira de Azeitão** is known for its wine, especially the Moscatel de Setúbal.

The **Estrada de Escarpa** (the N379-1) snakes across the top of the ridge and affords astounding views. A narrow road winds down to **Portinho da Arrábida**, a sheltered cove with a beach of fine white sand and crystal clear sea, popular with underwater fishermen. The sandy beaches of **Galapos** and **Figueirinha** are a little further east along the coast road towards Setúbal. Just east of Sesimbra, the Serra da Arrábida drops to the sea in the sheer 380-m (1,250-ft) cliffs of Risco, the highest in mainland Portugal.

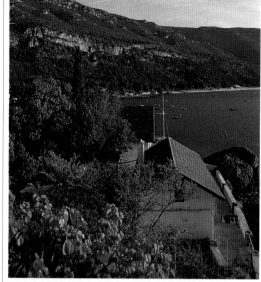

Portinho da Arrábida on the dramatic coastline of the Serra da Arrábida

⛪ Convento da Arrábida

Serra da Arrábida. **Tel** 212 197 620. **Open** 10am, 3pm Wed–Sun (by appt only). **Closed** Aug. 🖼

Half-hidden among the trees of the Serra, this 16th-century building was once a Franciscan monastery. The five round towers were probably used for meditation. The building now houses a cultural centre.

🏛 Museu Oceanográfico

Fortaleza de Santa Maria, Portinho da Arrábida. **Tel** 212 189 791. **Open** 10am–4pm Tue–Fri, 3–6pm Sat. **Closed** public hols, Sat in Aug. 🖼

This small fort, just above Portinho da Arrábida, was built by Pedro, the Prince Regent, in 1676 to protect local communities from attacks by Moorish pirates. It now houses a Sea Museum and Marine Biology Centre where visitors can see aquaria containing many local sea creatures, including sea urchins, octopus and starfish.

🍷 José Maria da Fonseca

Rua José Augusto Coelho 11, Vila Nogueira de Azeitão. **Tel** 212 197 500. **Open** 10am–noon, 2:30–5:30pm daily (Nov–Mar: to 4:30pm). **Closed** 1 & 2 Jan, 31 May, 24 & 25 Dec. 🖼 🎫 (prior appointment required) 🖼

The Fonseca winery produces quality table wines and is famous for its fragrant dessert wine, Moscatel de Setúbal *(see p129)*. Tours of the winery explain the process of making moscatel and visit a series of old cellars containing huge oak and chestnut vats. Tours last about 45 minutes and include a wine-tasting.

Key

▬▬ Major road
═══ Minor road
──── Other road

0 kilometres 5
0 miles 3

Map labels: Lisboa, Palmela, N379, N252, Lisboa, N10, Vila Fresca de Azeitão, N10, Vila Nogueira de Azeitão, Setúbal, N379, N379-1, N379-1, N10-4, Galapos, Figueirinha, Portinho da Arrábida, antana, Sesimbra, Baía de Setúbal

Manueline interior of Igreja de Jesus, Setúbal

⑯ Setúbal

🏠 92,000. 🚇 🚌 🚉 *i* Travessa Frei Gaspar 10 (265 539 130).

Although this is an important industrial town, and the third largest port in Portugal (after Lisbon and Oporto), Setúbal can be used to explore the area. To the south of the central gardens and fountains are the fishing harbour, marina and ferry port, and a lively covered market. North of the gardens is the old town, with attractive pedestrian streets and squares full of cafés.

The 16th-century **cathedral**, dedicated to Santa Maria da Graça, has glorious tiled panels dating from the 18th century, and gilded altar decoration. Street names commemorate two famous Setúbal residents: Manuel Barbosa du Bocage (1765–1805), whose satirical poetry landed him in prison, and Luísa Todi (1753–1833), a celebrated opera singer.

In Roman times, fish-salting was the most important industry here. Rectangular tanks, carved from stone, can be seen under the glass floor of the Regional Tourist Office on Travessa Frei Gaspar.

🏛 Igreja de Jesus

Largo de Jesus. **Tel** 265 520 964. **Open** 9:30am–1pm, 2–4pm Tue–Sat, 9am–12:30pm Sun. ♿ Museum: **Tel** 265 537 890. **Open** 9am–12:30pm, 2–5:30pm Tue–Sat. **Closed** public hols. Some parts of the museum are currently closed for restoration.

To the north of the old town, this striking Gothic church is one of Setúbal's architectural treasures. Designed by the architect Diogo Boitac in 1494, the lofty interior is adorned with twisted columns, carved in three strands from pinkish Arrábida limestone, and rope-like stone ribs decorating the roof, recognized as the earliest examples of the distinctive and ornate Manueline style.

On Rua do Balneário, in the old monastic quarters, a **museum** houses 14 remarkable paintings of the life of Christ. Painted in glowing colours, they are attributed to followers of Jorge Afonso (1520–30).

🏛 Museu de Arqueologia e Etnografia

Avenida Luísa Todi 162. **Tel** 265 239 365. **Open** 9am–12:30pm, 2–5:30pm Tue–Sat. **Closed** public hols.

The archaeological museum displays a wealth of finds from digs around Setúbal, including Bronze Age pots, Roman coins and amphorae. The ethnography display shows local arts, crafts and industries, including the processing of salt and cork over the centuries.

🏰 Castelo de São Filipe

Estrada de São Filipe. **Tel** 265 550 070. **Open** daily.

The star-shaped fort was built in 1595 by Philip II of Spain during Portugal's period under Spanish rule to keep a wary eye on pirates, English invaders and the local population. A massive gateway and stone tunnel lead to the sheltered interior, which now houses a *pousada (see p123)* and an exquisite small chapel, tiled with scenes from the life of São Filipe by Policarpo de Oliveira Bernardes (1695–1778). A broad terrace offers marvellous views over the city and the Sado estuary.

Environs

Setúbal is an excellent starting point for a tour by car of the unspoilt **Reserva Natural do Estuário do Sado**, a vast stretch of mud flats, shallow lagoons and salt marshes with patches of

Fisherman's boat on the shallow mud flats of the Reserva Natural do Estuário do Sado

pine forest, which has been explored and inhabited since 3500 BC. Otters, water birds (including storks and herons), oysters and a great variety of fish are found in the reserve. The old tidal water mill at Mouriscas, 5 km (3 miles) to the east of Setúbal, uses the different levels of the tide to turn the grinding stones. Rice-growing and fishing are the main occupations today, and pine trees around the lagoon are tapped for resin.

⊠ Reserva Natural do Estuário do Sado
ℹ Praça da República, Setúbal (265 541 157).

⓱ Península de Tróia

🚢 Tróia. 🚌 *ℹ* Travessa Frei Gaspar 10 (265 539 130).

High-rise holiday apartments dominate the tip of the Tróia Peninsula, easily accessible from Setúbal by ferry. The Atlantic coast, stretching south for 18 km (11 miles) of untouched sandy beaches, is now the haunt of sun-seekers in the summer.

Near Tróia, in the sheltered lagoon, the Roman town of **Cetóbriga** was the site of a thriving fish-salting business; the stone tanks and ruined buildings are open to visit. To the south, smart holiday villas and golf clubs are springing up along the lagoon.

Further on, **Carrasqueira** is an old fishing community where you can still see traditional reed houses, with walls and roofs made from thatch. The narrow fishing boats moored along the mud

View over Alcácer do Sal and the Sado river from the castle

flats are reached by walkways raised on stilts. From here to Alcácer do Sal, great stretches of pine forest line the road, and there are the first glimpses of the cork oak countryside typical of the Alentejo region.

🏛 Cetóbriga
N253-1. **Tel** 265 499 400. **Open** Oct–May: 10am–1pm, 3–5:30pm Tue–Sat (Jun–Aug: to 6:30pm). 🏛

⓲ Alcácer do Sal

🏙 14,000. 🚌 🚉 *ℹ* Largo Pedro Nunes 76 (265 247 013). 🏛 1st Sat of month.

Bypassed by the main road, the ancient town of Alcácer do Sal (*al-kasr* from the Arabic for castle, and *do sal* from its trade in salt) sits peacefully on the north bank of the Sado river. The imposing castle was a hillfort as early as the 6th century BC. The Phoenicians

made an inland trading port here, and the castle later became a Roman stronghold. Rebuilt by the Moors, it was conquered by Afonso II in 1217. The buildings have now taken on a new life as a *pousada (see p122)*, with views over the rooftops.

There are pleasant cafés along the riverside promenade and several historic churches. The 18th-century **Santo António** holds a marble Chapel of the 11,000 Virgins, while the **Cripta Arqueológica** exhibits finds dating from the Iron Age to the modern era. The bullring is a focus for summer events and hosts the agricultural fair in October.

🏛 Cripta Arqueológico
Castelo de Alcácer do Sal. *ℹ* 265 612 058. **Open** 9:30am–1pm, 3–6:30pm (summer); 9am–noon, 2–5:30pm (winter).

Thatched fisherman's cottage in the village of Carrasqueira

Birds of the Tagus and Sado Estuaries

Many water birds, including black-winged stilts, avocets, Kentish plovers and pratincoles, are found close to areas of open water and mud flats as well as the dried-out lagoons of the Tagus and Sado estuaries. Reed-beds also provide shelter for nesting and support good numbers of little bitterns, purple herons and marsh harriers. From September to March, the area around the Tagus estuary is extremely important for wildfowl and wintering waders.

Black-winged stilt, a wader that feeds in the estuaries

TRAVELLERS' NEEDS

WHERE TO STAY

Lisbon and its environs offer a variety of accommodation, from restored palaces and modern luxury hotels to comfortable chain hotels, old-fashioned guesthouses and family-run hostels. There are a number of nice places to stay around the main sightseeing areas of the city as well as along

the Lisbon Coast, where *pousadas*, often historic buildings converted into hotels and located in places of natural beauty, are an option. In the countryside, hotels are fairly scarce, though Sintra has a selection of places to stay and is a good base for exploring the area west of Lisbon.

Bedroom at the York House hotel in Lisbon, a converted 17th-century convent *(see p122)*

Choosing a Hotel

The majority of the modern, luxury hotels in Lisbon are centrally situated around Parque Eduardo VII, at the north end of Avenida de Liberdade. The Baixa district has a number of more modest guesthouses, with a wide choice of accommodation located around Rossio square.

Most of the city's older districts, including Chiado, Barrio Alto, Graça and Alfama, have small hotels that offer peace and quiet, if not always the top comforts. An increasing number of design and boutique hotels, as well as self-catering options, are springing up in these areas.

Types of Hotels

Hotels in Lisbon vary greatly in terms of quality, price and facilities. The Portuguese tourist authority classifies lodging into various categories.

Hotels are distinguished by the fact that they take up an entire building and are often purpose-built. However, visitors who prefer a family-style environment can choose to stay in a manor house, a palace, or a residence of architectural or historical significance. There are also aparthotels that offer tourists greater independence yet all the comforts of a hotel.

For those wishing to take part in a variety of leisure activities, resorts are a good option. Hostels offer great value for money, and can be found in the main cities as well as in the countryside. Some hostels even provide meals. *Pousadas* are either country inns or located in historic buildings such as mansions, castles and palaces. They are a state-owned chain run by **Pestana**.

Hotel Chains

International luxury groups are represented in Lisbon by such hotels as the Olissippo Lapa Palace *(see p122)*. Smaller luxury groups include **Sana Hotels**, **Tivoli Hotels**, which has three hotels in Lisbon and two in Sintra, and the **Pestana Group**, which owns the Pestana Palace Hotel *(see p122)* in Lisbon. **Heritage Hotels** runs five

smaller luxury hotels in the city, including the Solar do Castelo *(see p120)*.

Lower down the scale, **Ibis Hotel**, a part of the French-owned Accor Group, has six properties in the Lisbon area.

Gradings

The Portuguese tourist authority, **Turismo de Portugal**, grades hotels from one to five stars (five being the top rating). These ratings are based on a fixed set of criteria that cover most aspects of comfort. They do not take into account more subjective factors such as view or atmosphere. All graded establishments should have a sign showing their rating.

Prices

In Portugal, establishments are free to set their own prices, but tariffs must be displayed at reception and in the rooms. The cost of the room usually includes all taxes and a

The impressive façade of the luxurious Olissippo Lapa Palace *(see p122)*

◄ Cafés and stalls along Rua Augusta in the Baixa

View from the Tivoli Palácio de Seteais, Sintra, now a luxury hotel *(see p123)*

Continental breakfast. Other meals are charged separately. Cascais and Estoril can be expensive, but prices drop substantially out of season. Most hotels charge three rates: for low (Nov–Mar), mid (Apr–late Jul and mid-Sep–Oct) and high (late Jul–mid-Sep, Carnaval, Easter and New Year) seasons.

Booking

Travellers will need to book in advance for Estoril and Cascais in high season, when most accommodation is taken by tour operators. Book ahead for central Lisbon, which can also get full. Most hoteliers speak English so it should not be a problem to book by phone. Deposits are not usually required, but a written confirmation by email, including a credit card number, may be requested.

Pousadas can be booked through Pestana or on the **Pousadas de Portugal** website. The Portuguese tourist authority, Turismo de Portugal, publishes two official guides which are revised regularly, and are available in English, French and Spanish, as well as Portuguese: *Alojamento Turístico* (Tourist Accommodation) and *Turismo no Espaço Rural* (Tourism in the Country). These list all the establishments rated by the authority, but only the latter contains any description of individual settings.

For more information on hotels, see the **Portugal Hotel Guide**.

Travelling with Children

The Portuguese adore children and will welcome them warmly into hotels and restaurants. Travellers who have children with them will find an immediate point of contact with their hosts.

Disabled Travellers

Lisbon presents many obstacles for travellers with disabilities, but facilities and services are steadily improving. Tourists with specific requirements should check with individual hotels before booking. For more information, check **Accessible Portugal**.

Recommended Hotels

The accommodation options listed in this guide have been carefully selected to reflect a range of good-value lodgings available in and around Lisbon. **Historic** establishments include *pousadas* and charmingly well-preserved historic hotels. **Self-catering** options have either shared or private cooking facilities. **Modern** lodgings are generally comfortable and have standard modern conveniences while **Design** refers to the most fashionable of stylish hotels. The **B&B** category is used for guesthouses, which usually

include breakfast, but check the description or the website to be sure.

The hotels listed cover a variety of locations and price categories. They are arranged by area and then alphabetically within each price range, with the type of accommodation also indicated.

Look out for DK Choice lodgings which have earned a special mention for some exceptional feature, be it scenic location, impeccable service or innovative touches.

DIRECTORY

Hotel Chains

Heritage Hotels
Tel 213 218 200.
W heritage.pt

Ibis Hotel
W ibishotel.com

Pestana Group
Tel 210 193 029.
W pestana.com

Sana Hotels
W sanahotels.com

Tivoli Hotels
Tel 213 198 900.
W tivolihotels.com

Gradings

Turismo de Portugal
Rua Ivone Silva 6,
1050-124 Lisbon.
Tel 211 140 200.
W turismodeportugal.pt

Booking

Pousadas de Portugal
W pousadas.pt

Portugal Hotel Guide
W hotelguide.pt

Disabled Travellers

Accessible Portugal
Rua Jorge Barradas, 50–4º F,
1500–372 Lisbon.
Tel 351 926 910 989.
W accessibleportugal.com

Where to Stay

Lisbon

Alfama

The Keep €
B&B **Map** 7 C3
Costa do Castelo 74, 1100-179
Tel 218 854 070
The Keep offers great 360-degree
views over Lisbon, lovely rooms
and a terrace garden. Prior
booking suggested.

DK Choice

Memmo Alfama €€
Design **Map** 8 4D
Travessa Das Merceeiras 27,
1100-348
Tel 210 495 660
W memmoalfama.com
Housed in a sensitively
renovated 19th-century building, this boutique hotel offers
luxurious extras such as Egyptian
linen and iPad docking stations
in all rooms. Guests can admire
Lisbon's architecture and views
of the Tagus river from the
rooftop wine bar and terrace.

Olissippo Castelo €€
Modern **Map** 7 C3
Rua Costa do Castelo 126, 1100-179
Tel 218 820 190
W olissippohotels.com
Reliable four-star hotel below
Castelo de São Jorge. Luxurious
rooms, attentive service.

Senhora do Monte €€
B&B **Map** 7 D1
Calçada do Monte 39, 1170-250
Tel 218 866 002
W albergariasenhoradomonte.com
Definitely worth the steep climb
for the stunning views from each
room and the panoramic bar.

Solar do Castelo €€
Historic **Map** 7 C3
Rua das Cozinhas 2, 1100-181
Tel 218 806 050
W solardocastelo.com
Charming hotel built around
the courtyard of an 18th-century
mansion. Classic decor, original
stone walls and *azulejos*.

Palacete Chafariz del Rei €€€
Historic **Map** 8 4D
Travessa Chafariz del Rei 6,
1100-140
Tel 218 886 150
W chafarizdelrei.com
Ornate 19th-century family home,
with original stuccoed ceilings,
chandeliers and antique furniture.

Baixa and Avenida

Alegria €
B&B **Map** 4 F1
Praça da Alegria 12, 1250-004
Tel 213 220 670
W alegrianet.com
Cheerful family-run *residencial*
with lots of fresh flowers, large
windows and vibrant colours.

Florescente €
B&B **Map** 7 A2
Rua das Portas de Santo Antão 99,
1150-266
Tel 213 426 609
W residencialflorescente.com
Lovely rooms with facilities to
rival a three-star hotel. On-site
restaurant and souvenir shop.

Goodmorning Hostel €
Self-catering **Map** 7 A2
Praça dos Restauradores 65, 2°,
1250-188
Tel 213 421 128
W goodmorninghostel.com
Well-equipped hostel with
dormitory beds as well as private
rooms. Shared facilities are clean.

Lisboa Tejo €
Modern **Map** 7 B3
Rua dos Condes de Monsanto 2,
1100-159
Tel 218 866 182
W lisboatejohotel.com
Stylish hotel in an 18th-century
building with comfortable rooms.
Breakfast includes fresh fruit.

Lisbon Dreams Guesthouse €
Self-catering **Map** 5 B5
Rua Rodrigo da Fonseca 29, 1250-189
Tel 213 872 393
W lisbondreamsguesthouse.com
Elegant, contemporary rooms
with clean, shared bathrooms
and patio gardens. Well-equipped
kitchen. Breakfast included.

Spectacular views of the city from an
elegantly furnished room in Casa Balthazar

Price Guide
Prices are based on one night's stay in
high season for a standard double room,
inclusive of service charges and taxes.

€	under €100
€€	€100 to €250
€€€	over €250

Norte €
B&B **Map** 7 C3
Rua dos Douradores 161, 1100-205
Tel 218 878 941
Spotless rooms, some with
private bathrooms. Friendly
staff. Plenty of cafés nearby.

Roma €
B&B **Map** 7 A2
Travessa da Glória 22a, 1250-118
Tel 213 460 557
W residencialroma-lisbon.com
Pleasant rooms with en-suite
bathrooms and apartments for
families. Free Wi-Fi in the lobby.

Sana Capitol €
Design **Map** 5 C4
Rua Eça de Queiroz 24, 1050-096
Tel 213 536 811
W capitol.sanahotels.com
Restful rooms done in shades of
green with spacious, stylish public
areas. Breakfast is varied.

Shiado Hostel €
Self-catering **Map** 7 4A
Rua Anchieta 5, 3°, 1200-023
Tel 213 429 227
W shiadohostel.com
Private rooms with shared
bathrooms and dorm beds at this
bright cheerful hostel. Also offers a
shared kitchen. Buffet breakfasts.

Turim Suisso Atlântico €
Modern **Map** 7 A2
Rua da Glória 3, 1250-114
Tel 213 400 270
W turim-hotels.com
Traditional exterior with modern,
refurbished interiors. The frosted
glass bathroom doors limit privacy.

Beautique Hotels Figueira €€
Design **Map** 7 B3
Praça da Figueira, 16, 1100-241
Tel 210 492 940
W thebeautiquehotels.com
Stylish interiors with giant fig-leaf
and fruit motifs. Rooftop spa and
gourmet restaurant on site.

Britânia €€
Historic **Map** 5 C5
Rua Rodrigues Sampaio 17, 1150-278
Tel 213 155 016
W heritage.pt
Art Deco hotel with 1940s charm.
Chic rooms with all conveniences
and 24-hour room service.

DK Choice

Casa Balthazar €€
B&B
Map 7 A3
Rua do Duque, 26, 1200-159
Tel *917 085 568*
🌐 casabalthazarlisbon.com
Lovely 19th-century home of the
founder of Confeitaria Nacional,
Lisbon's oldest patisserie. Still
with the family, it exudes warmth
and personal attention to detail.
Breakfast – a real treat – comes
from the patisserie. Some rooms
also have a kitchenette.

A comfortably furnished room in the chic Hotel do Chiado

Executive Suites Éden €€
Self-catering
Map 7 A2
Praça dos Restauradores 24, 1250-187
Tel *213 216 600*
🌐 viphotels.com
Studio and double apartments
behind a 1930s Art Deco façade.
Rooftop pool and a terrace bar.

Hotel do Chiado €€
Design
Map 7 B4
Rua Nova do Almada 114, 1200-290
Tel *213 256 100*
🌐 hoteldochiado.pt
Prestigious boutique hotel with
Oriental and colonial influences.
Rooms with terraces offer castle
or river views. Rooftop bar.

Inspira Santa Marta €€
Modern
Map 5 C5
Rua de Santa Marta 48, 1150-297
Tel *210 440 900*
🌐 inspirahotels.com
Eco-friendly hotel with feng shui-
inspired rooms. Full spa and a
Mediterranean restaurant on site.

DK Choice

Internacional Design Hotel €€
Design
Map 7 B3
Rua da Betesga 3, 1100-090
Tel *213 240 990*
🌐 idesignhotel.com
Each floor of this smart hotel has
a different theme – urban chic,
Zen philosophy, and tribal and
pop culture – allowing guests
to choose a room that suits their
personality and size requirements. The delicious breakfasts,
a pillow menu and scenic location make for the perfect stay.

Lisboa Plaza €€
Historic
Map 4 F1
Travessa do Salitre 7, 1269-066
Tel *213 218 218*
🌐 heritage.pt
Family-run 1950s hotel with
classic decor and modern
comforts. Private library with a
nice collection of books, and a
fireplace. 24-hour room service.

Marques de Pombal €€
Modern
Avenida da Liberdade 243, 1250-143
Tel *213 197 900*
🌐 hotel-marquesdepombal.pt
Comfortable rooms adorned with
images of Lisbon's landmarks.
Hearty breakfasts. Friendly staff.

Metrópole €€
Historic
Map 7 B3
Praça Dom Pedro IV 30, 1100-200
Tel *213 219 030*
🌐 metropole-lisbon.com
Welcoming guests since 1917;
rooms with great views, Art Deco
furnishings and modern amenities.

Mundial €€
Modern
Map 7 B3
Praça Martim Moniz 2, 1100-341
Tel *218 842 000*
🌐 hotel-mundial.pt
Spacious rooms, some with
balconies. City views from the
terrace. Free city-centre parking.

NH Liberdade €€
Modern
Map 4 F1
Avenida da Liberdade 180b, 1250-146
Tel *213 514 060*
🌐 nh-hotels.pt
Well-located hotel with big
rooms and contemporary
furnishings. Rooftop pool.
Filling breakfasts.

Portugal €€
Design
Map 7 C3
Rua João das Regras 4, 1100-294
Tel *218 877 581*
🌐 hotelportugal.com
Beautifully refurbished four-star
hotel offering soundproofed
rooms and free city-centre parking.

Tivoli Jardim €€
Modern
Map 4 F1
Rua J César Machado 7–9, 1250-135
Tel *213 591 000*
🌐 tivolihotels.com
Family-friendly place with a leafy
garden and an outdoor pool.
Sidecar tours available.

Avenida Palace €€€
Historic
Map 7 B3
Rua 1 de Dezembro 123, 1200-359
Tel *213 218 100*
🌐 hotelavenidapalace.pt
Romantic 19th-century hotel with
modern comforts. The public
areas are perfect for afternoon tea.

Sofitel Lisboa €€€
Modern
Map 4 F1
Avenida da Liberdade 127, 1269-038
Tel *213 228 300*
🌐 sofitel-lisboa.com
Plush, deluxe rooms and suites.
Excellent restaurant and views
from the terrace. Attentive staff.

Tiara Park Atlantic Lisboa €€€
Modern
Map 5 B4
Rua Castilho 149, 1099-034
Tel *213 818 700*
🌐 tiara-hotels.com
Chic rooms, some with park
views and four-poster beds.
On-site gourmet restaurant.

Tivoli Lisboa €€€
Modern
Map 4 F1
Avenida da Liberdade 185, 1269-050
Tel *213 198 900*
🌐 tivolihotels.com
Big, luxurious rooms. Sweeping
vistas from the rooftop Skybar
and a lush garden with a pool.

Bairro Alto and Estrela

Casa do Carmo €
Design
Map 7 A3
Largo do Carmo 15, 1900-092
Tel *966 826 070*
Tastefully furnished rooms, some
with superb views. Bathrooms are
shared but clean. Great breakfasts.

Pensão Londres €
B&B
Map 4 F2
Rua Dom Pedro V 53, 1250-092
Tel *213 462 203*
🌐 pensaolondres.com.pt
Well-established B&B with friendly
service. Rooms on the fourth floor
offer splendid views of the city.

For more information on types of hotels *see page 119*

One of the designer Lisbonaire Apartments, available for short-term rental

Residencial Valentina €
B&B   **Map** 4 2E
Calçada Estrela 27, 1º, 1200-661
Tel *213 975 670*
Impeccable place with simple furnishings, shared bathrooms. Ask for a room away from the street.

DK Choice

Lisbonaire Apartments €€
Self-catering   **Map** 7 A2
Rua da Glória 16, 1250-116
Tel *912 769 797*
ⓦ lisbonaire.com
Stunning apartments designed by top Portuguese designers with extras such as long beds, iPad docking stations and independent cooking facilities. The basement allows a place to relax, read and play pool or board games.

Teatro Bed & Breakfast €€
B&B   **Map** 7 A3
Rua Trindade 36, 1200-468
Tel *213 472 024*
ⓦ teatrobb.com
Black-, white- and silver-themed B&B featuring theatrical and historical murals in a modern setup.

Altis Grand €€€
Modern   **Map** 4 F1
Rua Castilho 11, 1269-072
Tel *213 106 000*
ⓦ altishotels.com
Minimalist five-star hotel with a heated indoor pool, soundproofed rooms and business facilities.

As Janelas Verdes €€€
Historic   **Map** 4 D3
Rua das Janelas Verdes 47, 1200-690
Tel *213 968 143*
ⓦ asjanelasverdes.com
Romantic hotel in an18th-century mansion with Neo-Classical decor. Enjoy breakfast on the quiet patio.

Bairro Alto Hotel €€€
Modern   **Map** 7 A4
Praça Luis de Camões 2, 1200-243
Tel *213 408 288*
ⓦ bairroaltohotel.com
Cosmopolitan hotel with a range of rooms, gourmet restaurant, and bar with river views and live music.

Olissippo Lapa Palace €€€
Historic   **Map** 3 C3
Rua do Pau da Bandeira 4, 1249-021
Tel *213 949 494*
ⓦ olissippohotels.com
Graceful rooms with period decor that does justice to this former palace.

York House €€€
Historic   **Map** 4 D3
Rua das Janelas Verdes 32, 1200-691
Tel *213 962 435*
ⓦ yorkhouselisboa.com
Boutique hotel in a creatively renovated 17th century convent. Modern rooms with all amenities.

Belém

Jeronimos 8 €€
Modern   **Map** 1 C4
Rua dos Jerónimos 8, 1400-211
Tel *213 600 900*
ⓦ jeronimos8.com
Contemporary hotel designed around an urban chic theme. Secluded courtyard. Free Wi-Fi.

DK Choice

Pestana Palace Hotel €€€
Historic   **Map** 2 F3
Rua Jau 54, 1300-314
Tel *213 615 600*
ⓦ pestana.com
Splendid rooms and suites in a 19th-century palace. The sumptuous interiors are matched by the lovely landscaped gardens with a swimming pool and a Chinese pavilion. A truly regal experience in a refined oasis.

Further Afield

Residencial Roxi €
B&B   **Map** 6 5E
Avenida Almirante Reis 31, 2º e 3º, Anjos, 1150-009
Tel *218 126 341*
ⓦ residencialroxi.com
Spacious, traditionally furnished rooms with private or shared bathrooms. No lift. Friendly staff.

Real Parque €€
Modern   **Map** 5 C3
Avenida Luís Bívar 67, 1069-146
Tel *213 199 000*
ⓦ realhotelsgroup.com
Large, well-equipped rooms, some with terraces. Breakfast buffet.

Tivoli Oriente €€
Modern
Avenida Dom João II, 1990-083
Tel *218 915 100*
ⓦ tivolihotels.com
Rooms in a range of styles, many with river views. Lobby bar and indoor pool overlook the Oriente train station.

Sheraton Lisboa Hotel & Spa €€€
Modern   **Map** 5 C3
Rua Latino Coelho 1, 1069-025
Tel *213 120 000*
ⓦ sheratonlisboa.com
Chic rooms. The rooftop gourmet and bistro restaurants and bar offer sweeping views.

The Lisbon Coast

ALCÁCER DO SAL: Pousada
Dom Afonso II €€
Historic
Castelo de Alcácer do Sal, 7580-197
Tel *265 613 070*
ⓦ pousadas.pt
Converted century-old castle with sweeping views of the Sado river and valley. Well-appointed rooms.

CASCAIS: Dolce Cascais
Guest House €
Modern
Rua Joaquim Ereira 1114, Bairro do Rosário, 2750-390
Tel *911 508 665*
ⓦ dolcecascaisguesthouse.com
Lovely place with a pretty garden and bright rooms. Cooking lessons and massage therapy offerred.

DK Choice

CASCAIS:
Pérgola Guest House €€
Historic
Avenida Valbom 13, 2750-508
Tel *214 840 040*
ⓦ pergolahouse.com
A beautiful 19th-century Mediterranean mansion with stucco ceilings, marble floors and ornate furnishings. Original hand-painted tiles decorate the house and grounds. Gorgeous landscaped gardens. Guests are served a complimentary glass of port. Dinner available on request.

CASCAIS: Solar Dom Carlos €€
Historic
Rua Latino Coelho 104, 2750-408
Tel *214 828 115*
ⓦ solardomcarlos.pt
This former royal cottage from the 18th century has a chapel in the garden and magnificent frescoes in the dining room.

CASCAIS: Farol Design Hotel €€€
Design
Avenida Rei Humberto II de Itália 7, 2750-461
Tel *214 823 490*
🆆 farol.com.pt
Chic, stylish hotel in a 19th-century mansion.

CASCAIS: Miragem €€€
Modern
Avenida Marginal 8554, 2754-536
Tel *210 060 600*
🆆 cascaismirage.com
Opulent hotel with lovely bay views, an infinity pool, a kids' play area and a range of restaurants.

CASCAIS: Onyria Marinha Edition Hotel €€€
Design
Quinta da Marinha, 2750-715
Tel *21 486 01 50*
🆆 onyriamarinha.com
Boutique hotel with stunning views from the balconies. World-class spa and fitness facilities.

COSTA DA CAPARICA: Hotel Residencial Mar e Sol €
B&B
Rua dos Pescadores 42, 2825-325
Tel *212 900 017*
🆆 residencialmaresol.com
Modern B&B with colourful rooms and an Italian restaurant. Excellent breakfast with fresh fruit.

COSTA DA CAPARICA: Quinta do Tagus Village €€
Modern
Quinta do Tagus, Montinhoso, Monte de Caparica, Almada, 2825-075
Tel *212 951 733*
🆆 quintadotagus-village.com
Luxurious retreat on a farm estate with river views. Rooms with modern decor and artistic touches.

ERICEIRA: Vila Galé Ericeira €€
Modern
Praça dos Navegantes, 2655-320
Tel *261 869 900*
🆆 vilagale.com
Well-equipped rooms, most with sea views. Regional-style restaurant and saltwater pools on site.

ESTORIL: Hotel Inglaterra €€
Historic
Rua do Porto 1, 2765-271
Tel *214 684 461*
🆆 hotelinglaterra.com.pt
Renovated early-20th-century palace. Lovely mix of old and new.

ESTORIL: Palácio €€€
Historic
Rua da Particular, 2769-504
Tel *214 648 000*
🆆 palacioestorilhotel.com
Elegantly furnished rooms in this five-star hotel from the 1930s.

GUINCHO: Fortaleza do Guincho €€€
Historic
Estrada do Guincho, 2750-642
Tel *214 870 491*
🆆 fortalezadoguincho.pt
Renovated fortress with curved stone staircases, opulent decor and a Michelin-starred restaurant.

PALMELA: Pousada do Castelo de Palmela €€
Historic
Castelo de Palmela, 2950-317
Tel *212 351 226*
🆆 pousadas.pt
Luxury hotel in a former convent. Period furnishings and great views.

QUELUZ: Pousada Dona Maria I €€
Historic
Largo do Palácio Nacional, 2745-191
Tel *214 356 158*
🆆 pousadas.pt
Former 18th-century palace with individually decorated rooms.

SESIMBRA: Sana Sesimbra €€
Modern
Avenida 25 de Abril 11, 2970-634
Tel *212 289 000*
🆆 sesimbra.sanahotels.com
Classy hotel located right on the beach. Excellent sea views from the rooms. Rooftop hot tub.

SESIMBRA: Hotel do Mar €€€
Modern
Rua General Humberto Delgado 10, 2970-628
Tel *212 288 300*
🆆 hoteldomar.pt
Sprawling, cliffside beach hotel. Rooms are simply furnished but it has indoor and outdoor pools.

SETÚBAL: Quinta dos Moinhos de São Filipe €
Self-catering
Rua de São Filipe, 2900-670
Tel *265 228 278*
🆆 moinhossaofilipe.com
Remote estate with comfortable rooms. Stunning views of Tróia peninsula from the outdoor pool.

SETÚBAL: Pousada de São Filipe €€
Historic
Castelo de São Filipe, 2900-300
Tel *265 550 070*
🆆 pousadas.pt
Integrated within the castle, built in 1590. Five of the rooms are located in former cells.

SINTRA: Espaço Edla €
B&B
Rua Dr Alfredo da Costa 52, 2710-523
Tel *925 970 131*
🆆 espacoedla.pt
Modern rooms with artistic touches. Serves breakfast from the gourmet bakery downstairs.

SINTRA: Sintra Bliss Hotel €
Design
Rua Dr Alfredo da Costa 15–17, 2710-524
Tel *219 244 541*
🆆 sintra-b-hotels.com
Trendy rooms with balconies. Two-bed apartments also available.

SINTRA: Lawrence's Hotel €€
Historic
Rua Consigliéri Pedroso 38–40, 2710-550
Tel *219 105 500*
🆆 lawrenceshotel.com
Established in 1764, this hotel has rooms with four-poster beds. Friendly public lounges.

SINTRA: Penha Longa €€€
Modern
Estrada da Lagoa Azul-Linhó, 2714-511
Tel *219 249 011*
🆆 penhalonga.com
Luxury golf resort. Rooms have private balconies. Superb spa.

SINTRA: Tivoli Palácio de Seteais €€€
Historic
Rua Barbosa du Bocage 8, Seteais, 2710-517
Tel *219 233 200*
🆆 tivolihotels.com
Romantic 18th-century hotel in a stunning setting. Opulent rooms.

The plush Miragem in Cascais, with rooms overlooking the swimming pool

For more information on types of hotels *see page 119*

WHERE TO EAT AND DRINK

There are many restaurants dedicated to cooking all manner of freshly caught fish and seafood, particularly in Lisbon and along the coast. It may be grilled, pan-fried or turned into soup or a stew. However, meat dishes are also plentiful; some of the most popular are made of pork and lamb. The city has an abundance of inexpensive places to eat, as well as more expensive ones. There are typically Portuguese restaurants in Lisbon, along with Chinese, Indian, Brazilian and African restaurants, reflecting Portugal's colonial past. This section gives tips on the different types of restaurants and cafés, as well as advice on menus, drinks and ordering your meal. The listings found on pages 130–35 are a selection of the best restaurants in all price ranges that are to be found throughout the capital and the Lisbon Coast area.

Types of Restaurant

Eating venues in Lisbon come in all shapes and sizes and at all price levels. Among the most reasonable is the local *tasca* (tavern), often just a room with half-a-dozen tables presided over by a husband-and-wife team. *Tascas* are often frequented by locals at lunch time, which is a good indication of quality food. A *restaurante* is more formal and offers a wider choice of dishes. At a typical *marisqueira*, the emphasis is on seafood and fresh fish. A *churrasqueira*, originally Brazilian, specializes in spit-roasted foods. A *cervejaria* is the ideal place to go for a beer with a steak, seafood or simply a snack. *Petiscos* are Portuguese tapas and several restaurants specialize in them. *Pousadas (see p118)* offer a network of traditional restaurants, with the focus on local gastronomic specialities.

Eating Hours

Lunch is usually served between 12:30pm and 3pm, when many restaurants get very crowded. Dinner is served from 7pm until at least 10pm. Lisbon locals tend to dine after 9pm on weekends. An alternative for late dinner would be a *fado* house (see pp144–5).

Shaded alfresco tables in Café Fábulas, a popular eatery in Bairro Alto

Reservations

It is a good idea to book ahead for up-market restaurants and for those in popular locations during high season. Disabled people should check in advance on facilities and access. Special facilities are generally lacking, but most places will try to be helpful.

The Menu

Some restaurants offer an *ementa turística*, a cheap, daily-changing set menu. This is served with coffee and a drink (a glass of wine or beer, a soft drink or water) and provides a full meal at a good price with no hidden costs. *Almoço* (lunch) generally consists of a soup or starter and a fish or meat dish with potatoes or rice. To sample a local speciality, ask for the *prato do dia* – dish of the day. *Jantar* (dinner) may be two or more courses, perhaps rounded off with ice cream, fruit, a simple dessert or cheese. Casserole-style

The impressive interior of Cozinha Velha *(see p135)* in Queluz

Eating outside in Cascais, along the Lisbon Coast

dishes, such as *cataplana* (a kind of tightly sealed wok in which the food is steamed, often used for fish and seafood) or *porco à alentejana* (pork with clams), are brought to the table in a pot for diners to share. This is similarly done with large fish, such as sea bass, which are sold by weight. One serving is large and can usually be shared by two people, and it is perfectly acceptable to ask for a *meia dose* or half-portion instead.

Peculiar to Portugal is the plate of assorted appetizers – perhaps olives, cheese and sardine pâté – which is served with bread at the start of a meal. However, these are not usually included in the price of the meal and an extra charge will be made for each item consumed.

Vegetarians

Vegetarians will not eat as well as fish-lovers, although local cheeses and breads can be excellent. Chefs are usually happy to provide something without meat, although this will probably mean just a salad or an omelette. A greater variety of vegetarian dishes can be found in the various ethnic restaurants.

What to Drink

It would be a pity to visit Portugal without sampling port *(see pp128–9)* and Madeira wines, the country's two most famous drinks. As far as house wine is concerned, it is usually of an acceptable quality to wash down your meal, whatever the standard of the restaurant. Otherwise, ask for the *carta de vinhos* (wine list) and choose a Portuguese wine *(see pp128–9)*. Mineral water is either *com gás* (sparkling) or *sem gás* (still). Beer drinkers should find Sagres and Super Bock to be good lagers, while artisan beers such as Sovina are becoming more popular. Lisbon also provides plenty of opportunities to try *ginja*, the local cherry liqueur.

Pastéis de nata, or custard pastries

Paying

It is common practice to add a five or ten per cent tip to bills. Note that not all restaurants accept credit cards.

Children

The Portuguese view children as a blessing rather than a nuisance, so Lisbon is an ideal city for families to eat out together. Special children's menus are not common but a *meia dose* can be ordered.

Smoking

Smoking is theoretically banned in restaurants and other public places in Portugal, unless the establishment has an efficient smoke-extractor system. In reality, many bars and some cafés allow smoking.

Recommended Restaurants

The restaurants listed in this guide have been selected for their atmosphere, quality and good value. Establishments range from simple to lavish and cater to different tastes, from traditional, home-cooked recipes to Michelin-starred gourmet cuisine. They are listed by area and then by price, with map references and an indication of the main type of cuisine offered. Standard closures are listed but it is always advisable to call ahead or consult a restaurant's website before visiting.

DK Choice restaurants stand out from the crowd, whether it is for outstanding service, stunning views, intimate atmosphere or renowned chefs. These special places are highly recommended by both local and visiting diners and reservations are strongly advised.

Drinking Coffee in Lisbon

Coffee is widely drunk and served in many forms. The most popular, *uma bica*, is a small cup of strong black coffee, like an espresso. For a weaker version, ask for *um carioca de café*. A strong *bica* is called *uma italiana*. *Uma meia de leite* is half-coffee, half-milk. Strong coffee with a dash of milk is known as *um garoto escuro* (*um garoto claro* is quite milky). If you like coffee with plenty of milk, ask for *um galão* (a gallon). It is served in a glass, and again you can order *um galão claro* (very milky) or *escuro* (strong).

Uma bica   *Um galão*

The Flavours of Lisbon

Gastronomically, the Lisbon region is immensely varied, bringing together many different foods from all over Portugal. There is roast suckling pig from the north, an excellent choice of fish and seafood from the Atlantic coastline, plus unique cheeses and hearty stews from the mountains. One popular dish, originating in the south of the country and reflecting this diversity, is *porco à alentejana*, a mixture of pork and clams spiced with paprika. Cuisines old and new, exotic and familiar, blend with one another in cosmopolitan Lisbon's many quality restaurants.

Sardines

Fresh cheeses on sale at Lisbon's celebrated Mercado de Ribera

Meat and Dairy

Pork is the most commonly eaten meat in Portugal. Spit-roasted suckling pig *(leitão)* is a traditional favourite, but pork meat is also popular roasted *(porco preto)* and in rich, hearty stews. Pigs' trotters with coriander *(pézinhos de coentrada)* are considered a delicacy. Cured pork products *(enchidos)* – spiced, salted or smoked – are an essential part of the national cuisine, from paprika-hued *chouriço* sausage to dark and intensely flavoured *Ibérico* ham (made from pigs fed on acorns) and *morcela* blood sausage seasoned with cloves and cumin. Kid *(cabrito)* is also popular as a roast or in stews. Beef is served less often but is of high quality (look for the names Barrosã, Mirandesa or Maronesa), while sheep tend to be kept more for cheese production than meat. Ewe's and goat's milk cheeses are of exceptional quality, and are as delicious when they are fresh and soft as when they are long matured, firm and piquant. Portugal's most famous cheese, the distinctive and buttery Serra, is made from ewe's milk, and the rounds are wrapped in muslin to maintain their shape.

Saloio   Serra da Estrela   Palhais   Queijo fresco   Alavão
Fine ewe's and goat's milk cheeses from Portugal

Local Dishes and Specialities

Much traditional Portuguese cuisine is that of a hard-working, frugal people who preserved and used everything they could produce. Hence the predominance of cured meats and dried bean stews (often incorporating ham or sausage for flavour). *Favas à Portuguesa* is a Lisbon favourite. The capital is not just the place where all the flavours of Portugal come together, but also where the influences of Portugal's 16th-century overseas expansion get their strongest expression. This applies equally to older influences, long since assimilated into local cuisine, as well as to newer ones, from Cape Verdean restaurants to sushi bars. *Frango à piri-piri,* barbecued chicken with chilli, is a favourite dish, originating from Portugal's former colonies in Africa.

Paprika

Feijoada is a paprika-spiced stew of beans, vegetables and cured meat (usually pork), with many local variations.

Lisbon's famed lettuces take pride of place on a vegetable stall

Fish and Seafood

With its long Atlantic coastline, it is no surprise that Portugal's fish dishes are unmissable. The range on sale at any fish market is vast. Squid *(lula)*, cuttlefish *(choco)*, sea bass *(robalo)*, gilthead bream *(dourada)*, sardines *(sardinhas)* and shellfish such as oysters *(ostras)* and cockles *(ameijoas)* are found in abundance and often come together in the rich, steamed fish stew *cataplana de peixe e mariscos*. Traditional salt cod *(bacalhau)* is still much in evidence, but today river fish are less commonly served – trout *(trutas)* is often farmed and the once-common lamprey *(lampreia)* may be imported. Snails *(caracóis)* sometimes appear in dishes, including *feijoada*.

Vegetables and Fruit

A visit to Lisbon's superb food market Mercado de Ribera (Avenida 24 de Julio, Cais do Sodré) will reveal just how fertile the inland regions are, with heaps of every kind of

Waiter with a tray of traditional *pastéis de nata* pastries

vegetable (peppers and tomatoes are especially flavourful) and ripe, perfumed fruits including figs, melons, grapes, greengages, apricots and citrus fruits. Portuguese olives and their oil are omnipresent – the essential trio of ingredients, key to many a dish, is olive oil, garlic and coriander. Both wheat and maize are grown for bread, which is often hard and long-lasting and used to give extra volume to soups. The nickname *alfacinhas* for natives of Lisbon may have a connection with *alface* (lettuce) – the city has long been famous for an especially delicious variety.

ON THE MENU

Açorda de marisco Thick shellfish broth thickened with bread and favoured with garlic.

Bacalhau à gomes de sá Salt cod layered with potato and onion, and garnished with egg and olives.

Caldo verde A popular, bright green soup made from a type of kale.

Pastéis de bacalhau Little salt-cod cakes eaten cold as a snack or hot as a main dish. A national addiction.

Queijadas de Sintra Cheese tarts spiced with cinnamon.

Sardinhas assadas Chargrilled fresh sardines.

Caldeirada de peixe, a fish stew, uses a selection of seafood along with potatoes, tomatoes and peppers.

Favas à Portuguesa combines broad *(fava)* beans with *morcela* (blood sausage) and chopped pork ribs.

Arroz doce is a delicious dessert of lemon zest-scented rice pudding topped with a decoration of cinnamon.

The Wines of Portugal

Although still overshadowed by the excellence and fame of port, Portuguese table wine deserves to be taken seriously. After years of investment in the industry, many of the reds, such as the full-bodied wines from the Douro (made with some of the same grapes as port), have established an attractive style all their own. Great whites are fewer, but most regions have some. And of course there is *vinho verde*, the usually white, light, slightly carbonated wine from the north.

Sparkling rosés, such as Mateus and Lancers, have been Portugal's great export success. But the country now has many excellent wines that reach beyond the easy-drinking charms of these.

Wine Regions

Many of Portugal's wine regions maintain their individual style by specializing in particular Portuguese grape varieties. The introduction of modern wine-making techniques has improved overall quality, and as yet the increasing use of imported grape varieties seems no threat to Portuguese individuality.

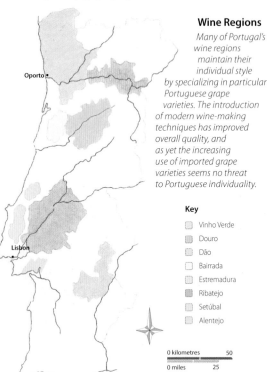

Oporto

Lisbon

Key

- Vinho Verde
- Douro
- Dão
- Bairrada
- Estremadura
- Ribatejo
- Setúbal
- Alentejo

0 kilometres   50
0 miles   25

Vinho verde vineyards in the village of Lapela, near Monção in the Minho

Cellar of the Bussaco Palace Hotel, near Mealhada, famous for its red wine

How to Read a Wine Label

Tinto is red, *branco* is white, *seco* is dry and *doce* is sweet. Beyond that, the essential information concerns the producer, the region and the year. Wines made to at least 80 per cent from a single grape variety may give the name of that grape on the front label. *Denominação de Origem Controlada* (DOC) indicates that the wine has been made according to the strictest regulations of a given region, but, as elsewhere, this need not mean higher quality than the nominally simpler *Vinho Regional* appellation. The back label often describes grape varieties and wine-making techniques.

The Sociedade Agrícola e Comercial dos Vinhos Vale da Corça, Lda, produced and bottled this wine.

This wine is from the Douro and is made according to DOC regulations for the region.

The name of this wine means "banks of the Tua river", further specifying its geographical origin.

Reserva means that the wine has been aged, probably in oak casks. It also implies that the wine is of higher quality than non-reserva wine from the same producer.

DOURO
DENOMINAÇÃO DE ORIGEM CONTROLADA
ENCOSTAS DO TUA
Reserva de 2000
VINHO TINTO
PRODUZIDO E ENGARRAFADO POR
SOCIEDADE AGRÍCOLA E COMERCIAL DOS VINHOS
VALE DA CORÇA, LDA
SEGURÃ - CARRAZEDA DE ANSIÃES - PORTUGAL
PRODUTO DE PORTUGAL
75 cl

Bairrada is a region where the small and thick-skinned Baga grape dominates.

Vinho verde, "green wine", from the Minho region, can be either red or white, but the fizzy, dry reds are generally consumed locally. Typical white *vinho verde* is bone dry, slightly fizzy, low in alcohol and high in acidity. A weightier style of white *vinho verde* is made from the Alvarinho grape, near the Spanish border. Among the best brands are Soalheiro and Palácio da Brejoeira.

It makes big, tannic wines, sometimes with smoky or pine-needle overtones and, like the older Dão wines, they need time to soften. Modern wine-making and occasional disregard for regional regulations have meant more approachable reds (often classified as *Vinho Regional das Beiras*) and crisper whites. Quality producers include Luís Pato and Caves Aliança.

Ribatejo is the fertile valley of the Tagus to the north and east of Lisbon. After Estremadura, it is Portugal's biggest wine region measured by volume, but its potential for quality wines has only just begun to be realized. As in Estremadura, *Vinho Regional* bottlings are frequently better than DOC ones. Producers to look for include Quinta da Alorna, Casa Branco and Fiuza & Bright.

The Douro region is best known as the source of port wine, but in most years about half of the wine produced is fermented dry to make table wine, and these wines are now at the forefront of Portuguese wine-making. The pioneer, Barca Velha, was launched half a century ago and is both highly regarded and among the most expensive. Other quality producers include Calheiros Cruz, Domingos Alves de Sousa, Quinta do Crasto, Niepoort and Ramos-Pinto.

Picking grapes for *vinho verde*

Setúbal, to the south of Lisbon, is best known for its sweet, fortified Muscat wine, Moscatel de Setúbal. In addition, the region also produces excellent, mostly red, table wine. Two big quality producers dominate the region: José Maria da Fonseca *(see p113)* and JP Vinhos. The co-operative at Santo Isidro de Pegões makes good-value wines, while interesting smaller producers include Venâncio Costa Lima, Hero do Castanheiro and Ermelinda Freitas.

The Dão region now offers some of Portugal's best wines. Small producers, such as Quinta dos Roques, Quinta da Pellada and Quinta de Cabriz, and the large Sogrape company make fruity reds for younger drinking; fresh, dry whites; and deeper, richer reds which retain their fruit with age – a far cry from the heavy, hard-edged, often oxidized wines of the past.

Estremadura is Portugal's westernmost wine area and has now emerged as a region in its own right. Several producers make modern *Vinho Regional* wines with character; look for wines by DFJ, Casa Santos Lima, Quinta de Pancas and Quinta do Monte d'Oiro. The most interesting DOC is Alenquer, a full-bodied wine. Bucelas, to the south of the region, produces characterful white wines.

Alentejo wine has possibly made the biggest leap in quality in recent years. Long dismissed by experts as a region of easy-drinking house reds for restaurants, this area now produces some of Portugal's most serious red wines and a surprising number of excellent whites. Among the best producers are Herdade do Esporão, Herdade dos Coelheiros, Cortes de Cima and João Portugal Ramos.

Where to Eat and Drink

Lisbon

Alfama

Casanova €
Italian **Map** 8 F3
Avenida Infante Dom Henrique,
Cais da Pedra, 1900-264
Tel *218 877 532*
Trendy riverside restaurant
specializing in pizza; try the one
with chocolate-spread topping.
It gets busy, so arrive early. Open
till late.

Hua-Ta-Li €
Chinese **Map** 7 C4
Rua dos Bacalhoeiros 109–15,
1100-068
Tel *218 879 170*
Popular family-run eatery serving
a vast all-you-can-eat buffet for
lunch and dinner. Extensive à la
carte menu. Expect generous
servings of well-presented food.
Service can be a bit patchy.

Tentações de Goa €
Indian **Map** 7 C3
Rua São Pedro Mártir 23, 1100-555
Tel *218 875 824* **Closed** *Sun;*
Mon lunch; holidays
Cheerful, friendly place with
brightly painted walls. Serves
mouthwatering Goan cuisine.
Dishes can be very hot and
spicy, but the chef is happy
to accomodate guests' prefer-
ences if asked. Cash only.

Faz Figura €€
Portuguese/Fusion **Map** 8 F2
Rua do Paraiso 15b, 1100-396
Tel *218 868 981*
Stylish eatery that draws crowds
for its location as well as the
menu. The chef creates exquisite
dishes, adding a touch of the
international to traditional
Portuguese ingredients. Sit
on the covered terrace to
enjoy fabulous river views.

Restô do Chapitô €€
International **Map** 7 C3
Costa do Castelo 7, 1149-079
Tel *218 855 550*
Choose from three eating options
at this performing arts school: bar
snacks or grilled meats on the outdoor terrace that offers amazing
views, or à la carte fare in the
stylish restaurant. Reserve ahead.

Santo António de Alfama €€
Modern Portuguese **Map** 8 E4
Beco de São Miguel 7, 1100-538
Tel *218 881 328*
Popular place serving generous
portions of tasty Portuguese food.

Depending on the weather,
sit in the intimate indoor
dining area, which has black-
and-white photographs
decorating the walls, or relax
outdoors under grapevines.

DK Choice

Bica do Sapato €€€
Modern Portuguese **Map** 8 F3
Avenida Infante Dom Henrique,
Cais da Pedra, 1900-000
Tel *218 810 320* **Closed** *Sun*
dinner; Mon lunch
Vegetarians as well as
meat lovers get a choice
of mouthwatering dishes
at this trendy converted
riverfront warehouse with
minimalist decor. Eating
options include bistro, gourmet and Asian from the café,
restaurant or sushi bar. Book
ahead to avoid waiting.

Casa do Leão €€€
Traditional Portuguese **Map** 8 D3
Castelo de São Jorge, 1100-129
Tel *218 875 962*
Casa do Leão offers fine dining
within the castle walls, coupled
with spectacular city views.
Smart, attentive waiters advise
on wine pairings. The classic
decor works well with stone
walls and *azulejos* to make
for a romantic ambience.

Sr Fado de Alfama €€€
Traditional Portuguese **Map** 8 E3
Rua dos Remedios, 176, 1100
Tel *218 874 298* **Closed** *Sun,*
Mon & Tue
A favourite with locals and
tourists alike, this family-run

Stylish interiors of Bica do Sapato, popular
Portuguese eatery in Alfama

eatery serves tasty home-
cooked food and fine wines.
Live *fado* music in the evening.
Reservations recommended.

Via Graça €€€
Traditional Portuguese **Map** 8 D1
Rua Damasceno Monteiro 9b,
1170-108
Tel *218 870 830* **Closed** *Sat &*
Sun lunch
Enjoy hearty meals such as
fried cod, *empada de caça*
(game pie) or the wild mushroom risotto at this stylish
restaurant. The hilltop location
guarantees panoramic city
views. Ask for a window table.

Baixa and Avenida

Casa do Alentejo €
Traditional Portuguese **Map** 7 A2
Rua das Portas de Santo Antão 58,
1150-268
Tel *213 405 140*
Housed in a Moorish building
dedicated to the Alentejo
community, this place offers
authentic Alentejan fare such
as *porco alentejano* (pork
with clams). Sit in the 19th-
century ballroom or the
azulejo-lined canteen.

**Marisqueira Santa
Marta** €
Seafood **Map** 5 C5
Travessa do Enviado de Inglaterra
1d, 1150-139
Tel *213 525 638*
Down-to-earth family restaurant
with traditional furnishings,
serving home-cooked food
that keeps guests coming
back. Try the seafood rice,
stuffed crab or the *cataplana*
(seafood casserole).

Os Tibetanos €
Tibetan **Map** 4 F1
Rua do Salitre 117, 1250-198
Tel *213 142 038* **Closed** *Sun;*
holidays
Cheerful restaurant with a
leafy garden terrace. Serves
healthy Tibetan dishes such
as momos, as well as international options such as
tofu with pesto, pasta gratin
with seitan, and steaks of
tofu or seitan. Cash only.

Contemporary decor at Can the Can featuring a quirky lampshade at the entrance

Can the Can
International   €€
Map 7 5C
Terreiro do Paço 82–3, 1100-148
Tel *914 007 100*
For a novel take on canned food, try this modern eatery decorated with tins, including a giant lampshade made from sardine cans. All starters have at least one tinned ingredient. Live *fado* sessions.

Gambrinus
Seafood   €€€
Map 7 B2
Rua das Portas de Santo Antão 23, 1150-264
Tel *213 421 466*
Well-established favourite for seafood and meat dishes. Try the conch shell filled with seafood. The extensive wine list includes an array of vintage ports.

Restaurante 33A
Traditional Portuguese   €€€
Map 5 C5
Rua Alexandre Herculano 33a, 1250-008
Tel *213 546 079* **Closed** *Sat lunch; Sun*
A lovely interior with dark wooden beams as well as a beautiful shaded garden. Smart, formally dressed waiters served delicious, unpretentious cuisine in a relaxed atmosphere. Boasts a highly regarded wine list. Divine desserts.

DK Choice

Solar dos Presuntos
Traditional
Portuguese   €€€
Map 7 A2
Rua das Portas de Santo Antão 150, 1150-269
Tel *213 424 253* **Closed** *Sun*
Lively traditional restaurant popular with local celebrities as well as families. Known for its *presunto* (cured ham) as well as other superb meat and seafood dishes. The excellent wine list is presented on an iPad. Reservations are advisable.

Bairro Alto and Estrela

Bota Alta
Traditional Portuguese   €
Map 7 A3
Travessa da Queimada 35–7, 1200-364
Tel *213 427 959*
A lovely little traditional restaurant decorated with ceramics, paintings and a giant clay boot on the bar. Try the *costaletas fumadas à algarvia* (smoked ribs Algarve-style). Service can be slow during peak hours.

DK Choice

Café Fábulas
Modern Portuguese   €
Map 7 5B
Calçada Nova de São Francisco, 14, 1200-300
Tel *216 018 472* **Closed** *Sun*
Eclectic, vintage furniture complements quirky art and chandeliers amid the exposed brickwork and arches of Café Fábulas. The restaurant features an innovative menu based on Portuguese dishes with a modern twist. Popular with locals, but the service may be slow at peak hours.

Cantinho Lusitano
Petiscos   €
Map 4 E2
Rua dos Prazeres 52, 1200-355
Tel *218 065 185* **Closed** *Sun & Mon*
Run by a husband-and-wife team, this tiny restaurant specializes in Portuguese tapas. Reserve a table in advance and tuck into goat's cheese with honey, cod fritters, pork stew with sweet potato or meat rolls with mint and Greek yogurt sauce, among other dishes.

Decadente
Modern Portuguese   €
Map 4 F2
Rua São Pedro de Alcântara 81, 1250-238
Tel *213 461 381*
Chic decor but relaxed environs, with a menu full of inventive twists on Portuguese favourites. Reservations are essential on weekends. Weekday lunch menu offers three courses for €10. Fabulous cocktails.

Flor da Laranja
Moroccan   €
Map 4 F2
Rua da Rosa 206, 1200-390
Tel *213 422 996* **Closed** *Sun & Mon; lunch*
A small, welcoming restaurant decorated beautifully in Arabian style, serving delicious, authentic Moroccan cuisine. Reservations are essential, as is ringing the doorbell to gain entry. Go for the lamb with plums, chicken with artichoke or caramelised onions with raisins, along with the house wine.

Grapes and Bites
Petiscos   €
Map 7 A3
Rua do Norte 81, 1200-284
Tel *919 361 171*
With wine barrels for tables and bottles lining the walls, the extensive wine list at this restaurant should come as no surprise. Also on offer is a selection of tasty hot and cold *petiscos* (Portuguese tapas). Live music in the evening.

Pátio do Bairro
Modern Portuguese   €
Map 7 B5
Rua da Atalaia 35–37, 1200-037
Tel *213 431 822* **Closed** *Mon; lunch*
The walls of this eatery have been painted to create the illusion of an indoor courtyard. It serves inventive takes on meat, fish and pasta, as well as vegetarian options. Try the cold strawberry soup for dessert.

Xapuri
Petiscos   €
Map 7 A4
Rua Duques de Braganca 5G, 1200-162
Tel *211 993 966* **Closed** *Mon–Fri lunch*
Stone pillars, arched ceilings and terracotta-tiled floors provide a wonderful setting. Enjoy appetising *petiscos* such as sardines with avocado and mango or Portuguese sausages served on a bed of sweet potato.

Café Buenos Aires
Steak House   €€
Map 7 A3
Calçada Escadinhas do Duque 31b, 1200-155
Tel *213 420 739*
Two charming dining rooms in different buildings offering the same menu. The succulent steaks served are flown in twice a week from Argentina. Try the innovative and delicious starters and desserts. Cash only. Reserve ahead.

For more information on types of restaurants *see page 124*

An elegantly laid out table at Bistro 100 Maneiras

Casanostra €€
Italian **Map** 7 A3
Travessa do Poço da Cidade 60, 1200-334
Tel *213 425 931* **Closed** *Sat lunch*
Charming eatery with a friendly atmosphere and impeccable service. Serves a variety of tasty home-made pastas – try the squid ink pasta with shrimps. Superb wine list. Popular with both locals and tourists.

Clube de Jornalistas €€
International **Map** 4 D3
Rua das Trinas 129, 1200-857
Tel *213 977 138* **Closed** *Sun*
Housed in a lovely 18th-century building with a courtyard garden, this restaurant is a rare find well off the tourist trail. Those who venture here will be rewarded with a glass of sparkling wine on arrival and excellent food.

La Brasserie de l'Entrecôte €€
Steak House **Map** 7 A4
Rua do Alecrim 117, 1200-016
Tel *213 473 616*
Elegant restaurant famous for its perfectly tender steak served with French fries, salad and a sauce made of secret ingredients. Sit in the upper area to appreciate the charming Art Deco decor.

Madragoa Café €€
Traditional Portuguese **Map** 4 E3
Rua da Esperança, 134–6, 1200-659
Tel *213 978 567* **Closed** *Tue*
Run by a friendly husband-and-wife team, this little place serves a wonderful *cataplana* as well as traditional *açorda* (bread stew) and tasty meat dishes. Cash only. Book a table well in advance.

Picanha €€
Brazilian **Map** 4 D4
Rua das Janelas Verdes 96, 1200-692
Tel *213 975 401* **Closed** *Sun dinner; Mon*
Great option for all-you-can-eat quality Brazilian steaks grilled over an open fire, enjoyed with tempting *caipirinhas*. Blue-and-white *azulejo* panels decorate the walls. Reservations are recommended.

Real Fábrica €€
Cervejaria **Map** 4 E1
Rua da Escola Politécnica 275, 1250-101
Tel *213 852 090* **Closed** *Sun*
This former silk factory is now a spacious restaurant specializing in seafood, steaks and beer. The signature dish, *entrecote à Real Fábrica*, is steak fit for royalty. Excellent Mozambique prawns.

Sea Me €€
Seafood **Map** 4 F3
Rua do Loreto 21, 1200
Tel *213 461 564*
Fresh seafood prepared by a creative chef who specializes in Portuguese and Japanese cuisine. Go for the excellent sushi and seafood platters or the melt-in-the-mouth *prego* (steak sandwich).

Taberna Ideal €€
Modern Portuguese **Map** 4 E3
Rua Esperança 112, 1120-114
Tel *213 962 744* **Closed** *Mon & Tue; Wed–Sat lunch*
The inventive menu features dishes that are meant to be shared. The eclectic furniture and fading posters create a relaxed, informal ambience. Cash only. Reservations recommended.

Trivial €€
Traditional Portuguese **Map** 4 F2
Rua da Palmeira 44a, 1200-314
Tel *213 473 552* **Closed** *Sun; Mon–Sat lunch*
Loyal patrons return for superb food in an intimate setting. Try the chicken with Elvas plums. Smoking is permitted. Attentive staff.

Bistro 100 Maneiras €€€
International **Map** 4 F2
Largo Trindade 9, 1200-466
Tel *210 990 475* **Closed** *Sun*
This glamorous, fashionable bistro is the place to see and be seen, so dress up and book ahead, especially for the romantic dining area. The menu is creative, and the kitchen stays open until midnight.

Kais €€€
Portuguese/International
Map 4 D4
Cais da Viscondessa, Rua da Cintura do Porto de Lisboa, 1200-109
Tel *213 932 930* **Closed** *Sun & Mon*
Riverside warehouse, stripped to brick and steel, and filled with industrial-inspired furniture and lovely water features. Enjoy Portugese food in the Adega downstairs or international fare in the upstairs restaurant.

Pap'Açorda €€€
Traditional Portuguese **Map** 4 F2
Rua da Atalaia 57, 1200-037
Tel *213 464 811* **Closed** *Sun; lunch*
This elegant restaurant is named after its signature dish, *açorda*, a bread stew from the Alentejo region. It is frequented by both locals and tourists, so reserve a table well in advance.

Restaurante Lapa €€€
Mediterranean **Map** 3 C3
Olissippo Lapa Palace, Rua do Pau da Bandeira 4, 1249-021
Tel *213 949 494*
Housed in an opulent 19th-century palace, this refined place serves exquisite gourmet dishes including *leitão a Bairrada* (suckling pig, Bairrada-style) and fresh sea bass. Extensive wine list.

Belém

Belém 2 a 8 €
Traditional Portuguese **Map** 1 C4
Rua de Belém 2, 1300-085
Tel *213 639 055* **Closed** *Mon*
Spread across two floors and an outdoor patio, this bright eatery is right next door to the president's palace. The food is hearty, traditional fare and the emphasis is on homeliness and a warm welcome. Vegetarians and kids are well catered for.

Nosolo Italia €€
Italian **Map** 1 B5
Avenida Brasilia 202, 1400-038
Tel *213 015 969*
Glass-sided building with a terrace jutting out over the Tagus river. Serves excellent pizza and *gelati* as well as English breakfasts. There's a special children's menu. Parking can be tricky.

DK Choice

Vela Latina €€€
Modern Portuguese **Map** 1 B5
Doca do Bom Sucesso, 1400-038
Tel 213 017 118 **Closed** *Sun*
Set in lush gardens with views
of the river and marina, this
is a stylish venue for lunch or
dinner. Lobster-filled crêpes
and hake fillets are the main
draws. Attentive and efficient
waiters advise on suitable wines
to complement the meal.
Reservations are recommended,
especially for the garden tables.

Further Afield

António €
Modern Portuguese **Map** 5 C3
Rua Tomás Ribeiro 63, 1050-226
Tel 213 538 780 **Closed** *Sun*
Simple but modern, serving
well-cooked food in large
portions, with a choice of four
bacalhau (cod) dishes. The daily-
changing lunch menu is popular.

Himchuli €
Nepalese **Map** 3 C4
*Rua do Sacramento a Alcântara 48,
1350-278*
Tel 213 901 722 **Closed** *Sun lunch*
Delectable, spicy Nepalese cuisine,
brimming with flavours; imported
Nepalese beer is also available. Try
the shrimp with coconut cream,
and the pudding with cashew
cream and passion fruit for dessert. Reserve for peak times.

Cervejaria Portugália €€
Cervejaria **Map** 6 E5
Avenida Almirante Reis 117, 1115-014
Tel 213 140 002
The first in a chain of brewery
restaurants, this flagship eatery
continues to serve excellent
steaks and seafood. Try the
house specialities of *açorda*
with prawns or *bacalhau à bras*
(cod) and wash them down
with the house beer.

Cervejaria Ramiro €€
Cervejaria **Map** 6 E5
Avenida Almirante Reis 1, 1150-007
Tel 218 851 024 **Closed** *Mon*
Tuck into seafood specialities
such as *percebes* (goose barnacles) and steak sandwiches at
this ever-popular *cervejaria*. The
excellent food goes well with
the draught beer. Book ahead.

La Gôndola €€
Italian/Portuguese **Map** 5 B2
Avenida de Berna 64, 1050-043
Tel 217 970 426
Choose from a range of home-
made pasta dishes, or traditional

Portuguese fare. Also has
several options for vegetarians.
Patrons can sit in the pretty garden or in the bright, spacious
dining area. Features occasional
fado performances.

DK Choice

Laurentina €€
Traditional Portuguese
Map 5 B2
*Avenida Conde de Valbom 71a,
1050-067*
Tel 217 960 260
Also known as the "King of
Cod", this restaurant offers an
extensive range of perfectly
cooked *bacalhau* (salted cod)
dishes. A small selection of meat
dishes and Mozambican fare
is also available, along with a
carefully selected wine list. Live
fado music on Thursday evenings.

Mezzaluna €€
Italian **Map** 5 A4
Rua Artilharia Um 16, 1250-039
Tel 213 879 944 **Closed** *Sat lunch;
Sun*
Quiet, inviting dining room with
an elegant decor. The menu,
created by Italian-American
chef Guerrieri, features innovative
combinations as well as standard
favourites such as spaghetti
carbonara. Reserve ahead.

O Polícia €€
Traditional Portuguese **Map** 5 B2
*Rua Marquês Sá da Bandeira 112a,
1050-158*
Tel 217 963 505 **Closed** *Sat dinner;
Sun*
Award-winning family-run
restaurant known for its traditional
Portuguese meals, especially
the seafood. Don't miss the
cod dish, *Bacalhau à Zé do Pipo*.
The *sericaia*, a traditional egg
pudding served only in winter,
is delicious. Packed at lunch time.

Sessenta €€
Modern Portuguese **Map** 5 B3
Rua Tomas Ribeiro 60, 1050-231
Tel 213 526 060 **Closed** *Sun*
Eat well-prepared dishes such as
veal cheeks with parsnip purée
and greens, or seafood dishes like
octopus and sea bass in one of
two dining rooms. Attentive staff.

Casa da Comida €€€
Modern Portuguese **Map** 5 B5
Travessa das Amoreiras 1, 1250-025
Tel 213 860 889 **Closed** *Mon &
Sat lunch; Sun*
For a romantic meal in an
elegant setting, ask for a table
in or overlooking the garden.
The staff can help in choosing
from the extensive wine list
that accompanies the delec-
table *haute cuisine*.

Eleven €€€
International **Map** 5 B4
*Rua Marquês de Fronteira, Jardim
Amália Rodrigues, 1070-310*
Tel 213 862 211 **Closed** *Sun; holidays*
A refined atmosphere and
artistic decor add to the fine-
dining experience at one of
Lisbon's top gourmet restau-
rants. The various menus here
include tasting, à la carte and
lobster-themed.

DK Choice

Pabe €€€
International **Map** 5 C5
*Rua Duque de Palmela 27a,
1250-097*
Tel 213 537 484
A mock Tudor façade, beamed
ceilings and wooden walls
combine to create the feel
of a traditional English pub
at Pabe. The charcoal-grilled
baby goat, roasted sea bass
and breaded squid are delicious. Expect old-school
courtesy from the waiters.

Simply furnished dining area at Cervejaria Ramiro

For more information on types of restaurants *see page 124*

The Lisbon Coast

ALCÁCER DO SAL:
Dom Afonso II   €€
International
Pousada de Alcácer do Sal,
7580-197
Tel *265 613 070*
The gourmet menu in this
classy castle restaurant features
typical starters such as clam
soup; mains include eel stew. The
roast leg of lamb is a must-try.

CASCAIS: Ginginha
Trasmontana   €
Traditional Portuguese
Rua de Alvide 366 A, Fontainhas,
2750-288
Tel *214 832 655*   **Closed** *Sun*
Intimate, with a ceiling crammed
with pots, lamps and lanterns.
Try the *javali* (wild boar with
prawns), which is served, like
many other grilled meat and
fish dishes, on a curved roof tile.

CASCAIS: Mayura   €
Indian
Rua Freitas Reis 15b, 2750-357
Tel *214 846 540*
Friendly, popular place that has
gained a loyal following by ser-
ving quality Indian dishes. The
ceiling is decorated with colour-
ful Indian shawls. Cash only.
Reservations recommended.

CASCAIS: Casa Velha   €€
Seafood
Avenida Valbom 1, 2750-508
Tel *214 832 586*
With stone walls, a ceiling
draped with fishing nets and a
bougainvillea-covered terrace,
Casa Velha offers a rustic ambience. The *caldeirada de peixe*
(fish stew) and *cherne grelhado*
(grilled halibut) are superb.

CASCAIS: Dom Diniz   €€
Petiscos
Rua Alexandre Herculano 77,
2750-284
Tel *214 837 170*   **Closed** *Sun; lunch*
Sample Portuguese cured meats,
sausages and other tapas-style
dishes at this small eatery. The
seafood skewer and Alentejo-
style pork is highly recommended.
Very popular, book ahead.

CASCAIS: O Pescador   €€
Seafood
Rua das Flores 10b, 2750-348
Tel *214 832 054*   **Closed** *Sun*
Nautical-themed eatery with
wooden tables and fishing para-
phernalia. The emphasis here
is firmly on seafood and fresh
fish. The huge terrace is a great
dining spot on warmer days.

CASCAIS: Gourmet Restaurant
Hotel Miragem   €€€
International
Avenida Marginal 8554, 2775-536
Tel *210 060 600*   **Closed** *lunch*
Elegant fine dining with sea views
and a romantic ambience, perfect
for savouring the gourmet cuisine.
The menu and wine list are regu-
larly updated. Friendly staff.

DK Choice

CASCAIS: Hemingway   €€€
International
Marina de Cascais, 1º, 2750-800
Tel *916 224 452*   **Closed** *Wed*
This stylish restaurant overlooks
the boats moored at the marina
and offers gorgeous sea views.
The superb gourmet cuisine,
featuring dishes such as
caramelized tuna steak,
steamed lobster medallions
and braised stone bass, give
diners an unforgettable
experience. A knowledgeable
sommelier assists diners with
the extensive wine list.

CASCAIS: The Mix   €€€
International
Avenida Rei Humberto de Itália 7,
2750-461
Tel *214 823 490*
Modern restaurant with three
dining areas and fabulous ocean
views. Serves beautifully presented
dishes and offers a weekday exec-
utive lunch menu. Reservations
are essential in summer.

ESTORIL: Tertulia do Monte   €
International
Avenida Saboia 515, 2765-278
Tel *214 681 508*   **Closed** *Sat lunch*
& Sun
The house speciality, baked
turbot with coriander, is highly
recommended. A chalkboard
lists the daily lunch menu and
specials. It has themed menus,
as well as *fado* nights in winter.

ESTORIL: Estoril Mandarim   €€
Chinese
Casino Estoril, 2765-237
Tel *214 667 270*   **Closed** *Mon &*
Tue
Plush restaurant run by chefs from
Hong Kong and Macau. Offers the
best Chinese food in Portugal,
especially the Peking duck and
dim sum. Friendly service.

ESTORIL: Four Seasons Grill   €€€
Portuguese
Hotel Palácio Estoril, Rua Particular,
2765-000
Tel *214 680 400*   **Closed** *lunch*
One of Estoril's most sophisticated
dining venues. Serves superb
gourmet dishes, some of which
are cooked at the table. Excellent
wine list. Attentive service.

GUINCHO: Bar do Guincho   €
International
Estrada do Abano 547, 2755-144
Tel *214 871 683*   **Closed** *Mon in winter*
This beach eatery is ideal for
light meals and offers a range
of toasties and salads, as well
as burgers and heavier meat
dishes. Great sunset views.

GUINCHO: O Faroleiro   €€
Seafood
Estrada do Guincho, 2750-642
Tel *214 870 225*
Bright and spacious, with large
windows affording great sea
views. The menu focuses on
local seafood cooked to perfection. Sample the goose barnacles
or seafood rice with lobster.

GUINCHO: Furnas
do Guincho   €€€
International
Avenida Nossa Senhora do Cabo
1265, 2750-642
Tel *214 869 243*
Enjoy grilled and fresh seafood at
this modern, oceanfront restaurant. Go for the octopus and sweet
potato *cataplana* or choose from
the wide range of steaks.

Beautifully decorated interior of the oceanfront Furnas do Guincho

GUINCHO: Porto de Santa Maria €€€
Seafood
Estrada do Guincho, 2750-642
Tel *214 879 450*
Seaside establishment with classy furnishings. The delicious seafood is priced by the kilo. Book ahead and arrive in time for the sunset.

MONTE ESTORIL: O Sinaleiro €
Traditional Portuguese
Avenida de Sabóia 595, 2765-278
Tel *214 685 439* **Closed** *Wed*
Simple, family-run traditional bar and restaurant serving generous portions of excellent quality food. Some less common dishes feature on the largely typical menu.

PAÇO D'ARCOS: Aquarela do Brasil €
Brazilian
Praça 5 de Outubro 12, 2770-029
Tel *214 415 412*
Relish perfectly cooked Brazilian steaks at this outstanding eatery. The house cocktail, *caipirinha*, is a must-try. Features live music on some days.

PALMELA: Chico's €
Italian
Avenida Antoine Velge, Quinta da Gloria Lt 3, 2950-019
Tel *210 993 395*
Local family favourite known for excellent pizza, a range of pasta dishes and tender steaks. The champagne sangria with forest fruits is worth sampling.

PALMELA: Pousada do Castelo de Palmela €€
Portuguese
Pousada do Castelo de Palmela, 2950-317
Tel *212 351 226*
Romantic restaurant housed in a former monastery. Sit in the cloisters on warm days or the historical dining room. The partridge and wild mushroom pie is a speciality.

PORTINHO DA ARRÁBIDA: O Farol €
Seafood
Portinho da Arrábida, 2925-378
Tel *212 181 177* **Closed** *Mon; holidays*
Popular restaurant in a prime location, right at the water's edge. House favourites include rock lobster with rice and clams and sea bass straight off the boat. Try the *caldeirada* (fish casserole).

QUELUZ: Retiro da Mina €
Traditional Portuguese
Avenida da Republica 10, 2745-206
Tel *214 352 978* **Closed** *Mon dinner; Tue*
Cheerful meals of hearty portions of home-cooked Portuguese favourites like *cozido à Portuguesa* (meat and vegetable stew) and the house-style chicken.

QUELUZ: Cozinha Velha €€
Portuguese
Largo Palácio Nacional de Queluz, 2745-191
Tel *214 356 158*
Housed in the palace kitchens, with an original stone chimney. The creative menu features *bacalhau grelhado* (grilled salt cod). Live harp music on Friday evenings. Reserve a table in advance.

SESIMBRA: O Rodinhas €
Seafood
Rua Marques do Pombal 25, 2970-772
Tel *212 231 557* **Closed** *Wed*
Old-fashioned eatery known for its excellent seafood. Serves *petiscos* and *francesinhas* (steak, ham, cheese and sausage sandwich in a beer sauce) as well. Cash only.

SESIMBRA: Casa Mateus €€
Seafood
Largo Anselmo Braamcamp 4, 2970-654
Tel *918 790 697* **Closed** *Mon*
Top-quality seafood is cooked to perfection by the owner's wife at this friendly restaurant. Try the *caldeirada* (fish stew) and leave room for the superb desserts.

SESIMBRA: Ribamar €€
Seafood
Avenida dos Náufragos 29, 2970-637
Tel *212 234 853*
Colourful, roomy venue widely considered one of the best restaurants in the region. The creative chef regularly updates the menu with surprise concoctions. Service can be a bit slow.

SETÚBAL: Poço das Fontainhas €
Seafood
Rua das Fontainhas 96, 2910-082
Tel *265 534 807* **Closed** *Mon*
Situated in the original fishermen's part of town, this place can be hard to find. The *ensopado de enguias* (eel stew) is worth a try. Reservations are recommended.

SETÚBAL: Pousada de São Filipe €€
Portuguese
Pousada de São Filipe, Castelo de São Filipe, 2900-300
Tel *265 550 070*
Beautifully prepared regional delicacies at this historical venue. Magnificent views of the ocean from the terrace. Impressive wine list. Save room for the orange tart.

Well-stocked bar overlooking the dining area at Casa Mateus, in Sesimbra

SINTRA: Tulhas €
Traditional Portuguese
Rua Gil Vicente 4–6, 2710-568
Tel *219 232 378* **Closed** *Wed*
This lovely, cosy little place serves ample portions of home-made food as well as delicious cheeses and wines, including the house red. Best to reserve a table.

SINTRA: A Raposa €€
International
Rua Conde Ferreira 29, 2710-556
Tel *219 243 440* **Closed** *Mon*
Housed in a lovely 19th-century building, this place functions as a tea house during the day and gourmet restaurant at night. The food is worth the wait.

SINTRA: Monserrate €€
International
Hotel Tivoli Sintra, Praça de República, 2710-616
Tel *219 237 200*
Attractive place with stunning views of the Sintra valley. Try the award-winning cream of pumpkin soup with mussels, followed by the house steak. Reserve ahead.

SINTRA: Lawrence's €€€
International
Rua Consigliéri Pedroso 38–40, 2710-550
Tel *219 105 500*
Enjoy fine dining in this historic hotel frequented by celebrities. Outstanding à la carte menu and an extensive wine list. The *foie gras* is highly recommended.

SINTRA: Tivoli Palácio de Seteais €€€
International
Rua Barbosa du Bocage 8, Seteais, 2710-517
Tel *219 233 200*
Dining at this elegant palace hotel is a memorable experience. Well-known gourmet chefs create exquisite dishes and the service is smart.

For more information on types of restaurants *see page 124*

Cafés and Bars

Coffee is a vital element of the Portuguese way of life and a vibrant culture has developed around the simple pleasure of relaxing over a cup of coffee and a pastry in one of Lisbon's many cafés. The Portuguese have a complex classification system for coffee options (see p125), which modern coffee fashions will not change. Although shortcomings of service and gastronomy may be allowed to pass in a restaurant, a bad coffee at the end of the meal is a cardinal sin.

Bar culture is a younger phenomenon. While traditional drinking places such as ginjinha bars live on, the bars that make Lisbon's nightlife one of Europe's liveliest and most varied are rarely more than a decade or two old. Bairro Alto is the city's best-known bar territory and has the widest choice, but Santos, Bica/Santa Catarina and Cais do Sodré are good areas for bar-hopping too.

Classic Cafés

Foremost among the grand cafés from the turn of the last century is **A Brasileira**, perfectly sited at the top of one of Lisbon's best shopping streets. The intellectuals who made it famous are long gone (there is a café-table bronze of poet Fernando Pessoa on the popular esplanade), but the atmosphere is cosmopolitan. **Nicola**, down in Rossio, has an elegant Art Deco interior and a busy outdoor seating area with plenty to watch. Across the square is **Pastelaria Suiça**, another boulevard-style café where the long promenade is its main attraction. **Martinho da Arcada**, under the arcades in Praça do Comércio, has an illustrious history and a beautifully tiled interior. Traffic makes the tables outside less of a treat, unless you opt for the restaurant, which has tables further in.

Park/Garden Cafés

Those who appreciate a bit of greenery and no traffic with their coffee should seek out **Linha d'Água** at the top of Parque Eduardo VII. As with many Lisbon cafés it also serves meals at lunch time. The pond-side café in **Jardim da Estrela** is another attractive option. **Pão de Canela** is a small café with a terrace on Praça das Flores, a quiet square with a garden in one of Lisbon's cosiest neighbourhoods. **Este**

Oeste, in the modern complex of the Centro Cultural de Belém, is an open-air restaurant set in an attractive, minimalist garden overlooking the river, serving freshly made pizza and sushi. There is also a quieter upstairs bar, Terraço. Vegetarians will appreciate **Psi**, with its small garden and spiritual vibe.

Contemporary Cafés

A contemporary approach means more froth in your milky coffee (do not call it latte though), a wider range of sandwiches and a lighter touch with meals. It may also mean a lounge-like atmosphere, plenty of magazines and a serious take on music. Exponents of this approach include **Café no Chiado** with a very relaxed atmosphere; **Vertigo**, also in Chiado; and the inimitable **Pois, Café** with its cosy vaulted living room near the Sé. There is no Starbucks in Lisbon, but home-grown chains **LA Caffé** and **Orpheu Caffé** offer style and quality.

Pastry Shops

Pastelarias are a crucial institution in Lisbon. Less raucous and smoky than normal cafés and snack bars, they are the preferred haunt of ladies of a certain age. However, as with any other customer, they would not bother coming in if the

glass counter was not laden with freshly made pastéis de nata or amêndoas (custard or almond tarts), bolos de arroz (rice-flour cakes) or queijadas (cottage cheese tarts). **Benard** is next to A Brasileira and gets some of the surplus custom from there, but its pastries are fresher. **Confeitaria Nacional** has been around for nearly two centuries and still does a booming over-the-counter business. The café section gets crowded quickly. Uptown is **Pastelaria Versailles** which is airier and has an atmosphere of faded grandeur. By far the most famous pastry shop is **Antiga Confeitaria de Belém**, where the pastel de nata (known as pastel de Belém in Lisbon) is said to have been invented.

DJ Bars

Bairro Alto has more bars than most people can ever manage to remember, but among those where music is taken particularly seriously are **Clube da Esquina** and **O Bom O Mau e o Vilão**. In nearby Bica/Santa Catarina, **Bicaense** has a coolly informal groove. Closer to the river, **Lounge** is less low key than it was, but remains dedicated to non-mainstream sounds. With a prime location overlooking the river, **Clube Ferroviário** features top DJs, live concerts and outdoor film screenings.

Outdoor Bars

Good bars for sunset viewing, warm nights and occasional sunrises include **Meninos do Rio**, whose irresistible chaises longues on the quayside need to be grabbed early. **Op Art** is a beacon of good taste and music in the now up-market Docas area under the bridge. **Noobai** combines great music with great views from the Santa Catarina viewpoint, and is one of Lisbon's most popular spots on warm summer evenings. Below the Castle, **Bar das Imagens** is a long-standing, or leaning, terrace over the city.

Classics and Ginjinhas

Pavilhão Chinês is on every tourist's itinerary, but it is worth a visit for its curio-shop interior. It is also one of the few places that give cocktails proper respect. The **British Bar** is a remnant from a bygone era and its wall clock goes backwards, but it attracts a very present-day crowd. **Portas Largas** could be said to be the engine that runs Bairro Alto – its street party is electric (and gay, but far from exclusively so). *Ginjinha* bars are a uniquely Portuguese institution: small, hole-in-the-wall bars that serve morello-cherry liqueur – *ginjinha* – and almost nothing else. Pop into **A Ginjinha** or **Ginjinha Sem Rival** for a taste.

Wine Bars

There are surprisingly few bars that offer a good range of wines by the glass in Lisbon. Among the few that exist, **Enoteca** is perhaps the best, where tasty small dishes are served alongside an excellent selection of Portuguese and some foreign wines. In a similar vein, the **Wine Bar do Castelo** serves a selection of wines by the glass. And **Lux**, Lisbon's premier nightclub, now has a bar dedicated to Bacchus. Port by the glass can also be had at the **Solar do Vinho do Porto** (*see p56*), run by the Port Wine Institute of Oporto.

DIRECTORY

Classic Cafés

A Brasileira
Rua Garrett 120.
Map 7 A4.
Tel 213 469 541.

Martinho da Arcada
Praça do Comércio 3.
Map 7 C5.
Tel 218 879 259.

Nicola
Praça Dom Pedro IV 24–5.
Map 7 B3.
Tel 213 460 579.

Pastelaria Suíça
Praça Dom Pedro IV 96–101. **Map** 7 B3.
Tel 213 214 090.

Park/Garden Cafés

Este Oeste
Centro Cultural de Belém, Praça do Império.
Map 1 B5.
Tel 914 914 505.

Jardim da Estrela
Jardim da Estrela, Praça da Estrela. **Map** 4 D2.

Linha d'Água
Jardim Amália Rodrigues (top of Parque Eduardo VII). **Map** 5 B3.
Tel 213 814 327.

Pão de Canela
Praça das Flores 27.
Map 4 E2.
Tel 213 972 220.

Psi
Alameda Santo António dos Capuchos.
Map 6 D5.
Tel 213 590 573.

Contemporary Cafés

Café no Chiado
Largo do Picadeiro 10–12.
Map 7 A4.
Tel 213 460 501.

LA Caffé
Campo Grande 3A.
Map 4 F1.
Tel 217 967 713.

Orpheu Caffé
Praça do Príncipe Real 5.
Map 4 F1.
Tel 218 044 499.

Pois, Café
Rua São João da Praça, 93–5. **Map** 8 D4.
Tel 218 862 497.

Vertigo
Travessa do Carmo 4.
Map 7 A4.
Tel 213 433 112.

Pastry Shops

Antiga Confeitaria de Belém
Rua de Belém 84–92.
Map 1 C4.
Tel 213 638 077.

Benard
Rua Garrett 104.
Map 7 A4.
Tel 213 473 133.

Confeitaria Nacional
Praça da Figueira 18B.
Map 7 B3.
Tel 213 424 470.

Pastelaria Versailles
Avenida da República 15A. **Map** 5 C3.
Tel 213 546 340.

DJ Bars

Bicaense
Rua da Bica de Duarte Belo 42 A. **Map** 4 F3.
Tel 213 257 940.

Clube da Esquina
Rua da Barroca 30.
Map 4 F2. **Tel** 213 427 149.

Clube Ferroviário
Rua da Santa Apolónia 59.
Map 8 F2.
Tel 218 153 196.

Lounge
Rua da Moeda 1.
Map 4 F3.

O Bom O Mau e O Vilão
Rua do Alecrim 21. **Map** 7 A5. **Tel** 213 471 282.

Outdoor Bars

Bar das Imagens
Calçada Marquês de Tancos 1. **Map** 7 C3.
Tel 218 884 636.

Meninos do Rio
Rua da Cintura do Porto de Lisboa, Armazém 255.
Map 4 E4.
Tel 213 220 070.

Noobai
Miradouro de Santa Catarina. **Map** 4 F3.
Tel 213 465 014.

Op Art
Doca de Santo Amaro.
Map 3 A5.
Tel 936 240 981.

Classics and Ginjinhas

A Ginjinha
Largo de São Domingos 8. **Map** 7 B3.

British Bar
Rua Bernardino Costa 52.
Map 7 A5.
Tel 213 422 367.

Ginjinha Sem Rival
Rua das Portas de Santo Antão 7. **Map** 7 B2.

Pavilhão Chinês
Rua Dom Pedro V 89.
Map 4 F2.
Tel 213 424 729.

Portas Largas
Rua da Atalaia 105.
Map 4 F2.

Wine Bars

Enoteca
Rua da Mãe d'Água.
Map 4 F1.
Tel 213 422 079.

Lux
Cais da Pedra, Avenida Infante Dom Henrique.
Map 8 F3.
Tel 218 820 890.

Solar do Vinho do Porto
Rua de São Pedro de Alcântara 45.
Map 7 A3.
Tel 213 475 707.

Wine Bar do Castelo
Rua Bartolomeu de Gusmão 13. **Map** 7 C4.
Tel 218 879 093.

SHOPPING IN LISBON

Lisbon offers a wide variety of shops to the visitor, with its combination of elegant high-street shops, flea markets and modern shopping centres. The cobbled streets of the Baixa and the chic Chiado district have traditionally been Lisbon's main shopping areas, but the numerous indoor shopping centres are becoming increasingly popular. Markets in Lisbon, Sintra and Cascais provide more adventurous shopping. If you are after something typically Portuguese, the hand-woven tapestries and lacework are worth buying. Most of all, choose from a range of ceramics, such as *azulejos* or Vista Alegre Atlantis porcelain. For lovers of wine, Lisbon's wine merchants offer the best from all over the country.

A delicatessen in the Bairro Alto

Opening Hours

Traditional shopping hours are Monday to Friday 9am to 1pm and 3pm to 7pm, and Saturday 9am to 1pm.

However, in order to satisfy consumer demand, many shops, especially those in the Baixa, are now staying open during the lunch hour and on Saturday afternoons. Specialist shops such as hardware stores generally close for lunch at 12:30pm and reopen at 2:30pm. Shopping centres are open daily from 10am to midnight, with most shops closing at 11pm. Generally, convenience stores are open daily from 7am to 2am.

How to Pay

Most shops in Lisbon accept Visa and, to a lesser extent, American Express and MasterCard. Many smaller shops outside the main shopping areas will not. An alternative is to obtain a cash advance with a credit or debit card from one of the many *Multibanco* ATMs.

Note that these charge interest on the withdrawal from day one, in addition to a currency conversion fee.

VAT and Taxes

Non-European Union residents are exempt from IVA (Value Added Tax) in Portugal provided they remain in the country for no longer than 180 days. However, obtaining a rebate may be complicated in small shops or in areas less frequented by tourists. It is much simpler to buy in shops with a Global Blue Tax Free sign outside.

To get your rebate, ask the shop assistant for an *Isenção na Exportação* form. This must then be presented to a customs officer on your departure from Portugal. The original of the document will be returned to the vendor who is responsible for the reimbursement.

Shopping Centres

Large shopping centres are now very much part of the shopping landscape in Lisbon. They combine vast supermarkets, international chain stores and small specialist shops. All have restaurants and underground car parks; most also have cinemas. The oldest is **Amoreiras**, which has 230 shops and international chain stores, seven cinemas and 40 restaurants. **Dolce Vita Monumental** is one of three smaller centres clustered near Praça Duque de Saldanha. **Armazéns do Chiado** in the Chiado area has a historic façade but a modern interior. The huge **Colombo Shopping Centre** (see p76) in Benfica boasts a large children's leisure centre. The **Vasco da Gama** centre connects Oriente Station with Parque das Nações. The Spanish department store **El Corte Inglés** is at the top of Parque Eduardo VII. **CascaiShopping**, located between Estoril and Sintra, is one of many suburban centres.

Markets

There are markets of every variety in Lisbon, from municipal markets selling fresh produce to

The vast Amoreiras shopping centre

Shoppers browsing in the popular Feira da Ladra

the famous **Feira da Ladra** (Thieves' Market), a flea market on the slopes of the Alfama district. Although some stalls just sell junk, some bargains can be found among the array of bric-a-brac, second-hand clothes and general arts and crafts.

For more specialized markets, head to Praça do Príncipe Real, where the **Feira de Antiguidades, Velharias e Artesanato**, an antiques market, is held every last Saturday of the month, or to the Chiado district for the **Feira dos Alfarrabistas**, for old books. The **Feira de Coleccionismo** (collectors' market) takes place in Cais do Sodré every Sunday (9am–1pm).

Set in picturesque surroundings outside Lisbon, the **Feira de São Pedro**, in Sintra, is a wonderful market selling everything from new clothes and old bric-a-brac, to maturing cheeses and cackling fowl.

Along the Lisbon Coast, the **Feira de Cascais** has some good clothes bargains, as does the **Feira de Carcavelos**. Arrive early to beat the crowds.

Food Shops

It is almost impossible to window shop in Lisbon's delicatessens (charcutarias) without buying. Lined with a vast array of mouthwatering foods, from superb cheeses to tasty smoked meats and exquisite sweets, establishments such as **Espaço Açores** are a must for all seasoned gourmets.

Here you can buy almost all regional specialities, from cheeses such as serra and ilhas to wild game such as partridge. Smoked hams and spicy sausages are also popular. If you have a sweet tooth, try some delicious ovos moles (egg sweets) or an assortment of dried or crystallized fruits, including delicious Elvas plums.

Other good food shops include **Dom Pedro** and **Manuel Tavares**, which has a large selection of port and madeira. **Celeiro Dieta** is a good health food shop, and is well known for stocking organic foods.

Wines and Spirits

Portugal has a large variety of wines, fortified wines and spirits (see pp128–9), ranging from light vinhos verdes to powerful tintos (reds), from fruity young ruby ports to ancient tawny ports or madeira, from sweet amêndoa amarga (bitter almond liqueur) to fiery bagaceira (grapeskin distillate).

Napoleão, the best-known wine merchant in Lisbon, has outlets in many parts of the city, with its oldest shop in the Baixa. For port specifically, visit the **Solar do Vinho do Porto** (see p56) in the Bairro Alto: this slightly fusty institution is

Fresh fish for sale at one of Lisbon's municipal markets

actually a bar where you can sample a vast range of ports before deciding what to buy. **Garrafeira de Campo de Ourique** is one of Lisbon's best smaller wine merchants, and **Coisas do Arco do Vinho** has a good selection. Alternatively, large supermarkets are good for bargains, with frequent special offers on wines and spirits. You could visit the cellars of **José Maria da Fonseca** (see p113) in Azeitão, where you can taste and buy many of the wines.

Music and Multimedia

The music scene in Portugal is a lively mix of tradition and the very latest trends. Fado music remains hugely popular, while techno and trance dance music have a dedicated following. Lisbon is also an important centre for contemporary music from former African colonies such as Cape Verde.

FNAC operates two megastores in Lisbon, and these are widely regarded as the city's best music shops in terms of variety. FNAC also sells most kinds of electronic hardware and software as well as books. **Discoteca Amália** in the Baixa specializes in fado.

Frontage of Livraria Bertrand, one of Lisbon's oldest bookshops

Bookshops

Portugal enjoys a great literary tradition with a range of authors, past and present, including Luís de Camões, Eça de Queiróz, Fernando Pessoa and José Saramago. Translations of their works, and those of other well-known Portuguese writers, are available in most large bookshops.

Livraria Bertrand and **Aillaud & Lellos**, both in the Chiado, are among Lisbon's oldest bookshops. **Livraria Buchholz**, near the top of Avenida da Liberdade, was founded by a German and has a particularly large section of books in languages other than Portuguese, including travel guides, paperback fiction and history.

For an interesting selection of second-hand books, try visiting the **Feira dos Alfarrabistas** market, held in the Chiado district on the first Sunday of every month.

Rustic terracotta ware, on sale in abundant quantities in Setúbal

Clothes

Many of the large chain stores, have outlets in Lisbon, particularly in the shopping centres (see p138). Perhaps most noticeable is the Spanish **Zara** chain, whose shops sell affordable clothes for everyone.

More exclusive shops, including designer outlets, can be found on and around Avenida da Liberdade. **Rosa & Teixeira** sells classic menswear; **Loja das Meias** is a mid-range chain with several shops. **Ana Salazar** is one of an increasing number of known Portuguese designers.

Ceramics

Portugal's ceramics are famous for their quality and variety. In Lisbon you can find everything, from delicate porcelain to rustic terracotta, and from tiles to tableware.

The very fine **Vista Alegre Atlantis** porcelain tableware is internationally known. Also famous are hand-painted ceramics, including tiles from **Viúva Lamego**, **Santana** and **Cerâmica Artística de Carcavelos**. Known as *azulejos*, glazed tiles have long been used in Portugal to brighten up buildings. They may be plain, patterned or make up large figurative paintings. In Cascais, **Ceramicarte** is one of the largest ceramic centres. Perhaps the most ubiquitous pottery originates from Barcelos, famous for its decoratively painted cockerel which has become the unofficial national symbol.

Regional Crafts

Portugal has a long and rich history of fine regional craft-work (artesanato), in particular embroidery and fine lace, hand-knitted woollens, and delicate jewellery made from silver and gold thread. There are plenty of handicraft and gift shops in the Restauradores and Rossio areas of Lisbon, though these can be a little touristy. **Arte Rústica**, in the Baixa, is excellent for genuine crafts and a fascinating place to spend time browsing.

Regionália, in Estoril, and **Sintra Bazar**, in central Sintra, are also both good for arts. Between July and August a wide variety of crafts can be seen at the Estoril Craft Fair, at which artisans from all over Portugal gather to exhibit their work. Cork carvings and pottery can be found at **Santos Ofícios**.

Lisbon offers regional crafts from all over Portugal

Antiques

Antiques often tend to be overpriced in Portugal, especially in Lisbon where the shops are mostly geared to a fairly up-market clientele. You will generally find better value in towns outside the city. It is a good idea to look for shops that are members of APA (Associação Portuguesa de Antiquários). These are usually identified by a sign in the shop window.

The majority of Lisbon's antique shops are located either in Rua Dom Pedro V, at the top of the Bairro Alto, or in Rua de São Bento, by the Parliament building, and around the cathedral, in the Alfama. There are numerous religious artifacts to be found in the area and **Solar** specializes in 16th–20th-century tiles (azulejos). Beautiful prints (known as gravuras), sold at various second-hand bookshops in the Bairro Alto, are usually good value for money. **Livraria Olisipo** stocks books and also old prints of landscapes, fauna and maps. For a good range of quality antiques it is worth visiting the auctions held at **Cabral Moncada Leilões** (which are held every Monday evening) and also the Antiques Fair, which is held in Lisbon annually during April.

Size Chart

Lisbon uses both British and American systems.

Women's dresses, coats and skirts

Portuguese	34	36	38	40	42	44	46
British	8	10	12	14	16	18	20
American	6	8	10	12	14	16	18

Women's shoes

Portuguese	36	37	38	39	40	41
British	3	4	5	6	7	8
American	5	6	7	8	9	10

Men's suits

Portuguese	44	46	48	50	52	54	56	58
British	34	36	38	40	42	44	46	48
American	34	36	38	40	42	44	46	48

Men's shirts

Portuguese	36	38	39	41	42	43	44	45
British	14	15	15½	16	16½	17	17½	18
American	14	15	15½	16	16½	17	17½	18

Men's shoes

Portuguese	39	40	41	42	43	44	45	46
British	6	7	7½	8	9	10	11	12
American	7	7½	8	8½	9½	10½	11	11½

DIRECTORY

Shopping Centres

Amoreiras
Avenida Eng. Duarte
Pacheco, Amoreiras.
Map 5 A5.
Tel 213 810 200.
w amoreiras.com

Armazéns do Chiado
Rua do Carmo 2, Chiado.
Map 7 B4.
Tel 213 210 600.

CascaiShopping
Estrada Nacional 9,
Alcabideche, Estoril.
Tel 210 121 620.
w cascaishopping.pt

Colombo Shopping Centre
Avenida Lusíada, Benfica.
Tel 217 113 600/36.
w colombo.pt

Dolce Vita Monumental
Avenida Fontes Pereira
de Melo 51, Saldanha.
Map 5 C4.
Tel 213 510 500.

El Corte Inglés
Avenida António Augusto
Aguiar 31. **Map** 5 B5.
Tel 213 711 700.
w elcorteingles.pt

Vasco da Gama
Avenida Dom João ll,
Parque das Nações.
Tel 218 930 600.
w centrovasco
dagama.pt

Markets

Feira dos Alfarrabistas
Rua da Anchieta, Chiado
(10am–5pm Sat).

Feira de Antiguidades, Velharias e Artesanato
Praça do Príncipe Real.

Feira de Carcavelos
Carcavelos (Thu).

Feira de Cascais
Cascais.

Feira de Coleccionismo
Mercado da Ribeira,
Avenida 24 de Julho.
Map 4 F4.

Feira da Ladra
Alfama (Tue & Sat).
Map 8 E3.

Feira de São Pedro
Sintra.

Food Shops

Celeiro Dieta
Avenida António Augusto
de Aguiar 130, Saldanha.
Map 5 B3.
Tel 213 558 164.

Dom Pedro
Rua da Prata 241. **Map** 7
C4. **Tel** 213 460 361.

Espaço Açores
Rua de São Julião 58.
Map 7 C4.
Tel 218 880 070.
w espacoacores
gourmet.com

Manuel Tavares
Rua da Betesga 1, Baixa.
Map 7 B3.
Tel 213 424 209.

Wines and Spirits

Coisas do Arco do Vinho
Centro Cultural de Belém.
Map 1 B5.
Tel 213 642 031.

Garrafeira de Campo de Ourique
Rua Tomás de Anunciação
29a, Campo de Ourique.
Tel 213 973 494.

José Maria da Fonseca
Vila Nogueira de Azeitão,
Azeitão.
Tel 212 197 500.

Napoleão
Rua dos Fanqueiros 70,
Baixa. **Map** 7 C4.
Tel 218 872 042.

Solar do Vinho do Porto
Rua São Pedro de
Alcântara 45, Bairro Alto.
Map 7 A3.
Tel 213 475 707.
w ivdp.pt

Music and Multimedia

Discoteca Amália
Rua do Ouro, 272. Baixa.
Map 7 B4.
Tel 213 420 939.

FNAC
Rua Nova do Almada 102,
Chiado. **Map** 7 B4.
Tel 707 313 435.

Bookshops

Aillaud & Lellos
Rua do Carmo 82, Chiado.
Map 7 B4.
Tel 213 424 450.

Livraria Bertrand
Rua Garrett 73, Chiado.
Map 7 A4.
Tel 213 476 122.

Livraria Buchholz
Rua Duque de Palmela 4,
Marquês Pombal. **Map** 5
C5. **Tel** 213 563 212.

Clothes

Ana Salazar
Rua do Carmo 87, Chiado.
Map 7 B3.
Tel 213 472 289.

Loja das Meias
Rua Castilho 39.
Map 4 F1.
Tel 213 710 303.

Rosa & Teixeira
Avenida da Liberdade
204, Avenida. **Map** 5 C5.
Tel 213 110 350.

Zara
Rua Garrett 1, Chiado.
Map 7 B4.
Tel 213 243 710.

Ceramics

Cerâmica Artística de Carcavelos
Avenida Loureiro 47b,
Carcavelos.
Tel 214 563 267.

Ceramicarte
Largo da Assunção 3–4,
Cascais. **Tel** 214 840 170.

Santana

Rua do Alecrim 95,
Chiado.
Map 7 A5.
Tel 213 422 537.

Vista Alegre Atlantis
Largo do Chiado 20–21,
Chiado.
Map 7 A4.
Tel 213 461 401.
w myvistaalegre.com

Viúva Lamego
Largo do Intendente 25.
Map 7 C1.
Tel 218 852 408.
w viuvalamego.com

Regional Crafts

Arte Rústica
Rua Augusta 193.
Map 7 B4.
Tel 213 461 004.
w arterustica.pt

Regionália
Arcadas do Parque 87,
Estoril.
Tel 214 680 659.

Santos Ofícios
Rua da Madalena 87,
Baixa.
Map 7 C4.
Tel 218 872 031.

Sintra Bazar
Praça da República 37,
Sintra.
Tel 219 248 245.

Antiques

Cabral Moncada Leilões
Rua Miguel Lupi 12,
Estrela.
Map 4 E2.
Tel 213 954 781.
w cml.pt

Livraria Olisipo
Largo Trindade Coelho
7–8, Bairro Alto.
Map 7 A3.
Tel 213 462 771.
w livraria-olisipo.com

Solar
Rua Dom Pedro V 68–70,
Bairro Alto.
Map 4 F2.
Tel 213 465 522.

ENTERTAINMENT IN LISBON

For a smallish European capital, Lisbon has a good and varied cultural calendar. Musical events range from classical and opera performances to intimate *fado* evenings, and large rock concerts. Dance, both classical and modern, is well represented in Lisbon. The Gulbenkian Foundation, long the only major arts patron, has been joined by other private funds as well as state institutions.

Football is a consuming passion of the Portuguese, and Lisbon's Sporting and Benfica teams play regularly at home. Lisbon out-parties many larger capitals, with a nightlife known for its liveliness.

Booking Tickets

Tickets can be reserved by phoning the Agência de Bilhetes para Espectáculos Públicos (**ABEP**). Pay in cash when you collect them from the kiosk. Some cinemas and theatres accept phone or credit card bookings – it is best to check first.

ABEP kiosk selling tickets on Praça dos Restauradores

Listings Magazines

Previews of forthcoming events and listings of bars and clubs appear weekly in news-papers *(see p155)*. English-language events publications include the monthly *Follow Me Lisboa*, which is free and widely available throughout the city, including most hotel reception areas. The monthly *Agenda Cultural* is in Portuguese (www.agendalx.pt).

Cinema and Theatre

Movie-goers are very well served in Lisbon. Films are shown in their original language with Portuguese subtitles, and tickets are inexpensive. On Mondays most cinemas offer reductions. The city's traditional cinemas have now largely given way to modern multiplexes, usually in shopping centres such as Amoreiras or El Corte Inglés *(see p141)*. While these screen mainstream Hollywood fare, cinemas such as **Espaço**

Nimas show more European films. Classics and retrospectives can be seen at the **Cinemateca Portuguesa**, whose monthly programme is available at tourist offices.

Theatre performances are most often in Portuguese, but large institutions such as the **Teatro Nacional Dona Maria II** and the **Teatro da Trindade** occasionally stage guest performances by visiting companies. Less formally, **Chapitô** sometimes has open-air shows.

Classical Music, Opera and Dance

The **Centro Cultural de Belém** *(see p70)* and the **Fundação Calouste Gulbenkian** *(see pp78–81)* host national and international events, including concerts and ballet. The **Teatro Nacional de São Carlos** is Portugal's national opera, with a season that mixes its own productions with guest performances. The **Teatro Camões** hosts the Lisbon symphony orchestra and the Portuguese national ballet. The **Coliseu dos Recreios** offers a variety of events.

Circus performance at the Chapitô theatre, Alfama

World Music, Jazz, Pop and Rock

Lisbon's musical soul may be *fado (see pp144–5)*, but the city is no stranger to other forms of musical expression. African music, particularly that of former Portuguese colony Cape Verde, plays a big part in Lisbon's music scene. Venues include **B.leza**, which has frequent live performances.

The **Hot Club** has been Lisbon's foremost jazz venue

The house orchestra playing at the Fundação Calouste Gulbenkian

Jazz trio performing at the Hot Clube in Lisbon

for as long as anyone can remember, and has the right intimate atmosphere. **Speakeasy** is younger, slightly bigger, and varies live jazz with up-tempo blues, particularly at weekends. Large rock and pop concerts are held at outdoor venues such as football stadiums, or indoors at **MEO Arena** or Coliseu dos Recreios.

Nightclubs

Bairro Alto remains a lively area for Lisbon nightlife, although its mostly small bars don't usually have dance floors or keep very late hours. However, there are a few exceptions, such as the imaginative **Incógnito**, a veteran of the early 1990s that accommodates both a bar and a club.

Among the larger and more mainstream dance venues are **Urban Beach** and **Kapital**; the former is a nearly historic house club, while the latter is an up-market club right by the river.

Further along the riverfront are **Belém Bar Café** and **Station**, while eastwards along the river, near Santa Apolónia station, is **Lux**, the cream of Lisbon's current club scene.

Details of recommended bars in Lisbon, Estoril, Cascais and Sintra can be found on pages 134–5.

Spectator Sports

Lisbon's main football stadiums, built for the 2004 European Football Championship, are **Estádio José Alvalade** and **Estádio da Luz**.

The Portuguese football cup finals as well as other events, such as the Portugal Open tennis tournament, are held at the **Estádio Nacional-Jamor**. The MEO Arena is also used for indoor sporting events such as tennis, volleyball and basketball. Estoril's **Autódromo** Fernanda Pires da Silva is a motor-racing venue.

DIRECTORY

Booking Tickets

ABEP
Praça dos Restauradores.
Map 7 A2.
Tel 213 470 768.

FNAC
Colombo Shopping
Centre, Avenida Lusíada,
Benfica. **Tel** 707 313 435.

Cinema and Theatre

Chapitô
Costa do Castelo 7. **Map** 7
C3. **Tel** 218 867 334.

**Cinemateca
Portuguesa**
Rua Barata Salgueiro 39.
Map 5 C5.
Tel 213 596 262.

Espaço Nimas
Avenida 5 de Outubro
42b. **Map** 5 C3.
Tel 213 574 362.

**Teatro Nacional Dona
Maria II**
Praça Dom Pedro IV.
Map 7 B3.
Tel 213 250 800.

Teatro da Trindade
Largo da Trindade 9.
Map 7 A3.
Tel 213 423 200.

Classical Music, Opera and Dance

**Centro Cultural
de Belém**
Praça do Império.
Map 1 B5.
Tel 213 612 400.

Coliseu dos Recreios
Rua das Portas de Santo
Antão 92.
Map 7 A2.
Tel 213 240 580.

**Fundação Calouste
Gulbenkian**
Avenida de Berna 45.
Map 5 B2.
Tel 217 823 000.

Teatro Camões
Parque das Nações.
Tel 218 923 477.

**Teatro Nacional de
São Carlos**
Rua Serpa Pinto 9.
Map 7 A4. **Tel** 213 253
045 or 213 253 046.

World Music, Jazz, Pop and Rock

B.léza
Cais da Ribeira Nova,
Armazém B. **Map** 4 F4.
Tel 213 888 738.

Hot Clube
Praça da Alegria 48.
Map 4 F1.
Tel 213 619 740.

MEO Arena
Parque das Nações.
Tel 218 918 409.
ⓦ arena.meo.pt

Speakeasy
Cais das Oficinas,
Armazém 115, Rocha
Conde d'Óbidos.
Map 4 D4.
Tel 213 964 257.

Nightclubs

Belém Bar Café
Avenida Brasilia, Belém.
Map 3 A4.
Tel 213 624 232.

Incógnito
Rua Poiais de São Bento
37. **Map** 4 E3.
Tel 213 908 755.
ⓦ incognitobar.com

Kapital
Avenida 24 de Julho 68.
Map 4 E3.
Tel 961 553 745.

Lux
Avenida Infante Dom
Henrique. **Map** 8 D5.
Tel 218 820 890.

Station
Cais do Gás, Armazém A.
Map 4 F4.
Tel 210 116 546.
ⓦ station-club.com

Urban Beach
Cais da Viscondessa, Rua
da Cintura, Santos.
Map 3 C4.
Tel 961 312 746.

Spectator Sports

Autódromo Estoril
Alcabideche.
Tel 214 609 500.

Estádio José Alvalade
(Sporting) Rua Francisco
Stromp 2.
Tel 707 204 444.

Estádio da Luz
(Benfica) Avenida General
Norton Matos 1500.
Tel 707 200 100.

**Estádio Nacional-
Jamor**
Cruz Quebrada.
Tel 214 146 030.

Fado: the Music of Lisbon

Like the blues, *fado* is an expression of longing and sorrow. Literally meaning "fate", the term may be applied to an individual song as well as the genre itself. The music owes much to the concept known as *saudade*, meaning a longing both for what has been lost and for what has never been attained, which perhaps accounts for its emotional power. The people of Lisbon have nurtured this poignant music in back-street cafés and restaurants for over 150 years, and it has altered little in that time. It is sung as often by women as men, always accompanied by the *guitarra* and *viola* (acoustic Spanish guitar). *Fado* from Coimbra has developed its own lighter-hearted style.

A graphic depiction of the music's low-life associations from the 1920s

All female *fadistas* wear a black shawl in memory of Maria Severa.

The *guitarrista* plays the melody and will occasionally perform a solo instrumental piece.

Maria Severa (1810–36) was the first great *fadista* and the subject of the first Portuguese sound film in 1931. Her scandalous life and early death are pivotal to *fado* history, and her spiritual influence has been enormous, inspiring *fados*, poems, novels and plays.

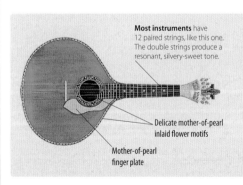

Most instruments have 12 paired strings, like this one. The double strings produce a resonant, silvery-sweet tone.

Delicate mother-of-pearl inlaid flower motifs

Mother-of-pearl finger plate

The Guitarra

Peculiar to Portuguese culture, the *guitarra* is a flat-backed instrument shaped like a mandolin, with eight, ten or twelve strings, arranged in pairs. It has evolved from a simple 19th-century design into a finely decorated piece, sometimes inlaid with mother-of-pearl. The sound of the *guitarra* is an essential ingredient of a good *fado*, echoing and enhancing the singer's melody line.

All kinds of themes may occur in *fado*. This song of 1910, for example, celebrates the dawning of the liberal republic. Such songsheets remained a favoured means of dissemination, even after the first records were made in 1904.

Alfredo Duarte (1891–1982) was a renowned writer of *fado* lyrics dealing with love, death, longing, tragedy and triumph. Affectionately known as *O Marceneiro* (the master carpenter) because of his skill as a joiner, he is still revered and his work widely performed.

A cultural icon for the Portuguese, Amália Rodrigues (1921–99) was the leading exponent of *fado* for over 50 years. She crystallized the music's style in the post-war years and made it known around the world.

The *viola* provides rhythm accompaniment, but the player will never take a solo.

The music has long inspired great writers and painters. *O Fado* (1910) by José Malhôa (1855–1933) shows it in an intimate setting with the *fadista* captivating his listener. The air of abandonment underlines the earthiness of many of the songs.

e Fado House

on's best fado *houses are
se run by* fadistas *themselves.
ed on a love of the music
on relationships with other
formers, such houses usually
r a truer* fado *experience
n the larger, tourist-oriented
ses. A good example is the
eirinha de Alfama, owned
rgentina Santos (shown
ve). Less slick, but more
otionally charged, are
ormances of* fado vadio,
erant" fado, *in humbler
aurants and bars such as
a do Chico in Bairro Alto.*

Where to Enjoy Fado in Lisbon

Any of these places offer good food, wine and music. Or visit the Museu do Fado for a fascinating exhibition on the history of *fado*.

Bacalhau de Molho
Beco dos Armazéns do Linho 2.
Map 8 E4. **Tel** 218 865 088.

Clube de Fado
Rua São João da Praça 92.
Map 8 D4. **Tel** 218 852 704.

O Faia
Rua da Barroca 54–6.
Map 4 F2. **Tel** 213 426 742.

Parreirinha de Alfama
Beco do Espírito Santo 1.
Map 7 E4. **Tel** 218 868 209.

Restaurante do Museu do Fado
Largo do Chafariz de Dentro 1.
Map 8 E4. **Tel** 218 823 470.

Senhor Vinho
Rua do Meio à Lapa 18.
Map 4 D3. **Tel** 213 972 681.

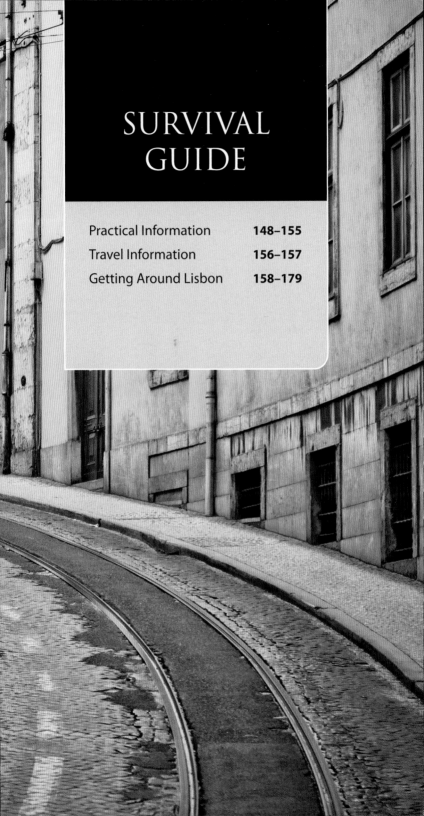

SURVIVAL GUIDE

PRACTICAL INFORMATION

Lisbon has become increasingly modern and cosmopolitan, with the advantages and disadvantages that this brings. The city is well equipped to receive visitors, and has professional tourist services, particularly at the Lisboa Welcome Center in the Baixa area and the Ask Me Lisboa tourist office in Restauradores. Visitors seeking the old-world Lisbon can still find it in the Alfama, or any of the city's smaller areas. One of the best ways to appreciate Lisbon is on foot, using trams or elevators for the steeper hills and pausing to enjoy the varied views.

Museu Nacional de Arqueologia, which is free to visit on the first Sunday of every month

Visas and Passports

Nationals of the EU need only a valid passport to enter Portugal, which is a signatory to the Schengen Convention; for stays longer than six months, a residence permit is required. Americans, Canadians, Australians and New Zealanders may stay for up to 90 days without a visa. All travellers from outside the EU should check with their nearest Portuguese embassy or consulate, as regulations may change.

UK passport holders should note that lost or stolen passports can no longer be replaced by the **British Embassy** in Lisbon; instead, you will need to apply to the British Embassy in the UK for a replacement.

Tourist Information

The opening hours of tourist offices in Lisbon are generally the same as those of local shops *(see p138)*. Those that are more centrally located, such as **Ask Me Lisboa** and the **Lisboa Welcome Center**, remain open throughout weekends. Offices in the centre of Lisbon are indicated on the Street Finder maps *(see pp172–9)*. Other offices may be found at Portela airport *(see p156)* and at Santa Apolónia station (Map 8 F3). Addresses of offices in the Lisbon Coast area are given in the information at the top of each sight entry. Portuguese tourist offices outside Portugal, such as those listed on page 149, can provide you with useful information before you travel.

Museum tickets

Language

Written Portuguese is fairly similar to Spanish, so if you know Spanish you should have little difficulty reading Portuguese text. Spoken Portuguese, however, sounds very different from Spanish. Although English is more widely spoken in Portugal than in neighbouring Spain, the Portuguese are proud of their language and appreciate visitors' efforts to communicate in Portuguese. A phrase book with some useful words and phrases is on pages 191–2.

Admission Prices

Most museums and monuments charge an entrance fee, which often increases in the summer. Entry is usually free on the first Sunday of every month. Pensioners and children under 14 are entitled to a 40 per cent discount. Visitors under 26 with a *Cartão Jovem* (youth card; www.geracao-c.com) or an ISIC card (International Student Identity Card; www.isic.org) are entitled to half-price entrance. Visitors can also buy a Lisboa Card *(see p158)*, which includes free or discounted entry to many of Lisbon's state museums, historic monuments and places of special interest, as well as discounted travel on the city's public transport.

Opening Hours

Most museums are open from 10am to 5pm Tue–Sun, with many closing for lunch from noon to 2pm or from 12:30 to 2:30pm. Smaller or privately owned museums may have different opening times. Note that state-run museums and some sights close on Mondays and public holidays. Major churches are open all day, although some may close from noon to 4pm. Smaller churches may only open for services.

◀ A typical yellow tram in the streets of Lisbon

Travellers with Special Needs

Facilities in Lisbon have improved greatly. Some buses (marked with a blue-and-white wheelchair logo at the front) can carry wheelchair-users, and ramps and lifts are common in many public places, including shopping centres, theatres, museums and across the rail and Metro network, though access to platforms is not always easy. Adapted toilets are available at airports and main train stations, and reserved car parking is clearly marked. The use of Braille to indicate directions and telephone numbers is on the increase. A number of tour companies, such as **Accessible Portugal** and **Access at Last**, offer specialist holiday packages to Lisbon or give advice on accessible accommodation for travellers with limited mobility.

Time

Portugal follows Britain in adopting Greenwich Mean Time (GMT) in winter and moving the clocks forward 1 hour in summer. The 24-hour clock is commonly used.

Electricity

Voltage in Portugal is 220 volts. Plugs have two round pins and most hotel bathrooms offer built-in adaptors for shavers only.

Conversion Chart

Imperial to Metric
1 inch = 2.54 centimetres
1 foot = 30 centimetres
1 mile = 1.6 kilometres
1 ounce = 28 grams
1 pound = 454 grams
1 pint = 0.6 litres
1 gallon = 4.6 litres

Metric to Imperial
1 millimetre = 0.04 inches
1 centimetre = 0.4 inches
1 metre = 3 feet 3 inches
1 kilometre = 0.6 miles
1 gram = 0.04 ounces
1 kilogram = 2.2 pounds
1 litre = 1.8 pints

Responsible Tourism

Lisbon is taking environmental issues seriously, as demonstrated by special "eco-points" for the correct disposal of rubbish. Colour-coded bins (blue for card/paper, yellow for plastic and tin, and green for glass) in strategic locations around the

Organic cakes at Quinoa, located near the Chiado area

city encourage the public to recycle their litter. The Inspira Santa Marta *(see p121)* is Lisbon's first eco-hotel. Awarded a Green Globe Certificate, it is constructed from ecologically sustainable building materials such as wood and stone, is designed to make maximum use of natural light and serves organic food in its restaurant.

Some shops have garnered green credentials too – for instance, the bread sold at **Quinoa**, a city-centre bakery, is 100 per cent organic. The Saturday market at Praça do Príncipe Real sells organic produce.

Slowly, Lisbon is reducing its carbon footprint, exemplified by its use of nearly 3 million energy-efficient light bulbs to illuminate its municipal Christmas decorations.

DIRECTORY

Embassies and Consulates

Australia
Avenida da Liberdade 200, 2°, 1269-121, Lisbon. **Map** 5 C5. **Tel** 213 101 500. **W** portugal. embassy.gov.au

Canada
Avenida da Liberdade 198–200, 3°, 1269-121, Lisbon. **Map** 5 C5. **Tel** 213 164 600. **W** canadainternational. gc.ca/portugal

United Kingdom Embassy

Lisbon
Rua de São Bernardo 33, 1249-082, Lisbon. **Map** 4 D2. **Tel** 213 924 000. **W** gov.uk/government/ world/portugal

United States
Avenida das Forças Armadas, 1600-081, Lisbon. **Tel** 217 273 300. **W** portugal.us embassy.gov

Tourist Information

Ask Me Lisboa
Palácio Foz, Praça dos Restauradores. **Map** 7 A2. **Tel** 213 463 314. **W** askmelisboa.com

Lisboa Welcome Center
Praça do Comércio (next to post office), 1100-038. **Map** 7 B5. **Tel** 210 312 810. **W** visitlisboa.com

Tourist Offices Abroad

W visitportugal.com

Canada
60 Bloor Street West, Suite 400, Toronto, Ontario M4W 3D8. **Tel** +1 416 921 4925

United Kingdom
11 Belgrave Square, London SW1X 8PP. **Tel** +44 20 7201 6666.

United States
866 Second Avenue, Eighth Floor, New York, NY 10017. **Tel** +1 646 723 0200.

Travellers with Special Needs

Access at Last
W accessatlast.com

Accessible Portugal
Rua Jorge Barradas, 50, 4°F, 1500-372, Lisbon. **Tel** 926 910 989. **W** accessible portugal.com

Responsible Tourism

Quinoa
Rua do Alecrim 54, Chiado, 1200-018, Lisbon. **Map** 7 A4. **Tel** 213 479 326.

Personal Security and Health

Lisbon does not have a serious crime problem, but simple precautions can and should be taken. Watch out for pickpockets in busy areas and on public transport, avoid carrying large amounts of cash and don't leave valuables in parked cars. The police are generally helpful, but bureaucratic; reporting a crime can take time. In case of a medical emergency, dial 112 and ask for an ambulance. For minor medical complaints, consult a pharmacist first.

Police

In Lisbon and other main towns in Portugal, the police force is the *Polícia de Segurança Pública* (PSP). A division of the PSP, a special Metro unit, patrols Lisbon's rail and Metro network, most notably at night. In rural areas, law and order is kept by the *Guarda Nacional Republicana* (GNR). The *Brigada de Trânsito* (traffic police) is a division of the GNR, and its members are recognizable by their red armbands. They are responsible for patrolling roads.

If you have any property stolen, you should contact the nearest police station at the earliest opportunity. Theft of a passport should also be reported to your embassy (see p149). Many insurance companies insist that policy holders report any theft to the police within 24 hours. The police will file a report; note that you will need this in order to claim from your insurance company on your return home.

There is a **Tourist Police Station** in the Foz Cultura building at Palácio Foz, in Praça dos Restauradores, manned by English-speaking officers, that deals exclusively with complaints from tourists. Rail and Metro carriages display dedicated telephone numbers for use in the event of emergencies.

In all situations, try to keep calm and be polite to the authorities to avoid delays. The same applies should you be involved in a car accident. In rural areas you may be asked to accompany the other driver to the nearest police station to complete the necessary paperwork. Ask for an interpreter if no one there speaks English.

What to be Aware of

Violent crime is fairly rare in Lisbon and in Portugal generally, and the majority of visitors will experience no problems whatsoever. Nonetheless, a few sensible precautions are worth taking: avoid quiet areas such as the Baixa after dark, and don't stroll alone through Bairro Alto, Alfama or around Cais do Sodré after bars have closed. In the daytime, be alert to the possibility of pickpockets or, more rarely, bag-snatchers. Be vigilant when withdrawing cash from an ATM (*Multibanco* or MB). Whenever possible, carry out the transaction in daylight and be aware of anyone standing too close behind you who could see your PIN number. Ideally, use an ATM together with someone you know and trust, or one that is housed within the bank's premises. Some poorer neighbourhoods and outlying slums see more serious daytime crime, but they are not on the typical visitor's itinerary.

Other general precautions include not carrying or showing large amounts of cash (carry only the amount needed for daily purchases), not leaving possessions visible in parked cars, not leaving bags unattended (especially at outdoor cafés and restaurants) and holding on to valuable equipment such as mobile phones and cameras. Beware of pickpockets on crowded Metro trains. If you are robbed, you are advised not to put up any resistance.

Vaccinations are not needed for visitors to Portugal although doctors recommend being up-to-date with tetanus, diptheria and measles jabs. Tap water is safe to drink throughout the country. If you are visiting during the summer, it is advisable to bring insect repellent, as mosquitoes, while they do not present any serious health problems, can be a nuisance. The use of a good sun block is also recommended, and try to drink plenty of water.

Traffic policeman

PSP officer

GNR officer

Ambulance

Fire engine

Police car

In an Emergency

The number to contact in the event of an emergency is **112**. Dial the number and then indicate which service you require – the police (*polícia*), an ambulance (*ambulância*) or the fire brigade (*bombeiros*). If you need medical treatment, the casualty department (*serviço de urgência*) of the closest main hospital will treat you. On motorways and main roads, use the orange SOS telephone to call for help should you have a car accident. The service is in Portuguese; press the button and wait for an answer. The operator will put you through.

Hospitals and Pharmacies

Social security coverage is available for all EU nationals in Portugal. To claim, you must obtain a European Health Insurance Card (EHIC) from the UK Department of Health or from a post office before you travel. The card comes with a booklet, *Health Advice for Travellers*, which explains exactly what health care you are entitled to and where and how to claim. You may find you have to pay and reclaim the money later. Not all treatments are covered by the card, and some are costly, so all travellers are advised to arrange for comprehensive medical insurance before travelling.

The **British Hospital** in Lisbon has English-speaking doctors, as do international health centres on the Lisbon Coast. Pharmacies (*farmácias*) can diagnose simple health problems and suggest appropriate treatment. Pharmacists can dispense a range of drugs that would normally be available only on prescription in many other countries. The sign for a *farmácia* is a green cross. They are open 9am–1pm and 3–7pm Mon–Fri and 9am–1pm Sat. Each pharmacy displays a card in the window showing the address of the nearest all-night pharmacy and a list of those that are open until late (10pm). Two centrally located pharmacies are **Farmácia Barral** and **Farmácia Estácio**.

Legal Assistance

An insurance policy that covers the costs of legal advice, issued by companies such as Europ Assistance or Mondial Assistance, will help with the legal aspects of your insurance claim should you have an accident. If you have not arranged this cover phone your nearest consulate or the **Ordem dos Advogados** (Lawyers' Association), who can give you names of English-speaking lawyers and help you with obtaining representation. Lists of interpreters are given in the local Yellow Pages (*Páginas Amarelas*) under *Tradutores e Intérpretes*, or contact **AP Portugal**, based in Lisbon.

Public Conveniences

The Portuguese for toilets is *casa de banho*. If the usual figures of a man or woman are not shown, look for the words *homens* (men) and *senhoras* (ladies). Toilet facilities are provided at motorway service areas every 40 km (25 miles) and at some drive-in rest areas. They can also be found in most modern shopping malls and at major transport hubs, such as coach and railway stations. In addition, a number of coin-operated toilets can be found in the streets. As a last resort, all cafés and restaurants provide toilet facilities; these, however, are often open only to customers – some are accessed by a key kept behind the counter.

Banking and Local Currency

Portugal is one of the founding members of the European Monetary Union and one of the countries that launched the euro in 2002. Credit and debit cards are widely accepted, and funds can be readily obtained from ATMs; those offering the best exchange rates are found mainly in the Baixa district. It is always a good idea to arrive with enough euros in cash to cover one or two days' expenditure. Both banks and bureaux de change offer exchange services but the latter may provide a faster service than banks.

Façade of a bank on the Rua do Ouro, in Baixa

Banks and Bureaux de Change

Banks are open between 8:30am and 3pm, Monday to Friday. Some branches stay open for longer, sometimes until 6pm – check at individual branches. Some banks are open on Saturday mornings, but most banks are closed throughout weekends, and all are closed on public holidays. ATM services, however, are available 24 hours daily. Money can be changed at banks, bureaux de change (*agências de câmbios*) and at many hotels. Be aware that in Portugal, larger denomination banknotes such as the €200 and €500 note have a limited circulation, and some establishments may not accept them.

There are several major banks, which have branches everywhere, but their rates of exchange and commission vary. Waiting times and bureaucratic practices at banks may also make them a slow option. There are many bureaux de change, such as **Nova Câmbios**, throughout the city. They often charge higher commissions than banks, but this is not always the case. It's worth shopping around, especially in and around Rossio, for the best rates. Bureaux de change also offer a speedier service, as well as longer opening hours (including weekends). As a rule, hotels have the worst rates of exchange.

Traveller's cheques are a safe but less commonly used way of carrying money; it is rare for shops or hotels to accept them as payment, and cashing them may be quite expensive. In general, bureaux de change are better for this than banks, where commissions may be high.

Funds may also be obtained using money-transfer companies like **Western Union**, which has several offices based in Lisbon. Recipients can pick up money at a participating Western Union agent in the city selected by the sender.

At banks, bureaux de change and money-transfer companies you may be asked to show your passport or some other form of photographic identification for exchange transactions.

Credit and Debit Cards

The most practical and convenient way to obtain cash is from an ATM (*Multibanco* or MB) using your credit or debit card. Note that many banks impose a small charge for international ATM transactions. Check the charges with your bank in advance. *Multibanco* machines for withdrawing cash are widely available, typically outside banks or in shopping centres.

Smaller, wireless chip-and-PIN *Multibanco* machines are found at shop counters and can be used to pay for a range of purchases including rail tickets, clothes, and meals and drinks in restaurants. Some are even used in taxis. Most *Multibanco* machines accept Visa, American Express, MasterCard, Maestro and Cirrus cards and operate in several different languages.

Be sure to notify your bank and credit card providers before leaving for Portugal. Some banks forbid foreign transactions for security reasons unless they have been notified ahead of time.

DIRECTORY

Banks, Bureaux de Change and Money-Transfer Services

Banco Bilbao Vizcaya Argentária
Avenida da Liberdade 222.
Map 5 C5. **Tel** 213 117 391.

Banco Espírito Santo
Avenida da Liberdade 195.
Map 5 C5. **Tel** 213 501 000.

Barclays Bank
Avenida da República 50.
Map 5 C1. **Tel** 211 112 346 or 707 505 050.

Caixa Geral de Depósitos
Praça Dom Pedro IV 36, Rossio.
Map 7 B3. **Tel** 213 264 080.

Nova Câmbios
Rua Augusta 283, Baixa.
Map 7 B3.

Western Union
Praça da Figueira 2, Rossio.
Map 7 B3.

Lost or Stolen Cards

American Express
Tel 707 504 050 (Portugal).

MasterCard Worldwide
Tel 800 964 767 (UK).

Visa
Tel 800 811 824 (Portugal).

The Euro

The euro (€) is the common currency of the European Union. It went into general circulation on 1 January 2002, initially for 12 participating countries, including Portugal. EU members using the euro as their sole official currency are known as the eurozone. Several EU members have opted out of joining this common currency.

Euro notes are identical throughout eurozone countries, each one including designs of fictional architectural structures and monuments. The coins, however, have one side identical (the value side), and one side with an image unique to each country. Both notes and coins are exchangeable in any country in the eurozone.

Banknotes

Euro banknotes, each a different colour and size, have seven denominations. The €5 note (grey in colour) is the smallest, followed by the €10 note (pink), €20 note (blue), €50 note (orange), €100 note (green), €200 note (yellow) and €500 note (purple).

€5 note

€10 note

€20 note

€50 note

€100 note

€200 note

€500 note

€2 coin

€1 coin

50 cents

20 cents

10 cents

Coins

The euro has eight coin denominations: €2 and €1; 50 cents, 20 cents, 10 cents, 5 cents, 2 cents and 1 cent. The €2 and €1 coins are both silver and gold in colour. The 50-, 20- and 10-cent coins are gold. The 5-, 2- and 1-cent coins are bronze.

5 cents

2 cents

1 cent

Communications and Media

Information and telecommunications technology in Portugal has advanced at a swift pace. Public telephones are widely available, and the country's mobile phone operators have roaming agreements with most international phone companies; there is good coverage across the city. Lisbon has numerous Internet cafés, and Wi-Fi access is available at the airport, most of the bigger hotels and in many public spaces. Foreign-language newspapers and magazines are on sale the same day of home publication. Portuguese terrestrial television is complemented by an array of foreign cable and satellite channels. Domestic radio broadcasts exclusively in Portuguese.

Mobile Phones

If you want to guarantee that your mobile phone will work in Portugal, make sure you have a quad-band phone. Tri-band phones are also usually compatible, but they may have limited global coverage. Contact your service provider to check your phone's compatibility.

To use your mobile phone abroad, you may need to request permission from your network provider before travelling so that they can set your phone to allow "roaming". Check roaming charges with your provider, as making and receiving calls can be very expensive.

A popular and cheaper option is to purchase a local SIM card (the electronic chip that links your phone to a particular network); this will use the local mobile phone networks and can be topped up with credit. There are three main mobile phone operators in Portugal: TMN, Vodafone and Nos. However, you can use a local SIM card only if your handset is "unlocked" – some operators lock their phones to specific networks. Visitors who intend to remain in the city for an extended period would benefit from hiring or even purchasing a mobile phone from one of the main phone operators' shops, such as **TMN** or **Vodafone**, listed opposite. The cost of both local and international calls will be significantly cheaper.

It is worth keeping your network operator's helpline number to hand in case of difficulties.

Public Telephones

Public telephones are plentiful in Lisbon, with options to pay by coin, phonecard or credit card. They are found in booths in the streets as well as in bars, cafés and shopping centres. Card-operated phones are more common and more convenient, accepting a variety of phonecards that can be purchased from post offices, newsagents, tobacconists (*tabacaria*) and Portugal Telecom company outlets. They also tend to be cheaper, charging about 3 cents for a local call. Some phones also accept credit cards, although that incurs a small extra charge.

International calls and calls to mobile phones are more expensive. An alternative is to phone from a post office, without having either change or a card. You simply step into a free booth, make your call, and pay the cashier afterwards. The cost per unit is relatively low. Some cafés, restaurants and bars have a units meter connected to their phone that calculates the cost of your call, for which you pay afterwards. They charge more than the post office but less than hotels.

For international calls and calls to mobile phones in particular, bear in mind that rates are lower between 9pm and 9am, at weekends and on public holidays. All Lisbon landlines start with 21 and mobile numbers start with a 9.

Accessing the Internet at an Internet café in Lisbon

Internet Access

Internet access is widely available in Lisbon, where an abundance of Internet cafés can be found in every major district, especially in tourist enclaves such as Bairro Alto and Chiado. Charges vary, but expect to pay between €1 and €3 per hour. Public Internet facilities can also be found at the city's coach and rail terminals, most of the large hotels, some guesthouses and the city's main youth hostel, Lisboa Central Hostel on Rua Rodrigues Sampaio (just off Praça Marquês de Pombal, Map 5 C5), as well as some other newer youth hostels.

Wi-Fi hotspots, such as those found at Lisbon airport and some modern shopping malls, enable users to log in on the go, but this facility is not always free.

People using mobile phones, laptop computers or palmtops and wishing to access the Web while abroad need to check that their Internet service provider offers a global roaming option.

A public phone booth outside a café in Lisbon

Postal Services

The postal service in Portugal is known as the *Correios* (the sign depicts a horse and rider in red). A letter sent to a country within the EU should take five to seven days to arrive, and a letter sent to the USA or further afield should take about seven to ten days.

First-class mail, known as *correio azul*, is posted in blue postboxes; second-class mail, or *normal*, in red ones. Post offices may have separate slots for national and international mail. There is also an express mail service *(EMS)* and a recorded delivery service *(correio registado)* for valuable letters.

Pre-paid Easy Mail envelopes for domestic and international destinations are available. They do not need to be stamped or weighed, thus allowing for immediate dispatch. Stamps *(selos)* can be bought from post offices, from any shop displaying the *Correios* sign and from vending machines found at the airport, in railway stations and the larger shopping malls.

Post offices are usually open 9am–6pm Monday to Friday; larger post offices open 8:30am–10pm Monday to Friday and 9am–6pm on Saturday and Sunday.

If mailing larger items, use an international courier company. **FedEx** and **DHL** both have offices in Lisbon but are not centrally located.

Lisbon's Addresses

Lisbon's addresses often include both the storey of a building and the location within that floor. The ground floor is the *rés-do-chão* (r/c), the first floor *primeiro andar* (1°), the second floor is expressed as 2°, and so on. Each floor is divided into left, *esquerdo* (E or Esqdo), and right, *direito* (D or Dto).

Newspapers and Magazines

English-language newspapers printed in Europe, including the *International Herald Tribune*, are available at larger newsagents on the day of publication except following a public holiday. The same is true of various other European newspapers and periodicals. Foreign newspapers and magazines are more expensive, and some sections, notably weekend supplements, are not included.

Portuguese daily newspapers include *Diário de Notícias* and *Público*. The weekly *Portugal News*, published on Friday, is the country's main English-language publication. Catering to the expats living along the Estoril coast, it provides news and information on local events. Listings magazines available include the weekly *Time Out Lisbon*, published in Portuguese. A special edition, *Lisbon for Visitors*, is printed annually in English (see p142).

Lisbon's Postboxes

First-class letters should be posted in blue *(Correio Azul)* boxes, and second-class letters in red boxes.

Portuguese newspapers

Radio and Television

Portugal has two state-owned TV channels, RTP1 and RTP2, and two privately owned ones, SIC and TVI. Most foreign programmes are broadcast in their original language, with Portuguese subtitles. Other English-language channels, such as the BBC and CNN, are available via satellite and cable. RDP radio (10 723 MHz) broadcasts in English in summer only.

DIRECTORY

Mobile Phones

TMN
Loja 4.09, Armazéns Chiado, Rua do Carmo 2. **Map** 7 B4.

Vodafone
Praça Dom Pedro IV 4–5, Rossio. **Map** 6 D3.

Internet Access

Fábulas
Calçada Nova de São Francisco 14 (off Rua Garrett), Chiado. **Map** 7 B4.

Lisboa Welcome Center
Praça do Comércio. **Map** 7 B5.
Tel 210 312 810.
🅦 visitlisboa.com

Unicâmbio
Praça da Figueira 2, Rossio. **Map** 7 B3.

Postal Services

DHL
Avenida Marechal Gomes da Costa 27, Olivais. **Tel** 707 505 606.

FedEx
Avenida Severiano Falcão 12, Prior Velho, Lisbon. **Tel** 707 244 144.

Main Post Office
Praça dos Restauradores. **Map** 7 A2. 🅦 ctt.pt

Information on collection times

First-class postbox

Second-class postbox

TRAVEL INFORMATION

Lisbon has an international airport, good rail links and a port that is popular with cruise liners. Its road network has improved greatly, with ring roads, motorways and a second bridge across the Tagus; however, traffic can be slow at rush hour. Trams provide fascinating trips through some of the city's oldest neighbourhoods; no other form of public transport can negotiate their steep hills and narrow streets. For the rest of the city, the Metro is the best way to get around. The bus network is huge, but buses do get held up in traffic. The Lisbon Coast and Sintra are easily accessible by train, and ferries are a pleasant way of crossing the Tagus to reach Caparica's beaches.

Arriving by Air

Lisbon has regularly scheduled flights from European capitals and major cities, including London, Paris, Madrid, Rome, Frankfurt, Munich, Zurich and Milan. Airlines with regular flights include **British Airways**, **Air France**, **Iberia** and **Lufthansa**. Most of these are daily, and in many cases there are several connections. **TAP Portugal**, Portugal's national carrier, currently operates five daily flights from London (three from Heathrow and two from Gatwick) to Lisbon.

Travellers from North America will usually have to change at a European hub. **Delta** flies to Lisbon via Paris (using a partner airline) once or twice daily. **United Airlines** flies to Lisbon direct from Newark, New Jersey, daily. **Aer Lingus** operates a daily summer schedule to Lisbon from Boston and New York via Dublin. TAP's only direct flights from the US are also out of Newark.

South America is better served thanks to Portugal's ties with Brazil: TAP has direct flights to and from several Brazilian destinations.

There are no direct flights to Lisbon from Canada, Australia or New Zealand; London is a popular hub for flights from these countries.

TAP Portugal (code-sharing with PGA Portugália Airlines) also flies to domestic destinations, including Oporto, Faro and Funchal. **SATA**, in partnership with TAP, serves the Azores. A number of budget airlines, including **easyJet** and **Monarch**, serve Lisbon. Charter airlines' tickets have fixed outward and return dates, but as they are often cheaper than a regular one-way ticket, many one-way passengers buy a return ticket but only use the outward flight. Some charter companies re-sell empty return seats at lower prices. Students can get reduced rates through specialist travel agencies such as STA, and it is also worth checking Internet travel companies such as Expedia.com for deals. Tickets tend to be pricier during high season in summer.

Signs at Lisbon's
Portela Airport

Lisbon Airport

Portela Airport is located 7 km (4 miles) north of Lisbon's city centre. It has two terminals linked by a bus service: Terminal 1 handles international flights (and TAP Portugal flights to Porto, Faro, Madeira and the Azores), and Terminal 2 is largely used for domestic flights, and also easyJet flights. Airport facilities include a bank and a post office.

Connections with the Airport

The airport's proximity to the city centre means that it is reasonably fast and cheap to get to the heart of Lisbon. Taxis are available from the taxi rank just outside the arrivals hall. Fares to the city centre are metered and cost between €10 and €15, with a small extra charge for luggage.

The Carristur-operated AeroBus and AeroShuttle bus services depart every 20–30 minutes between 7am and 11pm from the airport bus stop immediately beyond the taxi rank. They stop at major points in the city centre near to many hotels, such as Oriente, Entrecampos, Sete Rios, Saldanha, Marquês de Pombal, Restauradores, Rossio, Praça do Comércio and Cais do Sodré station. Tickets cost €3.50 and are then valid for the rest of the day for travel on buses, trams and funiculars.

Cheaper regular city buses can be caught at stops a little further to the right as you exit the arrivals hall. Tickets can be bought on boarding. Bus numbers 705, 722, 744 and 783 stop at numerous locations around central Lisbon.

Aeroporto de Lisboa

The exterior of Lisbon's large and well-maintained Portela airport

Entrance to the Ponte 25 de Abril, one of the main routes into Lisbon

Arriving by Rail

To the east of the Alfama district, on Avenida Infante Dom Henrique, is **Santa Apolónia**, the main station for long-distance trains from Coimbra, Oporto and the north, as well as from Madrid and Paris. It is 15 minutes' walk east of Praça do Comércio and is served by a Metro station. There is a tourist information office in the station and a taxi rank outside the main entrance.

The impressive, modern **Gare do Oriente** is another international terminus for trains from Madrid and Paris. Although located much further north of the centre, at Parque das Nações, it has excellent links into the city by both bus and Metro.

Trains from the south and east of the city cross the Tagus via the Ponte 25 de Abril and connect with **Entrecampos** and Gare do Oriente stations. **Cais do Sodré** station serves the resort towns of Cascais and Estoril. Use **Rossio**, **Roma Areeiro** and Entrecampos stations for trains to Queluz and Sintra. The Fertagus rail link is a commuter service to the south bank of the Tagus and Costa da Caparica. For further information *see p163* and visit the **Caminhos de Ferro** (state railway) website.

Arriving by Road

There are seven major entry routes into Lisbon: two from the south and east, two from the north and three from the west. Those arriving from the Algarve and the south on the A2 (E1) motorway or the IC1, as well as from Madrid and the east (A6), can cross to central Lisbon via the busy Ponte 25 de Abril, or to the north-eastern part of the city via the newer Ponte Vasco da Gama. Both are toll bridges; Vasco da Gama costs considerably more.

From Oporto and the north, the A1 (E1) motorway brings you to Lisbon's north-eastern outskirts. To reach central Lisbon, follow signs indicating Campo Grande and then Centro. If you wish to head to the coastal resorts of Estoril and Cascais without entering Lisbon, turn off the A1 (E1) on to the A9 at Alverca, 20 km (12 miles) north of the city, immediately after the toll. The A9, also known as CREL (exterior ring road), is signposted to Cascais and is also tolled.

Those arriving from Cascais and the Lisbon Coast enter via the tolled A5 motorway or the coastal N6 road, known as Avenida Marginal. From Sintra, you enter via the IC19, which links up with Avenida General Norton de Matos in the north of Lisbon. The A8 from northern Estremadura enters the city from the north. For information on driving in Lisbon *see p162*.

Lisbon's Bridges

One of Lisbon's most famous landmarks, the Ponte 25 de Abril provides the main link between Lisbon and Almada, on the southern bank of the Tagus. Built in the 1960s, when cars were still a rarity in Portugal, it became a bottleneck in the late 1980s. In the 1990s more lanes were added and a rail line slung underneath in the hope of easing the congestion. The toll, which is charged only on the way into Lisbon to lessen queuing, was raised to help pay for a second bridge.

This second bridge, the Ponte Vasco da Gama (*see p83*), links Lisbon's northeastern outskirts – Parque das Nações is right next to it – with Montijo, on the other side of the wide Tagus estuary. The toll is also charged only on the way into the city.

DIRECTORY

Arriving by Air

Aer Lingus
W aerlingus.com

Air France
W airfrance.com

British Airways
W britishairways.com

Delta
W delta.com

easyJet
W easyjet.com

Iberia
W iberia.com

Lisbon Airport
Tel 218 413 500.

Lufthansa
W lufthansa.com

Monarch
W monarch.co.uk

SATA (Azores Airlines)
W sata.pt

TAP Portugal
W tap.pt

United Airlines
W united.com

Arriving by Rail

Cais do Sodré
Avenida 24 de Julho, Lisbon.
Map 4 F4.

**Caminhos de Ferro
(State Railway)**
Tel +351 707 210 220.
W cp.pt

Entrecampos
Rua Doutor Eduardo Neves, Lisbon.
Map 5 C1.

Gare do Oriente
Avenida Dom João II, Parque das Nações, Lisbon.

Roma Areeiro
Avenida Frei Miguel Contreiras, Lisbon.
Map 6 E1.

Rossio
Praça Dom Pedro IV, Lisbon. **Map** 7 A3.

Santa Apolónia
Avenida Infante Dom Henrique, Lisbon.
Map 8 F3.

Getting Around Lisbon

An attractive city, Lisbon is a pleasure to explore, and walking can be one of the best ways to see it. However, the city is also hilly, and even the fittest of sightseers will soon tire. The trams and funiculars *(elevadores)* offer a welcome rest for the foot-weary as well as some great views. They are an essential Lisbon experience but may not always be the most efficient means of transport. For that, buses and the Metro are better choices. Driving around Lisbon is not generally recommended: the city suffers from quite a bit of congestion and its street plan is full of unexpected surprises. As a result, patience is in short supply among Lisbon drivers. Taxis offer a good alternative and are relatively cheap.

Red Tour electric buggy

Green Travel

Lisbon has, on the whole, embraced the notion of becoming an environmentally friendly city. Green initiatives are in place to help alleviate the city's chronic traffic problems. One such scheme, *Menos Um Carro* (One Less Car), launched by the public transport operator Carris on its website (www.carris.pt), encourages commuters to use public transport rather than drive into the city, or to consider sharing a car. Carris's online sustainable travel campaign *(Índice de Mobilidade Sustentável)* invites users to email their own ideas about how to improve Lisbon's congested transport infrastructure.

Gas-powered private vehicles that run on environmentally friendly liquefied petrol gas (LPG) are rare on Lisbon's roads due to their relatively high fuel consumption and a lack of service stations offering an LPG option. Rarer still are expensive gas-electric hybrid cars. However, Carris is slowly introducing a fleet of LPG-fuelled buses. Alternative fuel solutions remain high on the political agenda and Lisbon Town Hall is wooing potential converts by offering free parking for 30 minutes for drivers using these cleaner, alternative vehicles.

Increasingly, police officers are patrolling Lisbon's streets on Segways (two-wheeled electric vehicles). This eco-friendly mode of transport has also been adopted by sightseeing tour company Red Tour (tel 211 928 852; www.redtourgps.com), which offers self-guided tours in self-drive electric buggies and on Segway scooters.

The rail network in Lisbon and throughout Portugal is electrified and leaves a relatively small carbon footprint. It is also reasonably cheap to use and, for the most part, very efficient.

A number of electric trams trundle past some of Lisbon's most important cultural sights, and this "green" mode of transport offers excellent value for money.

Cycling is not popular in central Lisbon; its hilly geography simply does not make it a viable proposition. Cycle paths do exist along the Tagus river in areas such as Alcântara and Belém, and further afield at Parque das Nações, Parque Florestal de Monsanto and in Cascais. Some independent tourism companies, such as Lisbon Bike tour (www.lisbonbike tour.com) and Bike Iberia (www.bikeiberia.com), offer Lisbon cycle tours, but these, too, tend to avoid the capital's steeper areas.

Discovering Lisbon on foot requires a stout pair of legs and comfortable footwear, but this is one of the best ways to explore the city at leisure.

The Lisboa Card

This comprehensive tourist pass allows free access to most forms of public transport (not ferries) and reduced rates on some tourist tours (including the Carris open-top bus tour, the *Colinas* tour in the red trams,

Lisboa Card tourist pass

and Transtejo river tours). Additionally, admission charges are waived at 25 national museums and other sights, and are reduced at a number of others (20 per cent off at the Gulbenkian Museum, for instance). It is an impressive offer, and competitively priced, but with only 24, 48 or 72 hours in which to make use of it, you might be rushed off your feet. The Lisboa Card is on sale at the airport arrivals hall, tourist offices, selected hotels, travel agents and sights, as well as in Carris kiosks *(see p159)*.

Public Transport

Lisbon's public transport system provides access to all parts of the city by a variety of means: trams, lifts and funiculars, buses and the underground *Metropolitano*. The technological spectrum is vast, from early 20th-century trams and funiculars to modern Metro trains, sleek new trams and articulated buses. Buses have the most extensive network, while trams cover a smaller area but offer good sightseeing opportunities. Both are prone to delays due to traffic jams and are run, as are lifts and funiculars, by the state-owned Carris company. The Metro, run separately but also state-owned, is the most efficient form of public transport.

Tickets

Single-trip paper tickets for buses, trams and funiculars can be bought on boarding. Multi-trip paper tickets have been replaced with electronic passes such as the *7 Colinas*, *Viva Viagem* and *Lisboa Viva* smart cards. The *Viva Viagem* card is the most practical purchase for short-term visits. It can be topped up with credit whenever necessary and provides access to the Carris network and other public transport operators. It must be validated by holding it over a validator machine. Passes can be purchased at points of travel and from Carris kiosks in many parts of the city, including at railway stations, by the Basílica da Estrela, in Praça da Figueira and by Praça Marquês de Pombal, as well as at some post offices and newsagents.

Another option is the Lisboa Card *(see panel opposite)*, which includes unlimited free travel on the bus, tram, funicular/lift and Metro networks, and on the Sintra and Cascais railway lines. It can be purchased as a one-, two-, or three-day card and is validated on each trip by passing it over an electronic scanner.

Metro tickets are bought from machines (with multi-lingual instructions) or from ticket offices at Metro stations as reusable charge cards (there are no paper Metro tickets). The card costs €0.50 and lasts one year. A single trip costs €1.40, no matter what the zone. When purchasing your card you should keep the receipt and present it when necessary to change the card, for example if it is damaged. Cards must be validated on entering the platform area by passing them over an electronic

The Lisbon Metro and Rail Network

Key

— Azul Metro line
— Amarela Metro line
— Verde Metro line
— Vermelha Metro line
— Railway line
— Airport bus route
○ Interchange station

scanner to open the gate, indicated by a green light. Exiting a Metro station requires the same procedure.

Children between the ages of 4 and 12, adults over 65 and students all pay half-price on public transport. Children under the age of four travel free of charge. Fines for travelling without a valid ticket are severe.

Travelling by Metro

The fastest and cheapest way to get around town is by the *Metropolitano*. Metro stations are signposted with a red M, and the service operates from 6:30am to 1am every day.

There are currently 49 Metro stations operating on four lines: the Linha Azul (Blue Line), the Linha Amarela (Yellow Line), the Linha Verde (Green Line) and the Linha Vermelha (Red Line). These lines link the Metro to major bus, train and ferry services, and provide transport from Lisbon's suburbs to the commercial heart of the city, along the north bank of the river. Plans are under way to further extend the city's Metro system, and a number of stations

are currently under construction. Although the Metro does become quite packed during the morning and evening rush hours, there are frequent trains. The system is safe to travel on, even at night time, since the stations and trains are regularly patrolled by the police. All stations have automatic gates at the entrance to the platform areas and a valid ticket must be passed over an electronic scanner both on entering and leaving the station. Metro ticket inspectors can fine you up to 100 times the value of a single-trip ticket if you are caught travelling without a valid ticket.

Automated machine dispensing Metro tickets and passes

A *Colinas* sightseeing tram

Travelling by Tram

Trams (*eléctricos*) are one of the most pleasant ways of sightseeing in Lisbon. However, they only operate in a very limited area of the city, along the river to Belém and around the hilly parts of Lisbon. There are currently two types of tram operating in Lisbon: the charming, old, pre-World War I models and the much longer new trams with sleek interiors.

Single tickets for all rides are very cheap except for those on the red *Colinas* or *Tejo* trams, which provide special sightseeing rides for tourists and are much more expensive than the ordinary routes. These sightseeing services operate along a single giant loop throughout the year from Praça do Comércio, and take in all of the major historical sights through the hilly parts of Lisbon and along the Tagus. However, it is better value to catch either tram 25 or tram 28. The former runs from the Cemitério des Prazeres in Campo de Ourique, past the Basílica da Estrela to the attractive Lapa residential district, on a steep hill facing the river. It descends to the river then runs past Praça do Comércio to where the Alfama begins, ending its route in Rua da Alfândega. Tram 28 shares some of its route with tram 25, running via Estrela down past the Palácio de São Bento and up again to Bairro Alto and Chiado. It descends to the Baixa, passes Lisbon's cathedral, then climbs to Castelo de São Jorge. It offers an excellent sightseeing tour of old Lisbon – often most of its passengers are tourists.

Funiculars and Lifts

Due to Lisbon's hilly terrain, funiculars and lifts are a convenient and popular means of getting from river level to the upper parts of the city, particularly Bairro Alto. Although expensive in relation to distance covered, this form of transport certainly helps take the effort out of negotiating Lisbon's hills, and offers some superb views over the city.

Elevador da Bica climbs from the São Paulo area up to the lower end of Bairro Alto. Elevador da Glória goes from Praça dos Restauradores to the upper end of Bairro Alto (see p44). The walkway at Elevador de Santa Justa links the Baixa with the Bairro Alto (see p48). Elevador da Lavra climbs from Praça dos Restauradores up to the Hospital São José.

Travelling by Bus

Lisbon buses (*autocarros*) are usually yellow and are a bright feature around the city's streets. Most inner-city services run from 5:30am to 1am. A smaller number of night buses operate between 1am and 5:30am. The bus network is Lisbon's most extensive public transport system, and buses go just about everywhere. Their timetable suffers from Lisbon's traffic problems, which means you sometimes have to wait a long time to get on a very crowded bus. Most public vehicles are smooth-riding, air-conditioned buses that bend at the middle. Stops are indicated by a sign

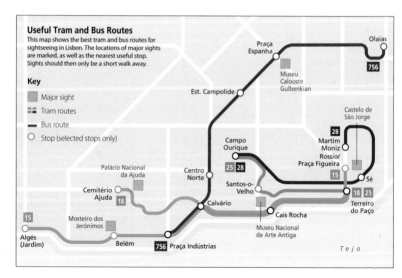

Useful Tram and Bus Routes
This map shows the best tram and bus routes for sightseeing in Lisbon. The locations of major sights are marked, as well as the nearest useful stop. Sights should then only be a short walk away.

Key

- Major sight
- Tram routes
- Bus route
- ○ Stop (selected stops only)

marked *Paragem*, where details of the specific route are shown. The final destination is shown on the front of the bus, along with its number. Paper tickets can be bought on boarding. If using a pre-paid smart card, remember to validate it by passing it over the electronic scanner machine by the driver. Buses, trams and funiculars use the same paper tickets.

A convenient way of getting between museums and other popular sights is to hop on and off a tour bus. **Carristur** *(see Directory, p165)* runs two excellent routes – the Tagus Tour, which takes in Belém, and the Olisip Tour, which passes by Lisbon's principal musems and visits Parque das Nações. Your ticket is valid for the whole day.

Lisbon's Elevador da Glória ascending to Bairro Alto

A typical yellow Lisbon bus, a common sight on the city's streets

Walking Around Lisbon

Lisbon is a delightful city to wander around, taking in the sights, especially in the old neighbourhoods such as the Alfama and Bairro Alto. Narrow cobbled streets, picturesque buildings and alleyways provide a charming setting to experience traditional Lisbon life.

For a more contemporary backdrop, take a stroll through Parque das Nações, a riverside district east of the city centre. The area, which is totally flat and easily reached by Metro, features some of the country's most striking examples of modern architecture, and it offers a wide array of attractions, including many restaurants and cafés with views over the Tagus.

Belém is another flat riverfront area and one of Lisbon's most historic neighbourhoods. It was from here that the great voyages of discovery departed, and monuments in tribute to intrepid navigators abound.

Walking tours, such as the day trips organized by Inside Tours (www.insidelisbon.com) and Lisbon Walker (www. lisbonwalker.com), are a great way to get to know the city more intimately. Many tours are themed to suit individual interests, and they are always conducted in English. Private walks in Portuguese, Spanish, French, German and Italian can usually be arranged under special circumstances.

Lisbon is built on a number of hills, and unless you are fairly fit, it is wise to take advantage of public transport for the uphill climbs. Tram 28 *(eléctrico)* goes almost all the way up to the Castelo de São Jorge; you can then walk down through the Alfama. The Elevador da Glória will take you from Praça dos Restauradores up to Bairro Alto.

Lisbon's most central shopping area is made up of the Baixa and Chiado, where pedestrianized streets are filled with shoppers, street performers and vendors, as well as a wide variety of shops, shopping centres, outdoor cafés and restaurants.

Taxis

Compared to the rest of Europe, taxis in Portugal are relatively inexpensive, and if costs are shared between two or more people, they can work out cheaper than travelling by bus or tram. Most taxis are now reverting to the older black and green, but some beige cabs are still in existence. All are metered, although costs depend on the time of day.

Taxis have their "TAXI" signs switched on when they are not available. Green lights indicate that the taxi is available: two green lights mean that the higher rate is being charged (10pm–6am, weekends and public holidays), one green light that the normal rate applies.

The starting rate for a taxi hailed in the street or taken at a taxi rank is €3.25 by day and €3.90 at night. A flat rate of €1.60 is charged for any luggage placed in the trunk. The meter should always be used, although the driver might suggest agreeing on a price for long trips.

Taxis can also be ordered by phone from companies such as **Autocoope**, **Retalis Rádio Táxis** and **Teletáxis**.

A pre-paid taxi voucher, available from tourist offices, guarantees fixed taxi prices.

DIRECTORY

24-Hour Taxi Services

Autocoope
Tel 217 932 756.

Retalis Rádio Táxis
Tel 218 119 000.

Teletáxis
Tel 218 111 100.

Driving Around Lisbon

Using a car to get around the busy city centre of Lisbon can be daunting. Finding your way around the complex street plan isn't easy, and traffic jams don't make it any easier. Parking can be very difficult to find. Lisbon's larger roundabouts have traffic lights; on those that don't, cars travelling around the roundabout have priority over cars waiting to enter it. At all other intersections, unless there are signs or lights to the contrary, traffic from the right has priority. If it is absolutely necessary for you to drive in Lisbon, try to avoid the rush hours (roughly 8–10am and 5:30–8pm). Also, be aware that driving at weekends is much easier than during the week. Always look out for pedestrians; crossings are badly marked.

Complexo das Amoreiras, which has an underground car park

Parking

On-street parking spaces are relatively few in central Lisbon and must mostly be paid for at parking meters. Pay-and-display parking spaces are marked by a P sign with a hand and a coin. Tickets are bought from machines along the pavement; the charge is quite low and only applies between 8am and 8pm on weekdays (and on Saturday mornings in some areas). However, there is a limit to the number of hours you can pay, and the machines don't give change, so come equipped with small coins. Illegally parked cars may be clamped or towed away, and will be released only upon payment of a fine.

Safer and longer-term parking is available in Lisbon's many underground car parks. These are marked by signs with a white P on a blue background and usually display whether there are spaces or not by means of a red full (*completo*) or green free (*livre*) light. Tickets are taken from a machine on entering and paid for before leaving. Car parks are more expensive than parking in the street. Some of the larger ones in Lisbon are beneath Praça Marquês de Pombal, Praça da Figueira, Praça dos Restauradores, Praça Luís de Camões and the Complexo das Amoreiras.

Car Hire

Most of the major car-hire companies have offices at the airport inside the arrivals hall (*see Directory*). To rent a car in Portugal you must have a driving licence (*carta da condução*). If you do not hold a driving licence from an EU member state you will need an international driving licence. Drivers must be over the age of 21 and have held their licence for at least one year.

It is usually more expensive to hire a car in summer. Most companies offer special off-peak and weekend deals. The price depends on whether unlimited mileage is included and if you want comprehensive insurance (*todos-os-riscos*). Normally, the car is provided with a full tank of petrol; it is best to return it with the tank full, since the agency will charge to fill it themselves.

Petrol (Gasoline)

Petrol, called *gasolina*, is relatively expensive in Portugal. Diesel (*gasóleo*) costs considerably less and is the cheapest vehicle fuel. Unleaded fuel (*gasolina sem chumbo*) comes in two types: 95-octane normal and 98-octane super. The latter is more expensive.

There are a number of petrol stations in central Lisbon, some of which are open 24 hours a day. They accept most major credit cards.

Travelling Around the Lisbon Coast

Lisbon and its surroundings offer numerous sightseeing opportunities, and the good road network means that most sights are only 30 minutes or so from the city centre. Buses, coaches and local trains are available for visiting Cascais and Estoril, buses and trains go to and from Sintra, and there are organized coach tours to the palaces and the glorious countryside around the town. There is also a frequent rail service operating from Rossio station to Sintra. To visit Sesimbra and other areas to the south of the Tagus, ferries depart from Terreiro do Paço (Estação Fluvial) and Cais do Sodré in Lisbon, and offer a more leisurely way to cross the river than the busy Ponte 25 de Abril. Alternatively, the Fertagus train also crosses the bridge on the lower level. Trains and buses can then be picked up on the south bank of the river.

High-speed train at Gare do Oriente in Lisbon

Travelling by Train

The state-owned railway company, **Caminhos de Ferro Portugueses (CP)**, is responsible for operating all trains in Portugal.

There are four main rail lines out of Lisbon. The most popular ones with tourists are the line that runs from Cais do Sodré to Cascais on the coast, and the line linking Rossio station to the town of Sintra. Trains to Sintra also leave from Entrecampos, Sete Rios, Oriente and Roma Areeiro stations, and the journey takes about 45 minutes. Santa Apolónia is the main station for trains travelling north, as well as for most international arrivals.

For those travelling east or south of Lisbon, trains depart from Gare do Oriente, Entrecampos and Sete Rios stations and cross the Ponte 25 de Abril road and rail bridge. The gleaming Gare do Oriente, near Parque das Nações, opened in 1998. It also serves as an alternative international terminus, in addition to operating as an interchange for local destinations.

To reach Estoril and Cascais, take the train from Cais do Sodré station. The journey follows the coastline and takes about 45 minutes. Check destinations on the screens at the station before you travel because some trains terminate at Oeiras, Parede or São João do Estoril during peak hours. You can also catch the train from Cais do Sodré to Alcântara-Mar, only 5 minutes away, or to Belém, 10 minutes away.

Ticketing System

Discounts of 50 per cent are available on all CP tickets for children from 5 to 12, students (with valid ID) and adults over 65. Children under four travel free. There are also discounts for groups of 15 people or more on urban trains in the Lisbon area.

Paper tickets have been discontinued and replaced with pre-paid smart cards that can be bought at vending machines in the station. They are validated electronically by passing them over a scanner at a gate to gain access to the platforms and on leaving the station. Single, return or multiple trips can be purchased on the Cais do Sodré–Cascais and Entrecampos/Sete Rios–Sintra lines. One- or three-day passes are also available for unlimited travel on the Sintra, Cascais and Setúbal lines. Bicycles are carried free of charge at any time of day on the Cascais and Sintra lines but only on specially marked carriages. Passengers without a validated card will be fined.

Façade of Rossio station, in Praça Dom Pedro IV

Travelling by Coach

Lisbon's main coach station is **Sete Rios**. There are several private enterprises operating coach services. Each operates its own ticketing system. As a rule, you buy your ticket from the driver when you board, although it is possible to get cheaper tickets, known as *módulos* or *bilhetes*, beforehand from the relevant coach company's kiosk. As on trains, there are no group discounts, though children between the ages of 4 and 12 pay half price.

At present, the best way to travel between Lisbon and Cascais is to catch an Aerobus coach to its terminus at Cais de Sodré railway station and then take the train to Cascais. The daily Aerobus service operates every 20 minutes from 7am to 11pm. From Cais de Sodré, regular trains run along the side of the Tagus estuary via Belém and Estoril, terminating at Cascais.

TST (Transportes Sul do Tejo) serves destinations south of the Tagus. Buses leave from Praça de Espanha (Metro Praça de Espanha) for destinations such as Costa da Caparica (1 hr) and Sesimbra (1 hr 45 mins).

For destinations northwest of Lisbon, contact **Rodoviária de Lisboa**, which operates from Campo Grande, among other places. **Rede Expressos** and **EVA** offer direct services to destinations all over the country. EVA covers the Algarve particularly well. Both are based at the Sete Rios bus terminal in Praça Marechal Humberto Delgado.

To date there is no coach link between Lisbon and Sintra.

Ferries crossing the Tagus river

However, **Scotturb** operates three routes to Sintra from Cascais and Estoril. The No. 403 departs from near Cascais railway station every 90 minutes, via Cabo da Roca. The No. 417 runs from Cascais via Alcabideche and the No. 418 departs hourly from outside Estoril train station. All three buses stop at Sintra station and in the town centre. In Sintra, Scotturb also runs a service from the train station to Palácio da Pena and Castelo dos Mouros (daily in summer; Tue–Sun in winter).

Coach Tours

There are many coach tours in the Lisbon area, offering a wide choice of destinations, from a local trip around the city's sights to longer trips to other cities in Portugal such as Oporto. For those who wish to tour Lisbon, short half-day tours are available. Sintra, Cabo da Roca, Estoril and Cascais are all easily reached in a day trip. Alternatively, head southwards to Sesimbra and Arrábida, or north to Mafra. Prices depend on whether meals or special events, such as *fado* or

bullfighting, are included. Most tours offer reductions to children under the age of ten. Tours can be booked directly with the tour operator, through a travel agent or at some hotels. If you are staying at one of Lisbon's major hotels, some tours will offer a pick-up service. For coach tour companies *see page 165*.

Ferries Across the Tagus

Most ferry services are run by **Transtejo**. There are several different points at which you can cross the Tagus. The trips are worth making purely for the fabulous views of Lisbon. From Terreiro do Paço (Estação Fluvial) there are crossings to Barreiro (5:45am–2am daily), taking 15 minutes, and to Montijo. Ferries operated by Transtejo also cross from Cais do Sodré to Seixal and Cacilhas, taking 20 and 15 minutes respectively.

From Belém, ferries go to Porto Brandão and Trafaria (7am–10pm weekdays, 7:30am–9:30pm Sat, 8:30am–9:30pm Sun & public holidays), where you can get a bus to the beaches at Caparica.

Travelling by Car

When driving, always carry your passport, licence, car insurance and rental contract. Failure to produce these *documentos* if the police stop you will incur a fine.

Drivers and passengers must don fluorescent yellow safety vests following a breakdown or an accident. In addition, a vehicle must carry a collapsible warning triangle in the trunk to

A long-distance coach from one of the many coach companies

be used in the event of such an emergency. These items are usually supplied by the car hire company.

The speed limit for driving on a motorway is 120 km/h (75 miles/h); on an open road it is 90–100 km/h (56–62 miles/h) and within a town, 50 km/h (30 miles/h).

The road network in and around Lisbon has seen much improvement in the last decade, with the construction of new ring roads and motorways. If you are heading west out of Lisbon towards the coast and Estoril and Cascais, take the A5 motorway and try to avoid rush-hour traffic (8–10am and 5:30–8pm). To get on to the A5, follow the road out from Praça de Espanha or from Praça Marquês de Pombal past Amoreiras. If you prefer to take the scenic coastal route (N6), follow the A5 out of Lisbon for 8 km (5 miles) and turn off at the sign to Avenida Marginal.

Local signs giving directions to Estoril, the south via the bridge and Sete Rios

To get to Sintra, the best routes are either the A5 motorway or the IC19 past Queluz. The A5 motorway passes through small areas of countryside.

To reach Caparica, Tróia and Setúbal, south of the Tagus, you can either cross the Ponte 25 de Abril at Alcântara or take the car ferry that departs regularly from Belém to Trafaria. Once across the river, follow the A2 south.

Roads and Tolls

Motorways around Lisbon have toll charges and most are privately owned by a company called **Brisa**. In general, they are the quickest way to travel around Portugal, as they have better surfaces than minor roads. There are also motorway rest areas where you can have something to eat and fill the car up with petrol.

There are two systems for paying tolls on motorways. Most drivers take a ticket (*título*) at the entrance and pay at the exit where the fee is displayed at the toll booth. The other system, known as *Via Verde*, is primarily for residents in the area and is not intended for general use. Drivers subscribing to this system drive through the *Via Verde* channel without stopping. Their passage is

registered automatically and billed later. It is strictly forbidden for anyone who does not subscribe to drive through the *Via Verde*, so make sure that you are in the correct lane as you approach the toll booths.

Breakdown Services

The local motoring association, the **ACP** (Automóvel Club de Portugal), has a reciprocal breakdown service with most other international motoring organizations. To qualify, drivers should take out European cover with their own organization.

Should you be involved in a road accident, the emergency services number is **112**. If you have simply broken down, call the ACP. There are SOS phones at regular intervals along motorways. Unless you state that you are a member of an ACP-affiliated organization, a private tow truck will be sent to help you.

Breakdown assistance will try to repair your car on the spot, but if it is a more serious problem, they will tow your car to a garage. Depending on your insurance, the ACP can make arrangements for you to have a hire car until yours is repaired.

In Portugal, international rules apply to breakdowns, including placing a red warning triangle behind the car to alert other drivers. Be sure to check that you have one before you travel.

DIRECTORY

Travelling by Coach

EVA
Praça Marechal Humberto Delgado, Rua das Laranjeiras, Lisbon.
Tel 707 223 344.
W eva-bus.com

Rede Expressos
Praça Marechal Humberto Delgado, Rua das Laranjeiras, Lisbon.
Tel 707 223 344.
W rede-expressos.pt

Rodoviária de Lisboa
Campo Grande 382c, 1º, Lisbon. **Tel** 217 928 180.
W rodoviariade lisboa.pt

Scotturb
Rua de São Francisco 660, Adroana, Alcabideche.
Tel 214 699 100/125.
W scotturb.com

Sete Rios Coach Station
Praça Marechal Humberto Delgado, Rua das Laranjeiras, Lisbon.
Tel 707 223 344.

TST
Rua Marcos de Portugal, Almada. **Map** 5 A2.
Tel 211 126 200.
W tsuldotejo.pt

Coach Tours

Carristur
Tel 213 478 030.
W carristur.pt

Cityrama
Tel 800 208 513 (toll free).
W cityrama.pt

Gray Line
Tel 800 208 513 (toll free).

Ferries

Transtejo
Tel 210 422 400.
W transtejo.pt

Travelling by Car

ACP (breakdown)
Tel 219 429 113.

Brisa (motorways)
W brisa.pt

LISBON STREET FINDER

Map references given in this guide for sights and entertainment venues in Lisbon refer to the Street Finder maps on the following pages. Map references are also given for Lisbon's hotels *(see pp120–23)* and restaurants *(see pp130–35)*. The first figure in the map reference indicates which Street Finder map to turn to, and the letter and number which follow refer to the grid reference on that map. The map below shows the area of Lisbon covered by the eight Street Finder maps. Symbols used for sights and useful information are displayed in the key below. An index of street names and all the places of interest marked on the maps can be found on the following pages.

Key to Street Finder

- Major sight
- Place of interest
- Railway station
- M Metro station
- Main bus stop
- Tram stop
- Funicular railway
- Ferry boarding point
- *i* Tourist information
- Hospital with casualty unit
- Police station
- Church
- Synagogue
- C Mosque
- Viewpoint
- Railway line
- Motorway
- Pedestrianized street
- Stepped Pedestrianized street

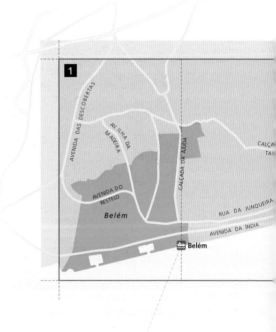

Scale of Map Pages 1–6

0 metres 250
0 yards 250

Scale of Map Pages 7–8

0 metres 200
0 yards 200

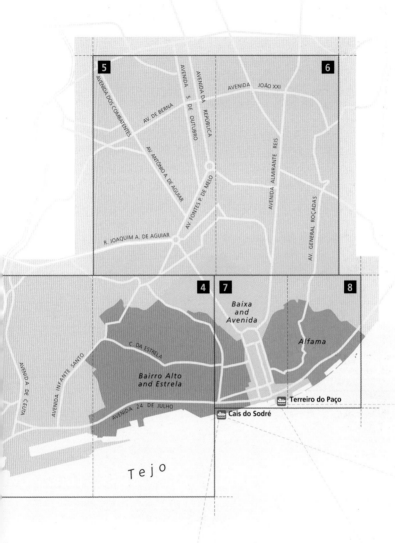

Street Finder Index

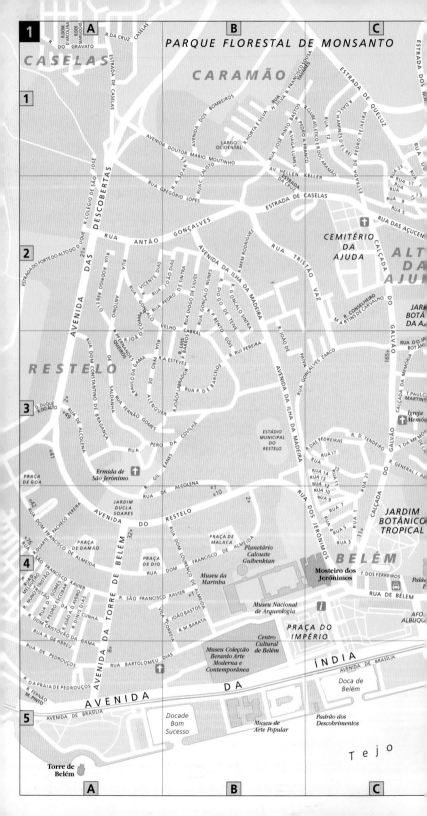

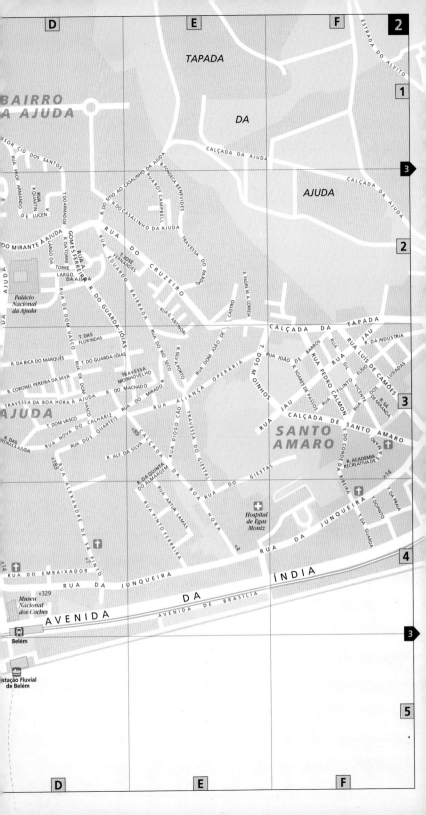

TAPADA

DA

AJUDA

BAIRRO
A AJUDA

CALÇADA DA AJUDA

CALÇADA DA AJUDA

ESTRADA DO ALVITO

SSOR CID DOS SANTOS

RUA PROF. ARMANDO
P QUADRIM
V
E LUCEN

RUA
P QUADRIM

T DO ARMADOR

DO MIRANTE À AJUDA
GOMES FERREIRA

R DA TORRE

LARGO DA
TORRE
LARGO
DA AJUDA

Palácio
Nacional
da Ajuda

AJUDA

RUA DE DOM VASCO

R DA BICA DO MARQUÊS

R. CORONEL PEREIRA DA SILVA

T. DAS
FLORINDAS

T. DO GUARDA-JÓIAS

RUA DO GUARDA-JÓIAS

RUA DO SÍTIO AO CASALINHO DA AJUDA

RUA DO CASALINHO DA AJUDA

RUA ROY CAMPBELL

R FONSECA BENEVIDES

RUA DO CRUZEIRO

T JOSÉ FERNANDES
EDUARDO

RUA BAIRRADA

RUA G ANTHORI

TRAVESSA DO PARA?

R PADRE M A CORREIA

CASTRO

CALÇADA DA TAPADA

JAU

RUA DA INDÚSTRIA

RUA LUÍS DE CAMÕES

LUSÍADAS

RUA
GIL

RUA JAU

R. SÃ DE MIRANDA

BARROS

RUA CFILINTO VICENTE

DOS
ELÍSIO

RUA PEDRO CALMON

RUA JOÃO DE

R. SOARES DE PASSOS

R SILVA PORTO

RUA DOM JOÃO DE

RUA DO RIO SECO

RUA ALIANÇA OPERÁRIA

T. DOS MOINHOS

RUA JAU

CALÇADA DE SANTO AMARO

SANTO
AMARO

T. DO CONDE DA RIBEIRA

R. ACADEMIA
RECREATIVA DE

T. DAS
FLORINDAS

TRAVESSA
MONHOVELHO

RUA DO MACHADO

RUA DO MIRADO

RUA CÃO DIOGO

T DOM VASCO

RUA NOVA DO CALHARIZ

RUA DOS QUARTÉIS

CALÇADA DA

R. ALF. DA SILVA

RUA DA QUINTA
DO ALMARGEM

RUA ARTUR LAMAS

RUA PINTO FERREIRA

TRAVESSA DO GIESTAL

BOA RUA HORA

RUA DO GIESTAL

Hospital
de Egas
Moniz

TRAVESSA DA BOA HORA À AJUDA

R. DAS
EIRAS À AJUDA

RUA ALEXANDRE DE SÁ PINTO

RUA DA JUNQUEIRA

T DO PINTO

T DA GUARDA

T DA PRAIA

RUA DO EMBAIXADOR

Museu
Nacional
dos Coches

AVENIDA

RUA DA JUNQUEIRA

AVENIDA DE BRASÍLIA

DA

ÍNDIA

Belém

Estação Fluvial
de Belém

«329

«14

«189

«89

«4

«47

«14

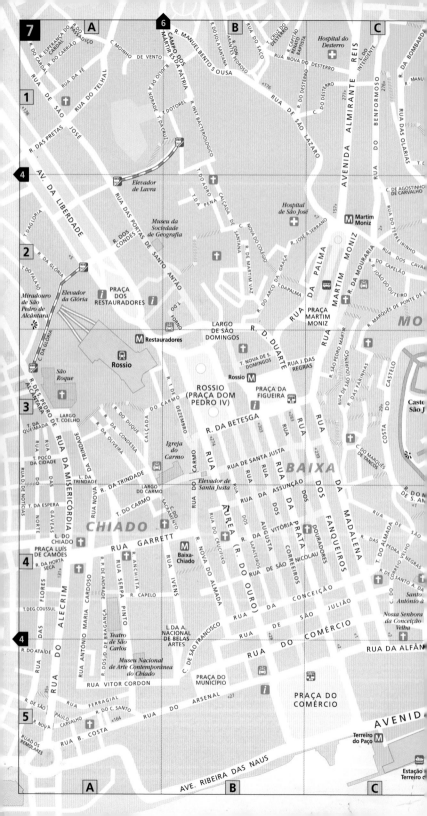

General Index

Acknowledgments

Dorling Kindersley would like to thank the following people whose contributions and assistance have made the preparation of this book possible.

Contributors
Susie Boulton studied History of Art at Cambridge University. A freelance travel writer, she is also the author of *Eyewitness Venice and the Veneto*.
Sarah McAlister is a freelance writer and editor for the *Time Out* guides. Her knowledge of Lisbon and the surrounding area is a result of extensive visits to the country.

Consultant
Martin Symington was born in Portugal and is a freelance travel writer. He contributes to numerous British newspapers including the *Daily Telegraph* and the *Sunday Telegraph*. He is the author of guides to *The Loire Valley* (Hodder and Stoughton), *Portugal* (AA) and *Denmark* (AA/Thomas Cook). He has also contributed to *The Algarve and Southern Portugal* (AA/Thomas Cook), *Portugal* (Insight), *Eyewitness Great Britain* and *Eyewitness Seville and Andalusia*.

Additional Contributors
Paul Bernhardt, Mark Harding, Paul Vernon, Edite Vieira.

Revisions and Relaunch Team
Ashwin Raju Adimari, Gillian Allan, Douglas Amrine, Gillian Andrews, Claire Baranowski, Paul Bernhardt, Uma Bhattacharya, Andrew Costello, Emer FitzGerald, Angela Marie Graham, Mark Harding, Vinod Harish, Mohammad Hassan, Paul Hines, Jasneet Kaur, Priyanka Kumar, Vincent Kurien, Esther Labi, Kathryn Lane, Maite Lantaron, Michelle de Larrabeiti, Nicola Malone, Bhavika Mathur, Caroline Mead, Sam Merrell, Adam Moore, Casper Morris, Reetu Pandey, Naomi Peck, Andrea Powell, Tom Prentice, Rada Radojicic, Mani Ramaswamy, Jake Reimann, Mihaela Rogalski, Ellen Root, Collette Sadler, Marta Bescos Sanchez, Sands Publishing Solutions, Azeem Siddiqui, Sadie Smith, Susana Smith, Christine Stroyan, Rachel Symons, Amanda Tomeh, Tomas Tranæus, Ingrid Vienings, Fiona Wild.

Indexer
Hilary Bird.

Additional Photography
Paul Bernhardt, Steve Gorton, Matthew Hancock, John Heseltine, Dave King, Martin Norris, Ian O'Leary, Roger Philips, Clive Streeter, Peter Wilson.

Photographic and Artwork Reference
Joy FitzSimmons, Veronica Wood.

Photography Permissions
Dorling Kindersley would like to thank the following for their assistance and kind permission to photograph at their establishments:
Instituto Português do Património Arquitectónico e Arqueológico (IPPAR), Lisboa; Instituto Português de Museus (IPM), Lisboa; Museu do Mar, Cascais; Museu da Marinha, Lisboa; Fundação da Casa de Alorna, Lisboa, and all other churches, museums, parks, hotels, restaurants and sights too numerous to thank individually.

Special Assistance
Emília Tavares, Arquivo Nacional de Fotografia, Lisboa; Luísa Cardia, Biblioteca Nacional e do Livro, Lisboa; Marina Gonçalves and Aida Pereira, Câmara Municipal de Lisboa; Caminhos de Ferro Portugueses; Carris; Enatur, Lisboa; Karen Ollier-Spry, John E. Fells and Sons Ltd; Maria Helena Soares da Costa, Fundação Calouste Gulbenkian, Lisboa; José Aragão, Turismo de Portugal, London; Instituto do Vinho de Porto, Porto; Simoneta Afonso, IPM, Lisboa; Mário Abreu, Dulce Ferraz, IPPAR, Lisboa; Pedro Moura Bessa and Eduardo Corte-Real, Livraria Civilização Editora, Porto; Metropolitano de Lisboa; Raquel Florentino and Cristina Leite, Museu da Cidade, Lisboa; Joao Castel Branco G. Pereira, Museu Nacional do Azulejo; and the staff at all the other tourist offices and town halls in Portugal.

Picture Credits
a-above; b-below/bottom; c-centre; f-far; l-left; r-right; t-top.

Works of art have been reproduced with the permission of the following copyright holders: *Terreiro do Paço* by Dirk Stoop 83b is reproduced by kind permission of the Museu da Cidade, Lisboa.

Dorling Kindersley would like to thank the following individuals, companies and picture libraries for permission to reproduce their photographs:

4Corners: SIME/Johanna Huber 2-3.

AISA: 20cra, 21tl/br, 68br; **Alamy Images:** Age Fotostock Spain, S.L 95b; David Angel 91tl; Luis Elvas 101tl; Peter Forsberg 127tl; John Warburton-Lee Photography/Ian Aitken 126cl; Reinhard Kliem 156br; Hideo Kurihara 4tr; Iain Lowson 163tr; Marka 44clb; Picture Contact/Jochem Wijnands 127c; Neil Setchfield 164bl; **Arquivo Internacional de Cor:** Neto Miranda 88cr, 89br, 89cla; **Arquivo Nacional de Fotografia-Instituto Português de Museus:** 21tc; Museu Conde de Castro Guimarães/Manuel Palma 16; Biblioteca da Ajuda/José Pessoa 18cl; Museu Grao Vasco/José Pessoa 22bl; Museu Nacional dos Coches/José Pessoa 21bc; Henrique Ruas 66br; Igreja São Vicente de Fora/Carlos Monteiro 21bl; Museu Nacional de Arte Antiga/Luís Pavão 20tr, 58cb/br, 59ca/cr/br, 61c; Francisco Matias 23tl, José Pessoa 23cra, 24–5t, 58tr, 60bl, 61br; Pedro Ferreira 60tr, 61t; Museu Nacional de Arqueologia/José Pessoa 67c; Arnaldo Soares 144tr, 145tl; Museu Nacional do Teatro/Arnaldo Soares 144cl; Luisa Oliveira 145tr; José Pessoa 144bl; **Tony Arruza:** 20ca, 24–5lc.

Bica do Sapato: Luisa Ferreira 130bc; **Bistro 100 Maneiras/Constantino Leite:** 132tl; © **Trustees of the British Museum, London:** 22br.

Café Fábulas: 124cl; Câmara Municipal de Lisboa: Antonio Rafael 24cl; Can the Can: 131tl; Casa Balthazar: 120bc; Casa Mateus: 135tr; Centro do Arte Moderna: José Manuel Costa Alves 82tl; Cephas: Mick Rock 128crb, 129c; Peter Stowell 28b; Cervejaria Ramiro: 133br; Chapitô: 142cr; Corbis: Klaus Hackenberg 36bc; Hans Georg Roth 5tl; Sylvain Sonnet 12br.

Dreamstime.com: Luis Alvarenga 56b; Alvaroennes 12tc; Fernando Batista 11tl; Anasztázia Batta 94; Artur Bogacki 13tr; Olena Buyskykh 46tr; Daniel M. Cisilino 8-9, 13bl; Henner Damke 50; Emicristea 62; Europhotos 30-1; Ghettog76 146-7; Ruslan Gilmanshin 42; Gvictoria 47bl; Karol Kozlowski 92-3; Lejoch 49br; Mario Savoia 10cla; Zts 32.

ECB: 153 all.

Fototeca Internacional, Lisboa: César Soares 20bl; Luís Elvas 29b/tr; Fundação Ricardo Do Espirito Santa Silva: Museu-Escola de Artes Decoratives Portuguesas 36c; Furnas do Guincho: 134br.

Getty Images: AFP/Michael Kappeler 21cra; AFP/Francisco Leong 150bc; Paul Bernhardt 143tl; DEA/G. DAGLI ORTI 19clb; Sean Gallup 21cr; Holger Leue 37cl; Stone/Hugh Sitton 90cla; Giraudon: 22cl; Glowimages: SuperStock 116-7; GoLisbon.com: Mario Fernandes 149tr; Guarda Nacional Republicana: 150br; Calouste Gulbenkian Foundation, Lisboa: 138br.

Hemispheres Images: Maurizio Borgese 11br; Bertrand Gardel 90br; Jean-Baptiste Rabouan 10br; Hotel do Chiado: 121tr.

Ideal Photo: N. Adams; The Image Bank: José Manuel 4br, 27bl; Moura Machado 28cr; Instituto Nacional de Emergência Médica: 151tl; Instituto da Biblioteca Nacional e do Livro, Lisboa: 17b, 18br, 111bc.

Jardim Zoológico de Lisboa: 86tr.

Lisbonaire Apartments: 122tl; Lusa: Luís Vasconcelos 54br; André Kosters 55tl; António Cotrim 145cra.

José Manuel: 25br; Mary Evans Picture Library: 25tc, 107b; Metropolitano de Lisboa: 159br; Miragem: 123br; Museu Calouste Gulbenkian, Lisboa: 78tl/cb/bl, 79tl/ca/cb/bl, 80tr/c/bl, 81tr/clb/br; Enamelled Silver Gilt Corsage Ornament, Rene Lalique, © ADAGP, Paris and DACS, London 2011 78cla; Museu da Cidade, Lisboa: Antonio Rafael 24bl/br, 25cr/bl; Museu da Marinha, Lisboa: 20br, 70bc.

Nationalmuseet, Copenhagen: 22tr; Naturpress: Juan Hidalgo-Candy Lopesino 26tc.

Oronoz, Madrid: 20bc.

Palácio Nacional de Queluz: Carlos Pombo 111tl; Palacio de Pena: 106cl; Pictures Colour Library: Photolocation Ltd 91br; Policia de Segurança Pública: 151cl.

Red Tour GPS Electric Move: 158tr; Dias dos Reis: 83tl, 152cla; Rui Santos: www.photographersdirect.com: 151cla, 161cl.

Symington Port & Madeira Shippers: Claudio Capone 129cl; Sogrape Vinhos S.A.: 128tr; SuperStock: Prisma 74.

Transtejo: 164tr; Turismo de Lisboa: www.visitlisboa.com: 48tr, 76b, 158bc.

Peter Wilson: 46tl, 55bl, 138b, 139cr, 140cr; Woodfall Wild Images: Mike Lane 115b; World Pictures: 27tc.

Front endpapers: Dreamstime.com: Anasztázia Batta lcra; Henner Damke rbc; Emicristea lbr; Ruslan Gilmanshin rbr; Mario Savoia; Zts rtr; SuperStock: Prisma rtc.

Map cover: AWL Images: Carlos Sanchez Pereyra.

Jacket
Front: AWL Images: Carlos Sanchez Pereyra; Dorling Kindersley/Linda Whitwam bl.

All other images © Dorling Kindersley. For further information see www.DKimages.com

Phrase Book

In Emergency

Help!	Socorro!	soo-**koh**-roo
Stop!	Páre!	pahr'
Call a doctor!	Chame um médico!	shahm' ooñ meh-dee-koo
Call an ambulance!	Chame uma ambulância!	shahm' oo-muh añ-boo-lañ-see-uh
Call the police!	Chame a polícia!	shahm'uh poo-lee-see-uh
Call the fire brigade!	Chame os bombeiros!	shahm' oosh bom-**bay**-roosh
Where is the nearest telephone?	Há um telefone aqui perto?	ah ooñ te-le-**fon'** uh-**keepehr**-too
Where is the nearest hospital?	Onde é o hospital mais próximo?	ond' eh oo ohsh-pee-**tahl'** mysh **pro**-see-moo

Communication Essentials

Yes	Sim	seeñ
No	Não	nowñ
Please	Por favor/ Faz favor	poor fuh-**vor** fash fuh-**vor**
Thank you	Obrigado/da	o-bree-**gah**-doo/duh
Excuse me	Desculpe	dish-**koolp'**
Hello	Olá	oh-**lah**
Goodbye	Adeus	a-**deh**-oosh
Good morning	Bom-dia	boñ **dee**-uh
Good afternoon	Boa-tarde	boh-uh tard'
Good night	Boa-noite	boh-uh noyt'
Yesterday	Ontem	oñ-**tayñ**
Today	Hoje	ohj'
Tomorrow	Amanhã	ah-mañ-**yañ**
Here	Aqui	uh-**kee**
There	Ali	uh-**lee**
What?	O quê?	oo keh
Which?	Qual?	kwahl'
When?	Quando?	**kwañ**-doo
Why?	Porquê?	poor-**keh**
Where?	Onde?	oñd'

Useful Phrases

How are you?	Como está?	**koh**-moo shtah
Very well, thank you.	Bem, obrigado/da.	bayñ o-bree-**gah**-doo/duh
Pleased to meet you.	Encantado/a.	eñ-kañ-**tah**-doo/duh
See you soon.	Até logo.	uh-**teh loh**-goo
That's fine.	Está bem.	shtah bayñ
Where is/are …?	Onde está/estão …?	ond' shtah/ shtowñ
How far is it to …?	A que distância fica …?	uh kee dish-**tañ**-see-uh **fee**-kuh
Which way to …?	Como se vai para …?	**koh**-moo seh vy puh-ruh
Do you speak English?	Fala inglês?	**fah**-luh eeñ-glehsh
I don't understand.	Não compreendo.	nowñ kom-pree-**eñ**-doo
Could you speak more slowly please?	Pode falar mais devagar por favor?	pohd' fuh-lar mysh d'-va-**gar** poor fuh-**vor**
I'm sorry.	Desculpe.	dish-**koolp'**

Useful Words

big	grande	grañd'
small	pequeno	pe-**keh**-noo
hot	quente	keñt'
cold	frio	**free**-oo
good	bom	boñ
bad	mau	**mah**-oo
quite a lot/enough	bastante	bash-**tañt'**
well	bem	bayñ
open	aberto	a-**behr**-too
closed	fechado	fe-**shah**-doo
left	esquerda	**shkehr**-duh
right	direita	dee-**ray**-tuh
straight on	em frente	ayñ freñt'
near	perto	**pehr**-too
far	longe	loñj'
up	para cima	pur-ruh **see**-muh
down	para baixo	pur-ruh **buy**-shoo
early	cedo	**seh**-doo
late	tarde	tard'
entrance	entrada	eñ-**trah**-duh
exit	saída	sa-**ee**-duh
toilets	casa de banho	**kah**-zuh d' **bañ**-yoo
more	mais	mysh
less	menos	**meh**-noosh

Making a Telephone Call

I'd like to place an international call.	Queria fazer uma chamada internacional.	kree-uh fuh-**zehr** oo-muh sha-**mah**-duh in-ter-na-**see**-oo-nahl'
a local call.	uma chamada local.	oo-muh sha-**mah**-duh loo-**kahl'**
Can I leave a message?	Posso deixar uma mensagem?	poh-soo day-shar oo-muh meñ-**sah**—jayñ

Shopping

How much does this cost?	Quanto custa isto?	**kwañ**-too **koosh**-tuh **eesh**-too
I would like …	Queria …	**kree**-uh
I'm just looking.	Estou só a ver obrigado/a.	shtoh sohuh vehr o-bree-**gah**-doo/uh
Do you take credit cards?	Aceita cartões de crédito?	uh-**say**-tuh kar-**toinsh** de **kreh**-dee-too
What time do you open?	A que horas abre?	uh **kee oh**-rash **ah**-bre
What time do you close?	A que horas fecha?	uh **kee oh**-rash **fay**-shuh
This one	Este	ehst'
That one	Esse	ehss'
expensive	caro	**kah**-roo
cheap	barato	buh-**rah**-too
size (clothes/shoes)	tamanho	ta-**man**-yoo
white	branco	**brañ**-koo
black	preto	**preh**-too
red	vermelho	ver-**mehl**-yoo
yellow	amarelo	uh-mah-**reh**-loo
green	verde	vehrd'
blue	azul	uh-**zool'**

Types of Shop

antique shop	loja de antiguidades	**loh**-juh de añ-tee-gwee-**dahd'sh**
bakery	padaria	**pah**-duh-**ree**-uh
bank	banco	**bañ**-koo
bookshop	livraria	lee-vruh-**ree**-uh
butcher	talho	**tah**-lyoo
cake shop	pastelaria	pash-te-luh-**ree**-uh
chemist	farmácia	far-**mah**-see-uh
fishmonger	peixaria	pay-shuh-**ree**-uh
hairdresser	cabeleireiro	kab'-lay-**ray**-roo
market	mercado	mehr-**kah**-doo
newsagent	quiosque	kee-**yohsk'**
post office	correios	koo-**ray**-oosh
shoe shop	sapataria	suh-puh-tuh-**ree**-uh
supermarket	supermercado	soo-**pehr**-mer-**kah**-doo
tobacconist	tabacaria	tuh-buh-kuh-**ree**-uh
travel agency	agência de viagens	uh-**jen**-see-uh de vee-**ah**-jayñsh

Sightseeing

cathedral	sé	seh
church	igreja	ee-**gray**-juh
garden	jardim	jar-**deeñ**
library	biblioteca	bee-blee-oo-**teh**-kuh
museum	museu	moo-**zeh**-oo
tourist information office	posto de turismo	**posh**-too d' too-**reesh**-moo
closed for holidays	fechado para férias	fe-**sha**-doo puh-ruh **feh**-ree-ash
bus station	estação de autocarros	shta-**sowñ** d'oh-too-**kah**-roosh
railway station	estação de comboios	shta-**sowñ** d' koñ-**boy**-oosh

Staying in a Hotel

Do you have a vacant room?	Tem um quarto livre?	tayñ ooñ kwar-too **leevr'**
room with a bath	um quarto com casa de banho	ooñ **kwar**-too koñ **kah**-zuh d'**bañ**-yoo
shower	duche	doosh
single room	quarto individual	**kwar**-too een-dee-vee-doo-**ahl'**
double room	quarto de casal	**kwar**-too d'kuh-**zahl'**
twin room	quarto com duas camas	**kwar**-too koñ **doo**-ash **kah**-mash
porter	porteiro	poor-**tay**-roo
key	chave	shahv'
I have a reservation.	Tenho um quarto reservado.	**tayñ**-yoo ooñ **kwar**-too-re-ser-**vah**-doo

Eating Out

Have you got a table for …?	Tem uma mesa para …?	tayñ oo-muh meh-zuh puh-ruh
I want to reserve a table.	Quero reservar uma mesa.	keh-roo re-zehr-var oo-muh meh-zuh
The bill please.	A conta por favor/ faz favor.	uh kohn-tuh poor fuh-vor/ fash fuh-vor
I am a vegetarian.	Sou vegetariano/a.	Soh ve-je-tuh-ree-ah-noo/uh
Waiter!	Por favor!/ Faz favor!	poor fuh-vor fash fuh-vor
the menu	a lista	uh leesh-tuh
fixed-price menu	a ementa turística	uh ee-mehñ-tuh too-reesh-tee-kuh
wine list	a lista de vinhos	uh leesh-tuh de veeñ-yoosh
glass	um copo	ooñ koh-poo
bottle	uma garrafa	oo-muh guh-rah-fuh
half bottle	meia-garrafa	may-uh guh-rah-fuh
knife	uma faca	oo-muh fah-kuh
fork	um garfo	ooñ gar-foo
spoon	uma colher	oo-muh kool-yair
plate	um prato	ooñ prah-too
napkin	um guardanapo	ooñgoo-ar-duh-nah-poo
breakfast	pequeno-almoço	pe-keh-noo-ahl-moh-soo
lunch	almoço	ahl-moh-soo
dinner	jantar	jan-tar
cover	couvert	koo-vehr
starter	entrada	eñ-trah-duh
main course	prato principal	prah-too prin-see-pahl'
dish of the day	prato do dia	prah-too doo dee-uh
set dish	combinado	koñ-bee-nah-doo
half portion	meia-dose	may-uh doh-se
dessert	sobremesa	soh-bre-meh-zuh
rare	mal passado	mahl'puh-sah-doo
medium	médio	meh-dee-oo
well done	bem passado	bayñ puh-sah-doo

Menu Decoder

abacate	uh-buh-kaht'	avocado
açorda	uh-sor-duh	bread-based stew (often seafood)
açúcar	uh-soo-kar	sugar
água mineral	ah-gwuh mee-ne-rahl'	mineral water
(com gás)	koñ gas	sparkling
(sem gás)	sayñ gas	still
alho	al-yoo	garlic
alperce	ahl'-pehrce	apricot
amêijoas	uh-may-joo-ash	clams
ananás	uh-nuh-nahsh	pineapple
arroz	uh-rohsh	rice
assado	uh-sah-doo	baked
atum	uh-tooñ	tuna
aves	ah-vesh	poultry
azeite	uh-zayt'	olive oil
azeitonas	uh-zay-toh-nash	olives
bacalhau	buh-kuh-lyow	dried, salted cod
banana	buh-nah-nuh	banana
batatas	buh-tah-tash	potatoes
batatas fritas	buh-tah-tash free-tash	french fries
batido	buh-tee-doo	milk-shake
bica	bee-kuh	espresso
bife	beef	steak
bolacha	boo-lah-shuh	biscuit
bolo	boh-loo	cake
borrego	boo-reh-goo	lamb
caça	kah-ssuh	game
café	kuh-feh	coffee
camarões	kuh-muh-roysh	large prawns
caracóis	kuh-ruh-koysh	snails
caranguejo	kuh-rañ-gay-joo	crab
carne	karn'	meat
cataplana	kuh-tuh-plah-nuh	sealed wok used to steam dishes
cebola	se-boh-luh	onion
cerveja	sehr-vay-juh	beer
chá	shah	tea
cherne	shern'	stone bass
chocolate	shoh-koh-laht'	chocolate
chocos	shoh-koosh	cuttlefish
chouriço	shoh-ree-soo	red, spicy sausage
churrasco	shoo-rash-coo	on the spit
cogumelos	koo-goo-meh-loosh	mushrooms
cozido	koo-zee-doo	boiled
enguias	eñ-gee-ash	eels
fiambre	fee-añbr'	ham
fígado	fee-guh-doo	liver
frango	frañ-goo	chicken
frito	free-too	fried
fruta	froo-tuh	fruit

gambas	gam-bash	prawns
gelado	je-lah-doo	ice cream
gelo	jeh-loo	ice
goraz	goo-rash	bream
grelhado	grel-yah-doo	grilled
iscas	eesh-kash	marinated liver
lagosta	luh-gohsh-tuh	lobster
laranja	luh-rañ-juh	orange
leite	layt'	milk
limão	lee-mowñ	lemon
limonada	lee-moo-nah-duh	lemonade
linguado	leeñ-gwah-doo	sole
lulas	loo-lash	squid
maçã	muh-sañ	apple
manteiga	mañ-tay-guh	butter
mariscos	muh-reesh-koosh	seafood
meia-de-leite	may-uh-d'layt'	white coffee
ostras	osh-trash	oysters
ovos	oh-voosh	eggs
pão	powñ	bread
pastel	pash-tehl'	cake
pato	pah-too	duck
peixe	paysh'	fish
peixe-espada	paysh'-shpah-duh	scabbard fish
pimenta	pee-meñ-tuh	pepper
polvo	pohl'-voo	octopus
porco	por-coo	pork
queijo	kay-joo	cheese
sal	sahl'	salt
salada	suh-lah-duh	salad
salsichas	sahl-see-shash	sausages
sandes	sañ-desh	sandwich
santola	sañ-toh-luh	spider crab
sopa	soh-puh	soup
sumo	soo-moo	juice
tamboril	tañ-boo-ril'	monkfish
tarte	tart'	pie/cake
tomate	too-maht'	tomato
torrada	too-rah-duh	toast
tosta	tohsh-tuh	toasted sandwich
vinagre	vee-nah-gre	vinegar
vinho branco	veeñ-yoo brañ-koo	white wine
vinho tinto	veeñ-yoo teeñ-too	red wine
vitela	vee-teh-luh	veal

Numbers

0	zero	zeh-roo
1	um	ooñ
2	dois	doysh
3	três	tresh
4	quatro	kwa-troo
5	cinco	seeñ-koo
6	seis	saysh
7	sete	set'
8	oito	oy-too
9	nove	nov'
10	dez	desh
11	onze	oñz'
12	doze	doz'
13	treze	trez'
14	catorze	ka-torz'
15	quinze	keeñz'
16	dezasseis	de-zuh-saysh
17	dezassete	de-zuh-set'
18	dezoito	de-zoy-too
19	dezanove	de-zuh-nov'
20	vinte	veent'
21	vinte e um	veen-tee-ooñ
30	trinta	treeñ-tuh
40	quarenta	kwa-reñ-tuh
50	cinquenta	seen-kweñ-tuh
60	sessenta	se-señ-tuh
70	setenta	se-teñ-tuh
80	oitenta	oy-teñ-tuh
90	noventa	noo-veñ-tuh
100	cem	sayñ
101	cento e um	señ-too-ee-ooñ
102	cento e dois	señ-too ee doysh
200	duzentos	doo-zeñ-toosh
300	trezentos	tre-zeñ-toosh
400	quatrocentos	kwa-troo-señ-toosh
500	quinhentos	kee-nyeñ-toosh
700	setecentos	set'-señ-toosh
900	novecentos	nov'-señ-toosh
1,000	mil	meel'

Time

one minute	um minuto	ooñ mee-noo-too
one hour	uma hora	oo-muh oh-ruh
half an hour	meia-hora	may-uh-oh-ruh
Monday	segunda-feira	se-goon-duh-fay-ruh
Tuesday	terça-feira	ter-sa-fay-ruh
Wednesday	quarta-feira	kwar-ta-fay-ruh
Thursday	quinta-feira	keen-ta-fay-ruh
Friday	sexta-feira	say-shta-fay-ruh
Saturday	sábado	sah-ba-doo
Sunday	domingo	doo-meen-go

Lisbon Transport Map

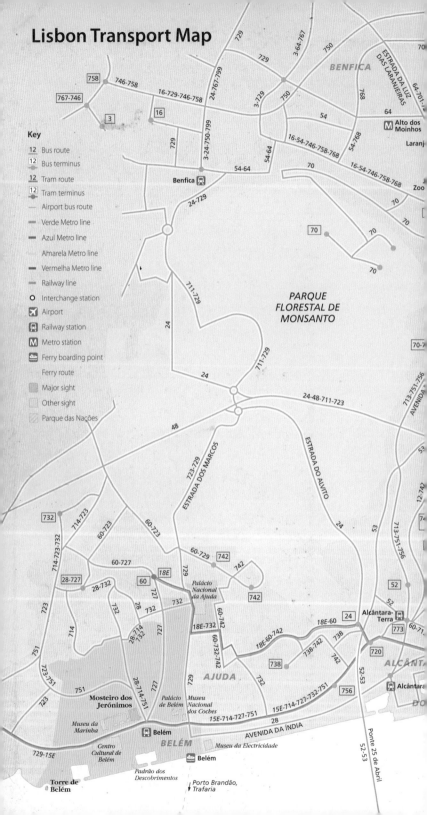

Key

- **12** Bus route
- **12** Bus terminus
- **12** Tram route
- **12** Tram terminus
- Airport bus route
- Verde Metro line
- Azul Metro line
- Amarela Metro line
- Vermelha Metro line
- Railway line
- O Interchange station
- Airport
- Railway station
- M Metro station
- Ferry boarding point
- Ferry route
- Major sight
- Other sight
- Parque das Nações

BENFICA

ESTRADA DA LUZ
DAS LARANJEIRAS

Alto dos Moinhos

Laranj

Zoo

Benfica

PARQUE
FLORESTAL DE
MONSANTO

AVENIDA

ESTRADA DOS MARCOS

ESTRADA DO ALVITO

Palácio Nacional da Ajuda

Alcântara-Terra

ALCÂNTA

AJUDA

Mosteiro dos Jerónimos

Palácio de Belém

Museu Nacional dos Coches

AVENIDA DA ÍNDIA

Alcântara

Ponte 25 de Abril

Museu da Marinha

Belém

BELÉM

Museu da Electricidade

Belém

Centro Cultural de Belém

Padrão dos Descobrimentos

Torre de Belém

Porto Brandão, Trafaria